GW00672428

The
Philosophers'
Secret Fire

PATRICK HARPUR

The Philosophers' Secret Fire

A History of the Imagination

IVAN R. DEE

CHICAGO 2003

First published in the United Kingdom by Penguin Books Ltd.

Library of Congress Cataloging-in-Publication Data:
Harpur, Patrick.
  The philosophers' secret fire : a history of the imagination / Patrick Harpur.
  p. cm.
  Originally published: London : Penguin Books, 2002
  Includes bibliographical references and index.
  ISBN 1-56663-485-7 (alk. paper)
    1. Imagination (Philosophy)—History. 2. Mythology—History. I. Title.

B105.I49 H37 2002
291.1'3--dc21   2002031260

To Mum and Dad

Contents

Contents

Contents

. . . Or let my lamp at midnight hour,
Be seen in some high lonely tower,
Where I may oft outwatch the Bear,
With thrice great Hermes, or unsphere
The spirit of Plato to unfold
What worlds, or what vast regions hold
The immortal mind that hath forsook
Her mansion in this fleshly nook;
And of those daemons that are found
In fire, air, flood, or under ground,
Whose power hath a true consent
With planet, or with element.

                John Milton: 'Il Penseroso'

Prologue

The English antiquarian Elias Ashmole records in his diary for 1653 that William Backhouse, 'lying sick in Fleet-Street, over against St Dunstan's Church, and not knowing whether he should live or die, about eleven o'clock told me in syllables the true matter of the Philosopher's Stone, which he bequeathed to me as a legacy'.[1]

Ashmole's 'true matter' was also often referred to as the secret fire of the Philosophers, as the alchemists called themselves. It was the one essential ingredient for making the *lapis philosophorum*, the Philosophers' Stone, which transmuted base metal into gold and, as the Elixir of Life, conferred immortality. However, the secret fire extends far beyond alchemy. It was a secret that was passed down from antiquity – some say, from Orpheus; others, from Moses; most, from Hermes Trismegistus – in a long series of links which constituted what the Philosophers called the Golden Chain. This august succession of Philosophers embodied a tradition which we have either ignored or labelled 'esoteric', even 'occult'; but it continues to run like a vein of quicksilver beneath Western culture, rising up out of the shadows during times of intense cultural transition.

Just as the Philosophers' Stone was known as the 'stone that is no stone', so the secret fire was more than a substance, more than a secret which could be communicated 'in syllables'. It is not a piece of information; nor is it a code to be cracked or a riddle to be solved. Nor, alas, is it a system of philosophy or body of knowledge which can be expressed directly. Geber, an alchemist probably writing in Spain around 1300, tried to reveal the secret plainly and, ever since, similar attempts have been pronounced by orthodox thinkers as Geber-ish. Gibberish, in other words, is the mode of communication naturally favoured by the secret fire itself, which subverts all efforts to speak of it in the usual Western style of discourse. Any book *about* the secret, and the Golden Chain which preserves it, necessarily becomes a book *in* the Golden Chain.

Thus the straight path of Apollonian lucidity I had planned to follow inevitably became a Hermetic labyrinth. The secret which cried out to be revealed at a single stroke, in a vision or work of art, could only be expounded in a roundabout way. The book proceeded less by logic than by analogy, each chapter connected to the next less by linear argument than by what the ancients called correspondence and sympathy. Ideally, the book may be thought of as a kind of revolving prism, in which each chapter presents in turn a facet of the whole. Better still, each may be imagined as a ray of diffracted light whose source – the secret fire – throws rainbows beyond this, or perhaps any, book.

The secret is, above all, a way of seeing. Although it is a way of seeing that Western culture has often lost sight of, it is central to those modern, tribal, pre-literate societies which I shall be calling 'traditional'. It is also a way of seeing taken for granted by the traditional European cultures of the past; and it is here that I will begin.

I

Shape-Shifters

THE BEGINNING OF ICELAND

One of the last European peoples to be converted to Christianity, around AD 1000, were those Norsemen who had settled Iceland more than a hundred years before. *The Book of the Settlement* describes the establishment of their new society, and so tells us a great deal about what old European cultures considered of fundamental importance.

The first thing they did was to find holy places which would serve as links to the Otherworld, then they set up shrines to the gods they had brought with them, such as Thor and Freyr, and organized annual feasts when sacrifices would be made to them. Lastly, they had to establish a harmonious relationship with the spirits of the new land.[1]

The mountains, hills, rocks, rivers, waterfalls and glaciers of Iceland were filled with elves, rock-dwellers and giants, collectively known as land-spirits. However, if the expression 'land-spirit' is taken to refer to something ethereal or spectral, it would be misleading. There is nothing insubstantial about the land-spirit Bard, for example, who was said to live at Snaefell in western Iceland. He was a tall figure in a grey cloak and hood, with a belt of hide, and he carried a stick to help him over the ice. He is clearly the model for Gandalf, the wizard in Tolkien's *The Lord of the Rings*. Young men were sent to Bard's cave beyond the glacier to be taught law and genealogies, 'two important branches of knowledge linked with the gods and the wisdom of the Otherworld'.[2]

The Icelandic land-spirits are very like another race of European beings called the Sidhe (pronounced 'Shee'). To paraphrase Lady Augusta Gregory, who described them at the turn of the nineteenth

3

century,[3] the Sidhe are shape-changers: they can appear small or large, or as birds, beasts or blasts of wind. They inhabit the forths and lisses, the ancient grass-grown mounds; but their own country is Tir-na-nOg, the Country of the Young. It is under the ground or under the sea, or it may not be far from any of us. They will eat what is left out for them or take for their feasts the best of what we have, but they will not touch salt. Fighting is heard among them, and music that is more beautiful than any of this world; if they are seen, they are often dancing or playing their ball games. The Sidhe will help a man with his work or even tell him where to find treasure; they will teach certain wise men and women where to find lost livestock, and how to cure the sick. They call many over to their world through the eye of a neighbour, the evil eye, or by a touch, a blow, a fall, a sudden terror. Those who have received such a stroke will waste away from this world, as their strength is lent to the Sidhe. Young men are taken to help with their games and their wars; young mothers are taken to suckle their newborn children; girls that they may themselves become mothers there. The dead are often seen among them. The Sidhe have been, like the angels, from before the making of the earth.

Lady Gregory compiled this description of the Sidhe's nature and attributes from reports, both of sightings and beliefs, gathered from the country people who lived on and around her estate in County Galway in the west of Ireland. The poet W. B. Yeats drew on her accounts for his stories and poems, sometimes accompanying her to the homes of her informants. He did not, however, speak the Irish language and had to rely on Lady Gregory for translations.

The Sidhe were also called the Tuatha de Danann, a race of mythological people who are as close as Irish myth comes to speaking of the gods. They are also called the Gentry and – more in hope than expectation – the Good People. Also, the fairies.

THE SECRET COMMONWEALTH

The idea that beliefs recorded in different parts of the world can be compared is currently frowned on in many academic circles.[4] But as Stewart Sanderson points out in his introduction to Robert Kirk's *The Secret Commonwealth*, it is uncontroversial to assert that 'there appears to be no country in the world where fairies by one name or another are not found, no traditional society, whatever its cultural patterns or historical development, where some such creatures do not figure in folk belief'.[5] The fairies were known to the Anglo-Saxons and Norsemen as elves, hulder-folk and land-spirits; to the Cornish as pixies; to the Bretons as corrigans; to the Welsh as Tylwyth Teg, the fair folk. Every county in England had a different name for the fairies, from the derricks of Dorset to the farisees of Norfolk.

In the ancient world, by the second century AD, 'virtually everyone, pagan, Jewish, Christian or Gnostic', notes Oxford Professor E. R. Dodds, 'believed in the existence of these beings and in their function as mediators, whether he called them daemons or angels or aions or simple "spirits" [*pneumata*]'.[6] The Romans, for example, conceived of 'an almost infinite number of divine beings . . . every grove, spring, cluster of rocks or other significant natural feature had its attendant spirit'.[7] They usually had personal names, but were generally known as *genii loci*, the geniuses of the place, such as the Fauni of the woods or the Lares and Penates of farms and houses. The latter 'had to be accorded honours by humans, to an extent much greater and more formal than those given by later Europeans to the fairies, pixies and elves whom these Roman beings resembled. Indeed, households were expected to offer food to the Lares and Penates at every meal.'[8]

Outside Europe, the belief in fairies or their equivalent is just as widespread. The Chinese, for instance, recognize a race of beings directly analogous to the Sidhe which can be transliterated as Kwei-shins. Kwei literally means 'that which belongs to man', and shin, 'that which belongs to heaven', suggesting a fusion of mortal and immortal.[9] Kwei-shin has many meanings, including the *genii* of hills and rocks; spirits presiding over land and grain; the spirits of the ancestors; the finer part of the human soul; and invisible beings in general.[10] They were accepted as being 'both superior and inferior to form, or between the two' as well as 'between the material and immaterial'.[11] In pre-Islamic Arabia the Jinn were 'haunting-demons of the deserts and wildernesses'.[12] Hairy, malformed or shaped like ostriches or serpents, they were dangerous to unprotected persons. The Prophet Mohammed acknowledged the existence of these beings in the *Koran* (37:158) and incorporated them into the religion he founded. Existing between angels formed of light and men formed of the dust of the earth, Jinn are composed of subtle fire, able to take on whatever shape they please and make themselves visible to mortals.[13]

In short, everyone outside modern Western culture has always believed, as the native American Ojibwa believe, in 'a universe of supernatural beings . . . Some are tied down to definite localities, some move from place to place at will; some are friendly to Indians, other [*sic*] hostile.'[14] Yet they are not entirely supernatural because, like the Sidhe, they are as natural a part of the world as humans are. They are analogous to humans, possessing similar intelligence and emotions, being both male and female, and in some cases having families of their own.

'Fairy' would be a suitable name for all these beings, particularly since the word embodies the very shape-shifting nature of what it describes – ninety-three different forms and spellings have been found prior to 1829. The word 'fairy' is 'neither an object with clear boundaries nor possessed of a meaning with clear boundaries'.[15] The clearest connotation that can be attached to it is the idea of *fatedness*, here defined as 'a quality in the world which can control and direct the actions of humanity'.[16] The fairies are believed to be connected to the destiny of the tribe whose well-being depends on a close, often propitiatory relationship with them. They are also linked to the fate of individuals, just like the personal *daimones*, described by Plato in *The Republic*, which are assigned to us at birth and control our destiny.[17] And I am going to follow Plato in calling all these fairy-like beings daimons (sometimes spelt daemons) – which are not of course to be confused with the *demons* Christianity turned them into. All daimons share the attributes of the Sidhe. They are emphatically not 'spirits' – the word anthropologists use, for want of a better, to describe them – because they are, like the land-spirit Bard, as much physical as spiritual. The notion that daimons are both material and immaterial is the most difficult of their many contradictions to grasp. The Reverend Robert Kirk who published in 1691 the first study of fairies, *The Secret Commonwealth*, wrestled with this paradox. He describes them as being 'of a middle nature betwixt man and angell', having 'light changeable bodies (like those called astral) somewhat of the nature of a condensed cloud and best seen in the twilight . . .'[18] The Kwei-shins are inscrutably described as 'incorporeal but not immaterial'.[19]

I am stressing the outstanding characteristics of daimons – elusive, contradictory, shape-shifting – because I hope to show that they provide root metaphors for certain central aspects of modern Western culture, aspects which are otherwise incomprehensible owing to our culture's exclusion of daimons. However, their exclusion is an illusion. True to their shape-changing nature, they continue to appear in our culture, but in a form so far removed from their traditional personified shape that we do not immediately recognize them.

FALLEN ANGELS

The banishment of the daimons in Europe began with Christianity. In the earliest of the New Testament writings, the epistles of St Paul, the gentiles are reproached for sacrificing 'to devils, and not to God'.[20] The word Paul used for devils was *daimonia*: daimons. The chief offence of the daimons was their intermediacy. All pagans recognized a multitude of daimons which mediated between them and their many gods. But for Christianity, there can only be one mediator between mankind and the one God: Jesus Christ.

Thus, throughout the Middle Ages, periodic attempts were made in the spirit of St Paul to cast out the daimons. For example, in one of Chaucer's *Canterbury Tales*, the Wife of Bath describes how an army of friars, 'as thick as motes in the sunbeam', was dispatched to bless everything from woods and streams, to cities and castles, to halls, kitchens and dairies 'that maketh that ther ben no fayries'.[21] Any daimons who escaped the net were demonized, as the Sidhe were, and dubbed 'fallen angels' who had been thrown out of Heaven along with Satan.

However, there was a gentler method of dealing with the daimons. They could be assimilated to Christianity by renaming them. The old daimons of hills, rivers and rocks, the *genii loci*, were Christianized into saints and the Virgin Mary – who supplanted many a nymph of stream and holy well. In this way, the daimons have retained their mediatory function in a Christian disguise, conciliating God on our behalf.

In both cases the demonizing and Christianizing of the daimons imply a polarizing of their essentially contradictory nature. Like all monotheistic religions, Christianity is intolerant of daimonic ambiguity. Daimons cannot, for instance, be allowed to be both benevolent and malign; they must be divided into either devils or angels. The man responsible for introducing angels into Christianity was the anonymous fifth-century mystic known as Dionysius the Areopagite. Although he was a Christian, his works were heavily indebted to the Neoplatonists, and particularly to Proclus, who taught in Athens around AD 430. Dionysius appropriated the Neoplatonic daimons, but did away with their ambiguity, making them into purely spiritual, angelic beings.

The Neoplatonic understanding of the daimons' ambiguity, and of their crucial role as intermediaries, goes back to Plato. In his dialogue, *The Symposium*, Socrates stresses that we have no contact with the gods or God except through the daimons who 'interpret and convey the wishes of men to the gods and the will of gods to men . . . Only through the daimons', he says, 'is there conversation between men and gods, whether in the waking state or during sleep.' Anyone who is an expert in such intercourse is 'a daimonic man'.[22]

WISE WOMEN AND CUNNING MEN

In the early centuries of the Christian era there were many types of daimonic men and women. *Prophetai* relayed messages from the Otherworld, though not necessarily predictions; while *ekstatikoi* (ecstatics) was a neutral psychological term applied to anyone in whom normal consciousness was temporarily or permanently disturbed. The early Fathers of the Church were either *prophetai* or *pneumatikoi*, 'filled with the spirit'.[23] *Entheoi*, 'filled with god', applied to any medium, seer

8

or *shaman* – as we now tend to call the wise woman and cunning man, the medicine-man and witch-doctor, who are so central to traditional cultures.

Shamans – the word comes from the Tungus of Siberia – are a combination of poet, priest and doctor. These three functions have in our culture been divided up among professionals who are no longer trained in daimonic intercourse. Priests usually mediate between us and God via the sacraments, without themselves seeing the need to enter an ecstatic trance; but there will always be charismatics and spiritualists who do.

Oddly enough, our nearest equivalent to the traditional shaman is probably the depth psychologist, who recognizes an autonomous and dynamic unconscious, analogous to the Otherworld of the daimons. The Swiss psychologist C. G. Jung, for example, was clearly a daimonic man. He dreamed of a daimon, a winged being sailing across the sky, who turned out to be an old man with horns.[24] He soon began to visit Jung during waking hours as well. 'At times he seemed to me quite real, as if he were a living personality', wrote Jung. 'I went walking up and down the garden with him . . . He brought me the crucial insight that there are things in the psyche which I do not produce, but which have their own life . . . like animals in the forest or people in a room . . . It was he who taught me psychic objectivity, the reality of the psyche.'[25]

We notice that Jung's daimon appears equally while he is asleep and awake, just as Plato described. It is during sleep, in dreams, that those of us who have no daimonic vocation nevertheless encounter daimons. We may not have many shamanic visions or those 'big dreams' which prophetically concern the whole tribe rather than just the individual; but we have all had, I suppose, one or two. Besides, as Jung has shown, there is a sense in which all dreams, no matter how personal, potentially open out into impersonal territory – that is, into myth.

THE LITTLE PEOPLE

In a previous book, *Daimonic Reality: A Field Guide to the Otherworld*, I recounted a great many reports of encounters by ordinary people with daimons in the form of strangely lit flying objects, large hairy monsters, white ladies, black dogs, tall angelic beings, small ugly 'aliens' – all of which have been regularly and globally sighted. My interest in this book is more to do with daimonic manifestation other than in this direct, visionary and apparitional, way. But since it should not be forgotten that daimons still appear in their traditional and, it seems, preferred personified form, it might be appropriate to provide a short reminder of the immediacy of daimonic encounters which, if we allow them, present such a challenge to our usual view of reality. I have deliberately chosen a category of daimon which has been most open to ridicule: the so-called Little People. But I am aware too that just as all attempts at categorizing the daimons are confounded by the shape-changing daimons themselves, this category is no exception. The Little People may not be so little; for, as a fairy once remarked to a Sligo man, 'I am bigger than I appear to you now. We can make the old young, the big small, the small big.'[26]

The Little People are about eighteen inches tall, perfectly proportioned, with hair that grows down to their heels. Some wear gold caps; others go bare-headed. Their footsteps and voices wake people at night, but if you get up you find nothing – although food may be missing. Sometimes, standing by a stream, you might hear what sounds like children laughing; but when you look, there is no one there, and you know it was the Little People.[27] This is how two Cherokee women described the Yunw Tsunsdi who live a hidden existence side by side with the Cherokee people of North Carolina. They are very like the daimons who inhabit all Europe but who have survived best, perhaps, in their Celtic strongholds from Brittany to Ireland, where the most detailed modern descriptions come from.

Marie Ezanno of Carnac described the corrigans of Brittany as mischievous little dwarves who lived under dolmens, danced in circles, made a whistling sound, and behaved brutally to anyone they had a grudge against.[28] Gwen Hubert wrote in 1928 that she had seen a pixy close to

Shaugh Bridge on Dartmoor in Devon. It was like a little old man, about eighteen inches high, with a little pointed hat, a doublet and 'little short knicker things. Its face was brown and wrinkled and wizened,' she said. 'I saw it for a moment and then it vanished.'[29]

In June 1952, Mrs C. Woods saw a little man standing beside some large boulders on Haytor, a rocky outcrop on the moors near Newton Abbot in Devonshire. 'He moved out from the rock and seemed to be watching her, shading his eyes from the sun . . .'[30] She approached him cautiously. 'He was dressed in what looked like a brown smock . . . [which] came almost to his knees, and his legs appeared to be covered in some brown material. If he had anything on his head it was a flat brown cap, or else he had brown hair. He appeared to be three or four feet tall and seemed elderly rather than young.'[31] When she was within forty yards of him, he dived out of sight under a boulder.

The Little People who helped the Inuit (Eskimo) shaman, described by the Danish explorer Knud Rasmussen, were called aua – little women no longer than an arm's length, with pointed caps, short bearskin trousers and high boots, which held upward-turned feet so that they seemed to walk only on their heels.[32] The Little People of Ghana, West Africa, are known as Asamanukpai. They are slightly bigger than a monkey; coloured black, white or red; and their feet are turned back to front. The older ones are the largest and have beards. They eat and dance on outcrops of smooth rock, which they polish. If you enter their haunts, it is advisable to propitiate them with offerings of rum placed against their dancing-stones and with pans of clear water in which they like to bathe and splash. If they are disturbed or annoyed, they will stone the offender, lead him into the depths of the forest and lose him there. Occasionally, however, they will teach him all they know. They will squeeze into his eyes, ears and mouth the juice of a plant which enables him thereafter to hear everyone's thoughts, to foresee all events, and to sing and talk with the Asamanukpai.[33]

In 1970, a forester called Aarno Heinonen and a farmer called Esko Viljo were out skiing in the woods near Imjarvi, southern Finland, when they came on a strange little man.[34] He was only about a metre tall, with thin arms and legs, a pale waxy face, small ears that narrowed towards the head and he was dressed in green with a conical hat. Aarno felt as if he had been seized by the waist and pulled backwards. Afterwards, his right side felt numb and his leg would not support him – Esko had to drag him home. He attributed these effects to a yellow pulsating light aimed at him from a black box the little man was holding.

This classic elf or fairy had appeared, however, in unfairy-like circumstances: moments before, the two men had been stopped in their tracks by a round craft which hovered above them. Then 'the huge disc began to descend', said Esko, 'so near I could have touched it with my stick'.[35] It sent an intense beam of white light downwards on to the forest floor. It was then that Aarno was pulled backwards. At the same moment he saw the little man standing in the light beam. Eventually the 'craft' gave off a red-grey mist which enveloped both the creature and the men, such that they could no longer see each other. When it dispersed, light, creature and craft had disappeared.

The intriguing thing about this encounter is the way it combines traditional European fairy motifs with modern ufological features, as if it were a transitional species. The so-called extraterrestrials who appeared in conjunction with 'spacecraft' to innocent bystanders in the 1950s were relatively benign; but they became smaller and darker with the passing of the decades until in the 1980s and 1990s there was an epidemic – in the USA, at least – of little grey aliens with skinny bodies and features which were at best rudimentary, apart from their enormous, almond-shaped and completely black eyes.[36] The 'greys' – or 'grays' – as they have come to be known may be a new species of daimon, peculiar to the very Western culture whose orthodox world-view denies the existence of daimons. But it is more likely that they are the old immortal daimons who masquerade in whatever guise suits the times. Banished from their original natural habitats, they return from outside Nature, from 'outer space', brandishing an 'advanced technology' which duplicates the supernatural power of the Sidhe.

2

The Seal-Woman's Skin

FEEDING THE DEAD

No matter how eccentric the aspect of daimons, they tend to appear as beings analogous to humans. But they can appear in three other ways: as the ancestors or the Dead; as animals; or as humans who are witches or witch-doctors, sorcerers or shamans. Each of these three categories can, in one culture or another, play the part of daimons and assume all their attributes; or else overlap with the daimons. For example, the Dead are sometimes seen among the fairies. Someone who has been 'taken' is as likely to have been abducted, taken by the fairies, as to have died, taken by God. In Brittany, the fairies have been completely replaced by the Dead, who are said to be more slender than the living; who have secret paths; who need food to be left out for them; who take people; who shape-shift – all exactly like the fairies.[1]

In traditional societies physical death is not thought of as a breach with the living. Life and death are not opposites; rather, it is birth which is the opposite of death, while life remains continuous. The Dead remain part of the tribe. Our words for describing the Dead – ghost, spirit, shade – distort the sense of the traditional term which is usually just 'dead man'.[2] Death merely signifies a change in the individual; it is only the last in the series of initiatory 'deaths' which have accompanied him or her through life. Just as the living can be considered essentially dead if their soul has been stolen by daimons or eaten by witches, so the Dead are thought of as still active in the community – often to an undesirable extent.[3] In the Far East the Dead often appear as 'hungry ghosts' who have to be fed – appeased and propitiated – in the same way that the

Sidhe have to be fed if they are not to grow importunate and even dangerous. This was especially important at Samhain, now Hallowe'en, when this world and the otherworld draw closer together.

Although literal food may well be left out for the daimons, there is no sense in which they literally need feeding. At most they are said to eat the likeness or essence of the food.[4] Afterwards, the milk or butter left out for the fairies has no nourishment left. The food given to the Dead in what used to be British New Guinea was consumed at the funerary feast; but it was understood that its goodness had been extracted.[5]

Feeding signifies heeding, the attention the daimons demand, and also the kind of vitality peculiar to humans. Sometimes the daimons need stronger stuff than milk and butter. When a Gol'd shaman of Siberia is possessed 'like smoke or vapour' by his daimon lover, his *ayami*, he drinks pig's blood, taboo for everyone else. But it is really the *ayami* who drinks it.[6] We remember too how Odysseus dug a trench and filled it with ox blood before summoning the spirits of the Dead, none of whom was substantial enough to speak until they had each drunk some of the blood.[7] There is always a touch of the vampire about the Otherworld. Daimons are hungry for this world, just as we are hungry for theirs. Not for their food – it is fatal to eat in fairyland or Hades alike lest we become trapped there – but for their psychic nourishment, as if they craved our bodily life as we long for the life of the soul.

The Chinese feed both the Kwei-shins who are the ancestors and those who are the daimons of hills and rivers. But they are explicit about the metaphorical nature of the feeding. The most important food for the ancestors is filial piety; and for the daimons, respect.[8] The 'first dictate of wisdom' according to Confucius, is to 'attend to the affairs of the people, respect the Kwei-shins, and keep them at a distance'.[9] They should be treated, he says, 'with stern dignity, not with undue familiarity'.[10] For there is always this sense that, as Yeats remarked, the fairies do not want too much to be known about them.[11] They are especially dangerous if they see you before you see them.[12]

THE PRINCESS AND THE DEER

It is extremely common for traditional cultures to believe that animals organize themselves into societies which mirror human society. Animals are also the ancestors: tribal clans from Canada to Australia claim descent from bears and seals, say, or kangaroos and wombats. Yet such animals tend in mythology to be anthropomorphized, not exactly animals, not quite humans – in other words, daimons. Indeed, any animal can suddenly seem not *right* as the Irish say – can seem, that is, uncanny. The deer that leads a knight through the forest to the enchanted castle is really the princess who lives there. Whereas the Irish say that such an animal is a fairy in the shape of an animal, it is more commonly believed to be a human being – either a dead one whose spirit has taken animal form, or a living witch or shaman who can change at will into animal form.[13] The strange children, or changelings, whom the fairies leave in exchange for the human child they have taken, are said in many tribal cultures to be the offspring of animals.[14]

Just as the dead man in Melanesia who comes back as a shark[15] is believed to be simultaneously in the land of the Dead, so a witch or shaman can be both at home in his or her hut and also roaming the forest as a wild beast. British witches changed into hares. Their familiars – black cats, for instance – were analogous to the 'spirit-animals' who assist shamans in their business of curing (or cursing). But there was always a sense in which the familiars were the emanation of the witch herself. Humans and animals are interchangeable. It is not so much that a human soul enters an animal; it is more that human and animal are a single being, but present in two places at once, whether as a wereleopard in West Africa, a werejaguar in Brazil,[16] a werewolf in eastern Europe ('wer' is the Anglo-Saxon word for 'man').

The anthropologist Bronislaw Malinowski tried to get to the bottom of Trobriand Island beliefs about witches. Called *yoyova* in everyday life, they became *mulukwansi* when they actively practised witchcraft. He established that they cast off their bodies – or, as they said, 'peeled off their skins' – which remained sleeping in their beds while the witch flew off naked. But he wanted to know more precisely: was it the witch herself who flew away or was it her 'emanation'? What exactly is *mulukwansi* that flies through the air as a firefly or a shooting star? Who is it that stays behind?[17] He never got definite replies to these questions, which I shall shortly be answering.

In the meantime, it is worth remembering that tales of skin-shedding are extremely widespread. For example, all along the northern seaboard of Europe the story is told of the young man who sees a flock of seals swimming towards a deserted shore under a full moon.[18] They step out of their skins to reveal themselves as beautiful young women who dance naked on the sand. The young man steals one of the skins, preventing its owner from resuming her seal form. He marries her and they have children. But she constantly searches for the seal skin her husband has hidden, until at last she finds it. 'One hot day', a Scottish version from North Uist tells us, 'her human child comes to her, saying "O mother, is not this the strange thing I have found in the old barley-kist, a thing softer than mist to my touch." Quickly, deftly, the seal woman put it on and took the straight track to the shore. And, with a dip down and keck up she went, lilting her sea-joy in the cool sea water.'[19]

In West Africa it is crocodiles who, the Toradjas believe, take off their skins when ashore and assume human shape.[20] The Dowayos of Cameroon believe the reverse: sorcerers take off their skins at night to become leopards.[21] Such beliefs are as old as they are widespread. In Norse mythology, for instance, the hero Sigmund and his nephew Sinfiotl find two wolf-skins in the forest and, putting them on, become wolves whose adventures seem to constitute an initiation for Sinfiotl.[22] Skin-shedding is a variation, rich in metaphor, for shape-changing; for it tells us, among other things, that there is only the softest, mistiest skin between this world and the Other.

DAIMON LOVERS

One of the chief expressions of our relationship with the daimonic is marriage. Union with the Dead is usually an unholy business in which, like hungry ghosts, like incubi, they return to drain our vitality or steal our souls, holding us in thrall. Union with animals, on the other hand, is usually fruitful. 'We know what the animals do,' said a Carrier tribesman of the Bulkeley River, '. . . because long ago men married them and acquired this knowledge from their animal wives.'[23]

In myth and folklore, men travel like Orpheus into the Otherworld. They go out of love or desire, voluntarily or in dread. A *leannan sidhe* can lure you against your will into Tir-na-nOg; in Irish mythology Oisin went of his own accord for the love of pearl-pale Niamh.[24] Sigurd, the Norse hero, braved a ring of fire to find the valkyr Brynhild. But just as mermaids and seal-wives can be held in this world, so heroes can remain trapped or enchanted in the otherworld, like Odysseus on Calypso's isle or mighty Heracles at the court of Omphale, queen of Lydia, where he grew soft and timorous and dressed in girl's clothing.

Analytical psychology talks of the need to unite masculine conscious-ness with the feminine unconscious, personified by the anima archetype. Poets talk less abstractly of a muse who is both a seductive source of inspiration and a dangerous, heartless and demanding sorceress. Keats describes her in *La Belle Dame sans Merci* and in *Lamia*. She is the personal daimon who, once awakened, will try to become the centre of the personality. From earliest times, she 'came to the poet as a god, took possession of him, delivered the poem, then left him', writes the poet Ted Hughes feelingly.[25] It was axiomatic, he goes on, that she lived her own life separate from the poet's everyday personality; that she was entirely outside his control; and that she was, above all, supernatural. Both W. B. Yeats and C. G. Jung speak of her in similar terms, as a daimon who ruthlessly had her way with them;[26] whom they had no choice but to follow, often to the detriment of their human life; and whom they struggled with and wooed all their days – 'for man and Daimon feed the hunger in one another's hearts'.[27]

Hughes explicitly relates poets to shamans, and their muses to the female daimons who, in Siberia for example, summon the shaman to his vocation, offer him love and even cohabit with him.[28] Among the Teleuts, the daimon lover like a fairy queen enchants the fledgling shaman with lavish hospitality, including delicious food served on gold and silver dishes. The male Siberian shaman's costume usually incorporates female symbols, while among the Chuckchi, shamans can take on the whole identity of their daimons, dressing as women, doing women's work and using the special language spoken only by women. They may even marry other men. There is a similar tradition of male transvestism among native Americans, who call it *berdache*. 'Among the Navajo the *berdache* is called *nadle* meaning "one who is transformed" . . . When *berdaches* became shamans they were regarded as exceptionally powerful.'[29]

The daimonic realm, then, is sometimes imagined as the Otherworld of the animal kingdom, or of the Dead, or of a separate race, like the Sidhe – but all of them have a reciprocal relationship with this world, expressed through metaphors of nourishing and marriage. Now that the human unconscious has become the locus of the Otherworld, psychotherapists might do well to keep these metaphors in mind: we feed the daimons in order to prevent them becoming unruly, and we maintain a close, even erotic relationship with them so that they need not relate to us by force, taking matters into their own hands. Indeed, the involuntary relationship with the Otherworld – daimonic abduction – is what I want to consider next.

3

Concerning Zombis

THE FATE OF THE REVEREND KIRK

The Reverend Robert Kirk, author of *The Secret Commonwealth*, was taking the air outside his manse at Aberfoyle in Scotland one night in 1692. Dressed only in his nightshirt, he wandered over to a favourite spot nearby – a fairy hill or 'fort'. He was only around fifty at the time, and in good health, but he suddenly collapsed. His body was carried home and in due course buried in Aberfoyle kirkyard.

Some time later, tradition has it, Kirk appeared to one of his relatives and gave him a message for his cousin, Graham of Duchray: Kirk declared that he was not dead but a captive among the fairies. He announced that he would appear again at the christening of the child his wife had borne him after his alleged death. As soon as he was seen, Graham was to throw a knife over him, thus breaking the fairy enchantment and restoring him to this world. Sure enough, while everyone was seated at the table for the christening feast, Kirk appeared. Graham, however, was so astonished that he omitted to throw the knife. Kirk retired, never to be seen again.[1]

The belief that Kirk is in fairyland endured. More than two hundred years later, the woman who kept the key to the churchyard told W. Y. Evans-Wentz, a young American researcher into fairylore, that Kirk's tomb contained a coffin full of stones. Kirk himself, she said, had been taken into the fairy hill, which she pointed out.[2] In 1943, the folklorist Katharine Briggs met a young woman at Methven who had rented the manse at Aberfoyle. Expecting a baby, the woman was anxious to get back to the manse before her baby was born because it was said that, if a baby was born and christened there – and providing a dirk was thrust into the seat of his chair – Kirk could yet be freed from fairyland.[3]

There is a strong intimation here that Kirk paid the price of looking too closely into the affairs of the fairies, who do not wish too much to be known about them.

Although tales of the abduction of mortals by daimons are perhaps most associated with the old Celtic areas, they are universal. But abductees are not always taken, like Kirk, for ever. Here are two accounts from the New World, one native and the other immigrant.

In his book *Myths of the Cherokees* (1901), James Mooney tells the tale of a hunter who discovered in the mountain snows some tiny footprints which the Cherokees had no trouble in identifying as those of the Yunw Tsunsdi. He followed the prints to a cave where little people were dancing and drumming. They took him in, gave him food and a place to sleep, and he stayed there for sixteen days. His friends, who had been searching for him, thought he must have died.

But, Mooney continued, 'after he was well rested, they had brought him a part of the way home until they had come to a small creek about knee deep, when they told him to wade across to reach the main trail on the other side. He waded across and turned to look back, but the Little People were gone, and the creek was a deep river. When he reached home, his legs were frozen, and he lived only a few days.'[4]

A miner called Tom from Bell Island, Conception Bay, Newfoundland, described how his buddy Jimmy had asked him to cover for him at work for ten minutes while he popped into the woods. It was eleven a.m. Jimmy did not come back. Search parties were sent out, the police were involved, everything, for two or three days. On the third day Jimmy reappeared 'a-beaming like an electric light bulb' and claiming to have been gone for only an hour. He had met 'the nicest little people' who 'had food and beer, and danced and played the accordion. Real friendly, he said . . . Yes sir, he was the only one that was ever treated that good by the fairies. But people always thought him a little queer after that. And you know, he swore it was the truth right up until he died. And you know something else, I believe him.'[5]

CHANGELINGS

The Sidhe most often take young adults or babies. A young man from County Donegal called Neil Colton was out picking bilberries with his brother and his female cousin when they heard music. 'We hurried around the rocks, and there we were within a few hundred feet of six or eight of the *gentle folk* [fairies], and they dancing. When they saw us, a little woman dressed all in red came running out from them towards us, and she struck my cousin across the face with what seemed to be a green rush. We ran for home as hard as we could, and when my cousin reached the house, she fell dead. Father saddled a horse and went for Father Regan [the priest]. When Father Regan arrived, he put a stole about his neck and began praying over my cousin and reading psalms and striking her with the stole; and in that way brought her back. He said if she had not caught hold of my brother, she would have been *taken* for ever.'[6]

Death is not as absolute in traditional cultures as it is in Christian, or other monotheistic, societies. It is more like a prolonged stay in the otherworld, and the Dead are always liable to come back in daimonic form. Abductees usually do come back, sometimes after a few hours, sometimes after a few years. Berry-pickers in Newfoundland, for instance, were often led astray by the Good People, to be discovered later in a state of dishevelment, bruising and amnesia[7] – very like those who claim to have been abducted by aliens after a UFO sighting. And like the UFO abductees, the berry-pickers only begin to remember after a time what happened: the unearthly music that lured them in the first place, the dance they were swept up in.[8]

Others returned after a longer time, hardly recognizable or terribly aged, scarred or simple-minded.[9] In Ireland the fairy abductees were sometimes allowed to return to their villages after a while, seven years perhaps, or multiples of seven. But they were only sent back when their years on earth had run out – 'old spent men and women, thought to have been dead a long time, given back to die and be buried on the face of the earth'.[10] The otherworld, whether of the daimons or the Dead, is at certain moments or places transparent to this world.

When babies are taken, changelings are left in their place. Human daimons also take babies: witches traditionally boil them up for salves and potions. But throughout history, whenever a group of people has been thought of as daimonic – marginal, uncanny, alien – it has also been immediately suspected of abducting babies. The Romans' accused the Christians, the Christians accused the Jews, everyone accused the Gypsies.[11] We are always quick to make daimons – and, more often, demons – of other people. It is common for a tribe to attribute to a neighbouring tribe all the activities usually associated with witches, such as baby-eating, incest and the evil eye.[12]

All over the world witchcraft is held responsible for the theft of souls. The victims fall ill, waste away and even die unless a good sorcerer or shaman can be found to travel into the Otherworld and retrieve the lost soul. The Sidhe similarly abduct young adults 'through the eye of a neighbour, the evil eye', perhaps, 'or by a touch, a blow, a fall, a sudden terror'.[13] Those who suffer such a 'stroke' waste away from this world, 'lending their strength to the invisible ones'.[14] A person taken by the Sidhe is said to be *away*. What remains, says Lady Gregory, 'is a body in their likeness, or the likeness of a body'.[15] It may be a log that is left, or a broomstick, or just a heap of shavings.

The Sidhe need human robustness, wrote Yeats,[16] while we need their wisdom. Just as they take young mothers to suckle their babies and young women for wives, so the modern 'aliens' – the so-called greys – take female ova or foetuses in order to strengthen their race.[17] The lack of reciprocity in early versions of this interesting folklore was later amended when it became widely believed that the aliens were in cahoots with the government, who sanctioned their activities in exchange for their 'wisdom' – in this case an advanced extraterrestrial technology.

Thus the motif of abduction by witches, fairies, the Dead – by any sort of daimon – seems to be universal, and even persists in the shadows of our own enlightened culture. Moreover it does not always appear in an obvious way, as my next example shows.

THE *BOKOS'* JARS

In Haiti, the stealing of souls by sorcerers is a crime under the Penal Code and is considered to be murder.[18] A *boko*, or sorcerer, extracts a person's soul by magic or else captures it after natural death. He keeps it in a bottle or jar. But he also – and this is a peculiarly Haitian innovation – steals the body from its tomb and revives it. The body retains its animating principle (*gwo-bon anj*) but has lost its agency, awareness and memory. In short, it has become a zombi which is easily enslaved and put to work in the *bokos'* slave camps. No one ever sees these camps, even though the mountains are said to be as full of *bokos* as any Nature daimons. No one ever stumbles across them, even though the population density of Haiti is very high. Yet these secret camps are believed to exist, holding vast numbers of zombis who cannot escape unless the *boko* dies or the jars containing their souls, or *zombi astrals*, break.

Notwithstanding, up to a thousand zombis are estimated to turn up every year. The population recognizes them immediately by their fixed stare, by their repeated, purposeless and clumsy actions and by their limited repetitive speech. They are objects of pity rather than fear, which is reserved for the *bokos*.

In 1997, Professor Littlewood and Dr Douyon investigated three cases of zombification, including Wilfrid Dorissant, the first zombi to be accredited by a Haitian high court. He escaped from his *boko*'s clutches nineteen months after his death of a sudden fever at the age of eighteen. He returned home as a zombi. He recognized his father and accused his uncle of zombifying him. He was tied to a log to stop him wandering off. Although he has a mannerism which Wilfrid possessed and a broken finger which his mother identified as Wilfrid's, his friends say he is different. He has had 'a change of soul'. His father is convinced that Wilfrid is his son, but says that 'he has lost his soul', as if he also acknowledged some essential change in the boy.[19]

The second case Littlewood and Douyon investigated was that of a woman known as F. I. She died at the age of thirty and was buried the same day in the family tomb next to her house. Three years later a friend recognized her wandering near the village. Her mother confirmed her identity by a facial mark – as did her daughter, siblings, husband and local priest. She could not speak or feed herself. Her husband was accused of zombifying her after she had had an affair. 'After the local court authorized the opening of her tomb, which was full of stones, her parents were undecided whether to take her home . . .'[20] She was placed in a psychiatric hospital in Port-au-Prince. Littlewood examined her and diagnosed catatonic schizophrenia. The people at a market where she was taken on an outing, on the other hand, immediately recognized her as a zombi.

The third case seems to have been solved. A girl called Marie Moncoeur died at the age of eighteen but reappeared thirteen years later, claiming to have been kept as a zombi in a village a hundred miles to the north, only to be released when the *boko* died. She did not seem to people like a typical zombi. She was recognized by her family, and especially by her brother.

When Littlewood and Douyon took her to the village where she claimed to have been kept, she was immediately named as a local woman, known to be simple, who had been abducted by a band of musicians. She was greeted by a daughter and a brother. Both this family and her 'first' family accused each other of zombifying her. DNA 'fingerprinting' suggested that she was related to neither of the men who claimed to be her brothers, but that she was likely to be the mother of the child she said was her daughter.[21]

THE SHADOW OF THE BODY

Later on, I shall describe the way myths, which may look very different from each other on the surface, turn out to be structured in much the same way underneath: they are symmetrical but inverted versions of each other. This is also true of zombi folklore, which is closer to European folklore than it seems.

A zombi's tomb when opened, for instance, is found to contain stones, just like the Reverend Kirk's. Mysterious scars are found on zombis like those found on alien abductees or on those 'touched' by the fairies. A corpse must be decapitated, like a vampire, to prevent it being zombified.

Salt is fatal to fairies and, usually, to the Dead; but it is not mentioned as dangerous to the *bokos*. Instead, it is positively helpful to the zombis – they escape enslavement if they are inadvertently fed it by their *boko* masters.

But zombis also invert the usual order of abductions. Instead of their souls being snatched while their bodies are left behind, their souls remain behind, as it were, in the *bokos'* jars while their bodies are abducted into the Otherworld of the slave camps. When they return they are recognized by strangers who believe they are relations, while, with fairy abductions, the people left behind are strangers, mere 'likenesses' scarcely recognized by their relations. Western culture regards both cases as delusional. Having debunked their literal reality, it is satisfied that they have no reality at all. It therefore misses the deeper reality of abductions which are working out at a collective level the perennial problem of the relationship between soul and body, and which are testimony to the generally held view that the soul is pre-eminent. No one expects a zombi to look like the person they were before the *boko* stole their souls. They are like the 'logs' left behind by the fairies when they steal the essence of the person, just as they steal the essence of food.

It is as if traditional cultures cannot decide whether the soul or the body is taken, or whether both are taken – certainly there is a reluctance to separate them, even while there is a sense that some sort of separation is inevitable. The same conundrum vexed the anthropologist Bronislaw Malinowski. His Trobriand Island witches 'peeled off their skins' and flew away naked. But in Africa there are Basotho who assert that witches in flight simply go in their entirety, both body and soul. The Thonga, however, say that the *noyi* (witch) is only part of the personality. 'When he flies away, his "shadow" remains behind him, lying down on the mat. But it is not truly the body which remains. It appears as such only to the stupid uninitiated. In reality what remains is a wild beast, the one with which the *noyi* has chosen to identify himself.'[22]

Victims of alien abduction usually believe that they were physically taken into a spacecraft by extraterrestrials, but sometimes they describe the event as an out-of-the-body experience. Western esotericists believe in a 'subtle' or 'astral' body, analogous to the 'ghost-body' or 'dream-body' of so many traditional cultures, which is the seat of consciousness in an 'out-of-the-body experience'. It may be that traditional cultures are wise, through their many different versions of such experiences, not to take this sort of body too literally. If you do, you are liable to mistake it for your physical body and so come to believe that you had, for example, been beamed up into a spaceship. On the contrary, it is more usual – almost universal outside our culture – to understand that the physical body is also 'subtle' and that it can therefore easily be taken into the Otherworld because it is not in the first instance a literal thing.

In other words, it is a purely Western peculiarity to confuse the literal and the physical. It is the result of the Christian polarizing of soul and body. Outside Christendom, and other monotheistic religions, the soul is as quasi-material as the body is quasi-spiritual – both forming a daimonic whole. We are fluid organisms, passing easily between this world and the other, between life and death.

We are like the seal-woman whom, in an inversion of fairylore, *we* abduct from *her* world. We do not take her soul and leave her body behind because no such distinction exists for a daimon. We take her 'skin'; and this stands for both soul and body because she is fully herself both with it and without it, but in the first case a seal and in the second, a woman. As traditional cultures suspect, we too may be not so much dual beings as single beings with dual aspects – we differ according to the element we are in. We too are daimonic.

When Christian saints are disinterred and found to have sweet-smelling uncorrupted bodies, the miracle is ascribed to their holiness and purity of life. But the bodies of shamans are similarly said not to decay.[23] Indeed, bad shamans or sorcerers are sometimes only detected after death when, continuing their nefarious activities, they are finally suspected and their bodies dug up – only to be found in a pristine state. In other words, those who traffic with the Otherworld become in some sense immune to death. Their souls continue to flit between worlds while their bodies, if not actually animate, are not actually dead either. They are 'undead', sympathetically echoing the life of the soul.

I shall return to the question of body and soul towards the end of the book, where I discuss the phenomenon known as 'loss of soul'. For the moment I want to consider the realm the daimons are said to inhabit: the Otherworld.

4

St Patrick's Purgatory

St Patrick's Purgatory was one of the most famous places of pilgrimage in Europe during the medieval period. It was a kind of cave, it seems, on an island in Lough Derg, County Donegal, in the north-west of Ireland. Thousands of pilgrims still visit the island every year to do penance. The present Basilica is said to have been built over the original cave which was demolished by Bishop Spottiswoode of Clogher in 1632. He called it 'a poor beggarly hole'.[1] But the earliest accounts represent the cave as 'a kind of pit with steps leading down to a considerable depth'.[2] In 1411, Antonio Mannini described the cave as being three feet by nine feet, and high enough to kneel but not to stand. According to one pilgrim, Knight Owen, who visited it in 1147, the cave appeared small from the outside but was cavernous within. He followed a long dark passageway towards a distant glimmer of light which finally brought him to a vast open cloister. Here he was greeted by fifteen men clothed in white who warned Owen that terrible demons would try to force him to return, but, if he succumbed to their threats, he would die.

Fortunately he is able to resist the demons and is given a tour of the punishments of hell: souls being 'devoured by dragons, set upon by serpents and toads, fixed to the ground with red-hot nails, baked in furnaces, immersed in boiling cauldrons'.[3] He has to walk the Bridge of Three Impossibilities – so high, so narrow, so slippery that it is almost impossible not to plunge into the stinking stream below, filled with tormented souls. On the other side, Owen finds himself in an earthly paradise where souls destined for Heaven are waiting. He is told that however much he wishes to stay, he must return and tell others of his experience. When he is released from the cave after twenty-four hours, he is more dead than alive.[4]

There are many records by pilgrims of visits to the Purgatory. While nothing happened to some of them, others attest to visions like Owen's. Mannini did not talk about his experience, saying only that he was 'marked for ever'. Raymond de Perelhos depicted the Purgatory as a dangerous underground labyrinth from which he was lucky to escape.[5] He also met the Dead, both King John of Arragon [*sic*] and a female relative who had been alive when he left home.[6] A French penitent called Louis de France, who made the pilgrimage in 1385, described his encounter with women of incredible beauty who tried to tempt him. He found them sitting in the shade of a great tree in a great field, playing chess.[7]

Throughout the Middle Ages similar itineraries through purgatory and hell, with a glimpse of paradise, were described – but all by people who had undergone what is nowadays called a Near-Death Experience.[8] The pilgrims to St Patrick's Purgatory underwent nothing of the kind. Mannini spoke, it is true, of having the office of the Dead spoken over him by the Augustinian Canons who took control of the site in 1135. This would have been a recognition of the death-and-rebirth nature of the experience; and it is possible that some kind of trance was induced, analogous to the visionary trances of shamanic initiation. But the legends would have us believe that you walked fully conscious into the Otherworld. This was no more than a continuation of the whole pilgrimage to Ireland which, situated in the extreme west of Christendom, was itself imagined as a kind of purgatory.

St Patrick's Purgatory is particularly fascinating because it represents a unique nexus between the physical and the non-physical, between the literal and the metaphorical and, lastly, between the Christian and the pagan. It is, for instance, the Christian equivalent of those portals into the Otherworld – usually prehistoric tumuli or 'forts' – through which the Sidhe pass.

GATEWAYS TO THE OTHERWORLD

In 1932, an Irish woman from County Longford described how, as a servant-girl, she had been sitting one day with some other girls by the gates to the 'Big House' when she heard the approaching clatter of horsemen. She sprang up at once, saying she must hurry back to the house as there was 'quality' coming, and her help would be needed.

'She had not run far when the party of riders came in sight, eight of them, men and young women, in bright clothes and with coloured bridles and saddles, the girls aside, the men astride, and all laughing and talking gaily. They were no more than forty yards from her when they swung to the right over a grassy bank, across a small field, and into the side of a small thorn-ringed fairy fort. Horses and all, they trotted into the earth as coolly and casually as humans would pass through a stable gate.'[9]

The girl went back to her companions. 'Ah, 'twas no quality at all. 'Twas only a pack of fairies going into the fort.'[10] Her matter-of-fact attitude is striking; a fairy sighting was nothing to wonder at.

Like the caves which are mentioned in Greek myth, and still exist, St Patrick's Purgatory is also a gateway to Hades. Instead of meeting beautiful 'fairy women' within, like the penitent Louis de France, you meet the unhappy Dead or even, like de Perelhos who described the Purgatory as a dangerous place, people you know. But there is always ambiguity surrounding Sidhe-ridden hills, and always an overlap between the daimons and the Dead. For example, Helgafell in Iceland – it means 'holy hill' – is near a natural landmark which resembles a small burial mound and is visible from miles away. One of the early settlers called Thorolf claimed that he and his family would pass into it at death. As it happened, his son Thorstein was lost at sea. Before the news reached the family, a shepherd out at night saw 'the rocky hill standing open with fires burning within, and heard the noise of merrymaking and men drinking together. He thought he saw the dead Thorstein welcomed along with his crew, who had drowned with him . . .'[11]

It is likely that St Patrick's Purgatory was a pre-Christian portal into the Otherworld. Once Christianized, men could enter where once only the Sidhe could pass. But there are of course daimonic men and women who can pass at will into the Otherworld. Perhaps the cave was a place of initiation for Celtic shamans who, if they were at all like other shamans, underwent intense ordeals. Typically, shamans' flesh is devoured by wild animals or is boiled in cauldrons, while new bones are hammered out of iron by unearthly smiths. This is so similar to the pilgrim Knight Owen's description of the souls in purgatory that we see at once that initiation has become, for Christians, punishment. The shaman returns from the dead remade, ready to heal; the Christian-penitent returns shaken at heart, ready to convert others.

WHERE THE DEAD LIVE

The Otherworld begins where this world ends. Traditionally it is imagined as a parallel society of daimons or animals or the Dead. It can be adjacent to us, in the forest or wilderness outside the sacred enclosure of the village. It can be underground, or in the sky, or in the west – or even, like the land of the Sidhe, in all of these places. Indeed, 'it may not be far from any of us'.[12] In Norse mythology there are nine parallel worlds, seven of them inhabited – by gods (Asgard), humans (Midgard), elves (Alfheim), dwarves (Svartalfheim), land- and sea-deities (Vanaheim), giants (Jotunheim) and the unheroic Dead (Hel).

Underworlds are usually balanced by skyworlds, and our human world becomes a middle realm between the two. Above, the gods dwell on Mount Olympus; below, the Dead wander aimlessly about Hades. Above, the Saved sit on the right hand of God the father; below, the Damned wail in torment. Sometimes the Norse cosmos is represented as a world-tree (Yggdrasil), in which case Asgard is placed at the top, Hel at the bottom, with Midgard in between.[13]

All traditional cultures believe that the Dead are living elsewhere, in places as variously located as those of the Sidhe. According to many Africans,[14] the Dead go to a subterranean village where life is easy and abundant. Otherwise they go to a far country to the east, or to the forest surrounding their earthly home. On the other side of the world, in the Torres Straits, the souls of the Dead typically go to an unknown island in the west; or to a place in the earth's interior; or to one of three spirit worlds.[15] Sometimes the Dead are held to go simultaneously to the 'underworld' and to 'heaven', in exactly the same way that Heracles (the Latin Hercules) was simultaneously promoted to Mount Olympus and sent down to storm gloomily around Hades.

The Otherworld of Christianity differs from the traditional realm in two main respects, both of which reflect the divisive tendency of monotheism. Firstly, just as it polarized the daimons into angels and devils, so it polarized the Otherworld into Heaven and Hell; and secondly, it removed the Otherworld altogether from the world to a transcendent Heaven beyond even the sky and a less important, vaguely subterranean Hell.

Moreover, the only way to enter the Christian Otherworld is by death. It may be possible to catch a glimpse of the afterlife, but only in exceptional circumstances such as a Near-Death Experience or by visiting St Patrick's Purgatory. The very term 'afterlife' is distinctively Christian. For pagans, life is continuous between this world and that Otherworld which may be above or below us, but never breaks entirely with this world as the Christian Otherworld seems to have done.

HEL AND VALHALLA

In traditional cultures, there is a widespread fear of being without enough *mana*, enough personal power to join the glorious ancestors who hunt and feast and dance in the Otherworld. Amongst the Greek heroes there was a dread of dying other than heroically, in battle, because it meant that you did not join your peers in the beautiful Elysian Fields but eked out your eternal life as a grey shade in the cold halls of Hades. Similarly, the Norse heroes who did not fall in battle were condemned to the dreary underworld presided over by the giantess Hel, instead of journeying to the halls of Valhalla where their fellow heroes made merry.

Christianity replaced the idea of the outstanding man with the idea of the good man, and its Otherworld is correspondingly determined by ethics: Heaven is not where the glorious hero goes by right, but the reward of the good. Hell meanwhile is a punishment of the sinful rather than the repository of the mediocre.

Christianity imagines the Otherworld as the opposite of this world. This is true of all cultures. 'One feature nevertheless is almost unvarying. The world of the Dead is the exact reverse of that of the living.'[16] For example, the sun and the moon typically travel in opposite directions; the Dead go head first downstairs and their language means the opposite of ours; their canoes, say the Inuit, float below the water, bottom uppermost; like the realm of the Sidhe, their summer is our winter; their day is our night, and that is why it is dangerous to go out at night when they are abroad.[17]

The idea of reversal points to the ambiguity of the Otherworld. It takes on its character in reciprocal relation to this world. If we think of this world as full of suffering and uncertainty, the Otherworld is a 'happy hunting ground' where we live in abundance and without care. Conversely, the Otherworld can seem a cold and joyless place when compared with the rich, sensuous life of this world.

In psychological terms, it is as if the Otherworld is determined by the attitude we bring to it and the view we take of it. To someone as passionately attached to this world as the Greek hero Achilles, 'we who are parted from earthly life have the strongest desire to return to it again'.[18] So he tells Odysseus who has summoned his shade back from beyond the grave. But to someone who communes with the Otherworld as deeply as William Blake, this world seems shadowy in comparison. To the orthodox Christian, wrote Blake, the 'joys of genius' in the Otherworld seem like 'devils and hellfire'.[19]

In his early poems, W. B. Yeats depicted fairyland as a realm of eternal beauty and the abduction of humans there as a desirable escape from mundanity. But this view is at odds with a more traditional one, in which abductees are loth to go and glad to return.[20] While Yeats recreates the realm of the Sidhe in all its sumptuousness, tradition offers little description of time spent with the fairies compared to the detailed accounts of the abductees' departure and return.[21] Yeats's poetry mentions no anxiety on the part of the parents or relations; but there are many descriptions of 'tradition-bearers weeping, sometimes after the passage of many years, as they narrated memorates [remembered events] dealing with the abduction of their children or other relatives'.[22] As one of Lady Gregory's informants concludes: 'This world's the best.'

PLATO'S CAVE

The dual fate of Heracles after death, dwelling simultaneously on high with the gods and below in Hades, reflects the Greek notion that we have two different kinds of soul. *Thymos* is warm, emotional and red-blooded; while *psyche* is colder, deeper and more impersonal.[23] From *thymos'* point of view, the Otherworld is the cold, grey, unsubstantial Hades full of 'pottering shades, querulous beside the salt-pits/And mawkish in their wits'.[24] From *psyche*'s perspective, it is our robust, red-blooded world which is unreal, while Hades who was called *Plouton* (Pluto), the Rich One, holds all the treasures of the imagination. The shades are not dim ghosts to *psyche*, but mythic images that erupt out of the Underworld like the laughing Sidhe, their silver eyes flashing. We can begin to understand what Heraclitus meant when he remarked that 'Dionysus and Hades are one.'[25] The god of creative life has a secret affinity with death.

Thymos has been assimilated into the robust ego-consciousness of Western man who believes in no reality other than his own. From the deeper psychic viewpoint, however, ego-consciousness is – as the Neoplatonists noticed[26] – a kind of unconsciousness. We are unaware of reality, claim the Romantics, except in moments of imaginative vision. The Otherworld lies all about us, an earthly paradise – if we would but cleanse 'the doors of perception', as Blake put it, and see the world as it really is, 'infinite'.[27]

Plato illustrated the unreality of our normal perception of the world by an extended analogy. We are like people in a cave, he says, who sit facing a wall with a fire burning behind them.[28] As people and objects pass to and fro in front of the fire, we see only their shadows, and the shadows of ourselves, as they are cast on the wall. We mistake these shadows for reality. (It is as if we mistake a film at the cinema for reality.) To achieve a truer perception of reality we have to turn around – to revert our point of view – and see both the fire and the objects in front of it directly. This is perhaps as close to reality as most of us ever come.

Yet even then we are still a long way from reality because we believe that the fire is the only source of illumination. The true philosopher goes further: he leaves the cave and sees the world in the light of the sun. It may look strange at first, and even unreal, until his eyes grow accustomed to the very different kind of light; but at last he sees this Otherworld truly and can turn and look directly at the sun, the source of all light. The allegory expresses the mental darkness in which we normally live, mistaking shadows for reality, unaware of the substance of things, mistaking light for enlightenment, ignorant of the real world presided over by the one divine Illuminator.

5

The Soul of the World

One of the distinctive innovations of Western thought has been to turn the Otherworld into an intellectual abstraction. It has been formulated in three main ways: as the Soul of the World; as the imagination; and as the collective unconscious. The latter two models of the Otherworld have the added eccentricity of locating it within us.

Historically, all three models have been largely ignored or outcast by Western orthodoxy, whether Christian theology or modern rationalism. But wherever they have as it were broken the surface and emerged from their 'esoteric' or even 'occult' underworld, they have been accompanied by extraordinary efflorescences of creative life. In Renaissance Florence, and again, among the German and English Romantics three hundred years later, imagination was exalted not only as the most important human faculty, but as the very ground of reality.

PRIMARY IMAGINATION

The parallel world of the Irish fairies was, for Yeats, synonymous with imagination.[1] He does not want, that is, to see imagination as a kind of abstract faculty which enables us vaguely to conjure up images of things which are not present to the senses. He means something almost the opposite by imagination: a whole world, peopled by fierce daimons, which has a life of its own. This is the defining characteristic of that imagination we call Romantic.

Yeats had been especially struck by William Blake, whose works he had spent years editing. For Blake seemed to have retained that traditional visionary view of the world which enabled him to see angels in a tree or a heavenly host in the sun; at the same time he entertained a complex and sophisticated notion of imagination as man's primary mode of grasping the world. This was something he shared with other great Romantic poets – Wordsworth, Keats, Shelley and above all Coleridge, who famously proclaimed:

The Primary Imagination I hold to be the living power and prime agent of all human perception, and is a repetition in the finite mind of the eternal act of creation in the infinite I AM . . .[2]

The only concern of the Primary Imagination, wrote another poet, W. H. Auden, is with sacred beings and events.[3] They cannot be anticipated, he says – they must be encountered. Our response to them is a passion of awe. It may be terror or panic, wonder or joy, but it must be awe-ful. Auden's sacred beings and events are our daimons, archetypal images which Imagination generates. They are chiefly personifications but Imagination can, of course, like fairy glamour, cast its spell over any object so that we suddenly see it as ensouled, as a *presence*, as if it were a powerful living person.

It must be emphasized that Imagination in the poetic, Romantic, true understanding is pretty much the opposite of what it has come to mean – something unreal and invented, what Coleridge called 'fancy'. 'The nature of Imagination is very little known', lamented Blake, '& the Eternal nature and permanence of its ever Existent Images is considered as less permanent than the things of Vegetative and Generative Nature.'[4] Yes, Imagination is independent and autonomous; it precedes and underpins mere perception; and it spontaneously produces those images – gods, daimons and heroes – who interact in the unauthored narratives we call myths.

This view of a mythopoeic – a myth-making – Imagination is so foreign to all but the most Blakean of us that it may help further to return to its prototype among the Neoplatonists. Like Plato, they understood that daimons are intermediate between mortals and gods; but they developed this insight, recognizing a whole daimonic state, partly physical and partly spiritual, which mediated between our sensory material world and the spiritual or 'intelligible' world of Forms – those abstract gods that provide the ideal models for everything that exists.

This intermediate world was called *Psyche tou Kosmou*, the Soul of the World – although it was better known in Latin-speaking Europe as *Anima Mundi*. It is where the daimons come from. Sometimes it was imagined hierarchically, with the intelligible world of the gods above and our world below – but all three emanating from an unknowable source simply called the One. At other times it was thought of as a single, dynamic realm with two aspects: one intelligible (spiritual) and one sensory (material). And this is how the Western esoteric tradition has generally pictured it. All Neoplatonists, Hermetic philosophers, alchemists and Kabbalists have asserted that the cosmos is animated by a collective soul which manifests now spiritually, now physically, now – daimonically – both at once; but which above all connects and holds all phenomena together. This is the true orthodoxy, they say, from which the erroneous orthodoxy of what the philosopher A. N. Whitehead has called 'the last three provincial centuries' has deplorably lapsed.

THE ANIMATED WORLD

According to the Neoplatonic tradition, *psyche* or soul is the underlying principle – the very stuff – of reality. It is, as we have just seen, ambiguous. It is imagined both as a macrocosm, 'great world', and as a microcosm, 'little world'. It is both a collective world-soul, containing all daimons, images, souls, including the human soul; and an individual soul containing a profound collective level, in which we are connected to each other and, indeed, to all living things. Depending on our perspective, then, we can see ourselves as either embracing the Soul of the World or as being embraced by it, although both are the case. Or we might say that soul manifests itself both impersonally, as world-soul, and personally as individual souls. At any rate, we can begin to see that the ancient laws of sympathy and correspondence which modern science has discredited are not primitive scientific laws at all, but profound psychic principles which express the way each microcosm – each of us – potentially reflects and participates in the entire cosmos.

In Plato's *Timaeus*, where the Soul of the World is first described, it is infused throughout the cosmos by the Demiurge, Plato's creator-god, who thus makes a living ensouled universe. (The Soul of the World remains the root metaphor for all conceptions of the world as organism, including modern ecological ideas.) In other words, as well as being transcendent, one level above our world, the Soul of the World is also immanent, just as traditional cultures imagine it. Not that they always have a concept for the world-soul – they do not abstract from the world but rather see it in the first instance as animate, instinct with soul. 'All things', according to the ancients, from Thales to Plutarch, 'are full of gods.'[5]

The very people who have emptied Nature of soul and reduced it to dead matter obeying mechanical laws, pejoratively call the traditional world-view *animism* – a term which effectively writes off what it claims to describe. To 'animistic' cultures there is no such thing as animism. There is only Nature presenting itself in all its immediacy as daimon-ridden. Every sacred object or place had its genius or jinn, numen or naiad, yes, even its boggart and hob, as the case may be.

The Romantics imagined Nature in this way. Imagination was co-extensive with Creation, just like the Soul of the World. They were identical. Every natural object was both spiritual and physical, as if dryad and tree were the inside and outside of the same thing. Thus every rock and tree was ambivalent: a daimon, a soul, an image. 'To the eyes of a man of Imagination', wrote William Blake, 'Nature is Imagination itself.'[6]

THE COLLECTIVE UNCONSCIOUS

The Soul of the World and Imagination are models of the same daimonic reality. Another model, and the most recent, emerged from depth psychology. Freud had already discovered the subconscious, the repressed contents of which appeared in his patients as recalcitrant symptoms. But these patients were neurotics, and their symptoms could be traced to some event in their personal history. One of Freud's followers, however – C. G. Jung – was treating patients who were more deeply disturbed, psychotic or schizophrenic. He noticed in their fantasies features that could on no account be explained by their personal lives – fragments of some arcane mythology, for instance – and concluded that there was a deeper level of the unconscious which was truly collective, common to us all.

Actually, as he later revealed in his autobiography, this insight was derived just as much from his own experience as from his patients'. In his late thirties Jung had been suddenly overwhelmed by a spate of violent and uncontrollable images, flooding up into his mind from the unconscious and threatening to drown him in a psychosis. He fought them off as long as he could, until he was forced to give in. He sat at his desk, closed his eyes and let himself go. He had the physical sensation of the ground giving way, of plunging into dark depths where he encountered, not the madness he expected, but . . . a *myth*. A mummified dwarf, a red crystal in a cave, a beautiful dead youth, a black scarab, a tide of blood – Jung recognized that he was participating in a Hero myth, 'a drama of death and renewal' which related not just to him but to the fate of Europe on the eve of the First World War.[7]

Jung initially conceived of the psyche as structured like a pyramid, or as a system of concentric circles: the ego was at the apex (or at the centre) with the 'field' of consciousness just below (or surrounding) it. Below consciousness comes the unconscious, which consists of two levels, the personal and the collective. The personal unconscious – Freud's subconscious – contains all those contents which can be retrieved at will by memory, and those which cannot – because they have been repressed. The more contents are denied conscious expression, the more deeply they are alienated from consciousness, sinking deeper and deeper until they become autonomous *complexes*. They assume, that is, a personality of their own which exerts an influence over us without our being aware of it. They can even erupt into consciousness and 'possess' it, as in the case of the psychosis which Jung himself had feared.

ARCHETYPES

Ego (Hero), persona, shadow, anima, animus, puer (eternal youth), senex (old wise man), trickster, Great Mother, significant animal, healer, divine child, self – this list just about covers the archetypes that Jung discovered in the collective unconscious. Like their historical precedents, Kant's *a priori* categories and Plato's Forms, they are abstract entities which never-theless constitute the substrate of reality. The archetypes are, said Jung, unknowable in themselves; but, paradoxically, they can be known because they manifest themselves in images. Unlike the complexes, these images cannot be traced back to our personal history; nor do they result from repression because they have never been conscious. They are, said Jung, 'endowed with personality at the outset'. They 'manifest themselves as *daimones*, as personal agencies . . . felt as actual experiences'.[8]

Thus the archetype of the anima, unknowable in herself, appears as a myriad female images, from nymph to *femme fatale* to crone and so on. The self (or Self) archetype, which represents the goal of psychic development – what Jung called individuation – might appear as a god, a tree, a circular pattern (mandala) or as a syzygy – a union of male and female, such as an old father and young daughter. The Neoplatonists put much of this more succinctly when they said that the gods who are in themselves 'formless and unfigured' appear as daimons, many of whom are different images of the same god.[9] Since Creation myths always place the gods prior to mankind, it seems just as likely that the gods imagine us as that we imagine them. And this is what Jung claimed for the archetypes: 'All we know is that we seem unable to imagine without them . . . If we invent them, then we invent them according to the patterns they lay down.'[10]

The archetypes do not only manifest as single images; they also appear as those structures and patterns which form the recurring motifs of every mythology, such as the death and rebirth of the hero, the quest for hidden treasure, the journey to the underworld and the abduction of a mortal by a god. Understanding that myths are the true stories of the soul, Freud drew instinctively on myth, notably that of Oedipus, when he wanted to describe the dynamics of the psyche. Jung went a step further and realized that *all* myths are alive in the collective unconscious. We may talk about the ego's struggle to break free of the matrix of the id; or the child's striving for independence from the mother; or the hero's slaying of the dragon – they are all variants of the same archetypal pattern. Like the daimons who inhabit them, myths shape-shift, cutting their cloth to suit the times. 'Mythology is a psychology of antiquity. Psychology is a mythology of modernity.'[11]

Jung's hierarchical scheme of the psyche looks much like the Neoplatonic cosmos, except that it is located inside us. He is describing the microcosm which mirrors the macrocosm. Sometimes he depicts it as geological strata; at others, as the successively 'older' layers of the brain; or as the floors of a house. He himself dreamt of discovering in his own 'house' prehistoric bones buried under the cellar floor, an image of the collective unconscious foundations on which our psyches are built.[12]

However, like the Neoplatonic scheme, the psyche is not really as static a hierarchy as Jung, attempting clarity, makes it sound. It is more like a dynamic flux, more like the parallel realm of daimons and gods who merge seamlessly into each other, in the same way as do the personal and collective unconscious, the complexes and the archetypes. As any analytical psychologist will attest, within a patient's affliction or symptom 'is a complex, within the complex an archetype, which in turn refers to a god'.[13] No fantasy or dream image is so personal that it has no archetypal content; no daimonic encounter or epiphany is without some trace of the personal.

Levels, layers, strata – these metaphors for the unconscious smack of that orderliness which consciousness wants to impose on an unconscious that has its own order. Its spontaneous representation of itself, in dreams and fantasies, is always by concrete images – an ocean, an abyss, a riotous party, a tidal wave, a dim primeval forest, a lunatic asylum.[14] In the Orient, it may be a river, forever changing, always the same; or a god, like Shiva, who dances the universe into existence. At the Renaissance it was often Proteus, offspring of the sea-god Poseidon, who took on any shape he pleased. For the old Gnostics it was the night sky itself, in which they saw a majestic series of bright spheres guarded by powerful daimons through which the soul, made ecstatic by fasting and prayer, journeyed back to its source in the One. Indeed, the cosmos which every culture inhabits is a self-portrait of its soul.

Given the affinity between the Romantic Imagination and Jung's collective unconscious, it is unsurprising that the post-Jungians who style themselves archetypal psychologists should make imagination the cornerstone of their thought and practice. Following the scholar of Sufism, Henri Corbin, they have adopted the word *imaginal* (from *mundus imaginalis*, 'imaginal world') to describe that in-between reality which Jung calls *psychic* and which I have been calling daimonic.

The leading archetypal psychologist, James Hillman, identifies the founder of his psychology as the pre-Socratic philosopher Heraclitus, who was the first to characterize soul by its depth. 'You could not find out the boundaries of soul [*psyche*]', he wrote, 'even by travelling along every path: so deep a measure does it have.'[15]

Hillman relates imagination unequivocably to soul. Soul is not a substance, he says, but a set of perspectives. It is 'the imaginative possibility in our natures, the experiencing through reflective speculation, dream, image and fantasy – that mode which recognizes all realities as primarily symbolic or metaphorical'.[16] Soul has no existence apart from the images by which it manifests itself; yet, in another sense, all existence is soul because 'to be in soul is to experience the fantasy in all realities and the basic reality of fantasy . . . In the beginning is the image: first imagination then perception; first fantasy then reality . . . we are indeed such stuff as dreams are made on.'[17]

DREAMING

Archetypal psychology helps us to understand that otherworld journeys are not the exclusive preserve of Romantic poets, Siberian shamans or alien abductees. We all have access every night to the Otherworld – through sleep. Like the daimons it contains, the Otherworld of dreams is shifting, elusive and ambiguous. Dreams take the stuff of our waking days and, in a work of pure imagination, transform it into imagery. That dreams are no longer regarded as being of crucial importance is a result of the very strength of our waking, Heraclean consciousness. They flee like Hades' shades from its muscular efforts to drag them up into daylight. They expire under the spotlight of analysis and interpretation.

Both Freud and Jung were guilty of translating dreams into 'waking language';[18] Hillman, on the other hand, insists on letting the dream be, on observing it in its natural twilight habitat, on attending deeply to it – but not extracting a message from it according to the presuppositions of the daylight world. 'For a dream image to work in life it must, like a mystery, be experienced fully as real. Interpretation arises when we have lost touch with the images . . .'[19]

Dream images have nothing to do with our normal sense images, so we cannot truly perceive them in the normal sensory way. We have to perceive them with the same psychic consciousness of which they are themselves composed – and this means perceiving with the imagination. Better still, 'we imagine rather than perceive them, and we cannot perceive with sense perception the depths that are not extended in the sense world'.[20] Thus a dream image may be ambiguous and fleeting in one way – visually, perhaps – but, in another way, it is always concrete and definite, even if only as a distinct sensation or powerful feeling.[21] A dream's vagueness, then, is as much a part of it as any overt content – the *way* a dream comes is part of its expression. Its ambiguity therefore needs no resolution. 'Do what we will, the dream presents itself in the robes of duplicity', writes Hillman in *The Dream and the Underworld*. 'If dreams are the teachers of the waking-ego, *this duplicity is the essential instruction they impart* . . . In fact, duplicity is a basic law of imagination . . .'[22]

If we should avoid interpreting our dreams, we should not be afraid to amplify them imaginatively, through association for example, and, above all, by *epistrophé* – a 'turning back' through likeness to the dream's archetypal background. We should ask ourselves: 'What archetype is at work in our unconscious? What god is covertly influencing our lives? What myth are we living without realizing it?'[23] The act of using the dream to see through the literal appearance of our waking lives to the larger imaginative narratives in which we live, releases us from whatever patterns we are stuck in. It is intrinsically healing and liberating for the soul to be told the stories, the myths, of its tribe.

When Tertullian wrote that 'it is to dreams that the majority of mankind owe their knowledge of God',[24] he was voicing the widespread belief among Christians and pagans alike that dreams are daimonic, mediating between us and the gods. This means that the images – for instance of friends and family – we meet in dreams are not literal. They do not refer exclusively to their waking counterparts. 'In dreams we are visited by the *daimones*, nymphs, heroes and Gods, shaped like our friends of last evening.'[25] Just as in Homer, the god can appear in the guise of a living friend.[26]

Nor are the dream people exclusively expressions of our own psyches:

'They are shadow images that fill archetypal roles; they are personae, masks, in the hollow of which is a *numen*.'[27] The reason the daimons do not appear as such, but disguise themselves as the friends of last evening is, says Hillman, that these dream persons are necessary for soul-making: 'They are necessary for the work of seeing through, of de-literalizing. Without any friends of last evening, a dream would be a direct communication with spirits. A dream is not a vision, however, as the psyche is not the spirit.'[28]

6

Inside Out

IN SEARCH OF TIR-NA-NOG

When Plato speaks of the daimons conveying the wishes of the gods to men 'whether in the waking or the sleeping state',[1] he is making no distincton between visions and dreams. Indeed the Greeks did not think of dreams as a private, internal matter. They always spoke of *seeing* a dream, not of *having* one, as we do.[2]

What we call the unconscious was, to the Greeks, the Otherworld. Although they understood that daimons might be encountered as inner impulses – fear, hope and jealousy for instance were considered daimons[3] – they tended to locate the daimons' Otherworld outside themselves.

Conversely, like all psychologists, Jung located the Otherworld exclusively within us, as the unconscious – until he was compelled by experience to conclude that 'there may well be a psyche "outside-the-body", a region so utterly different from *my* psychic sphere that one has to get out of oneself . . . to get there'.[4] He re-imagined the unconscious as an 'alien country outside the ego', an Otherworld of gods, ancestors and daimons just as traditional cultures describe. If it is within us, it is also as if, were we to travel deeply enough within, the unconscious turns inside out. 'At bottom', said Jung, ' "psyche" is simply the "the world" '.[5]

The whole debate about whether the unconscious is inside us or outside is a distraction. When Plato's Demiurge created the world, he did not create space. He found it already existing.[6] This is a metaphor for the fact that we cannot depict daimonic reality without space – without, that is, a spatial metaphor. Even those Christian mystics who denied all images in their desire for the unimaginable God, nevertheless

45

imagined His abode as an abyss of darkness, like a bottomless 'inner space'.

The unconscious, soul, imagination – whatever model we use – are in themselves non-spatial, just as they are timeless. Like the Hermetic definition of God they are each 'an intelligible sphere whose centre is everywhere and whose circumference is nowhere'. But in order to discuss them at all we find ourselves falling back on spatial metaphors, calling the unconscious for instance an 'inner realm' or 'an alien country outside the ego'. But the unconscious is not a literal place. Images are not 'contained' in it; images are the unconscious – 'image *is* "psyche" ',[7] said Jung – just as daimons do not literally 'inhabit' the Soul of the World, but are the many faces soul shows to us. The unconscious is itself an image, a metaphor for deliteralizing, and a tool for deconstructing, our conscious viewpoints so that we come to understand that the world we imagine we are in is only one among many ways the world can be imagined.

Now we can see the wisdom of traditional cultures which variously locate their Otherworlds, like the land of the Sidhe, underground or in the air, under the sea or on islands out to the west. Multi-spatiality stands for non-spatiality. This is why the Otherworld is perhaps the best metaphor for daimonic reality: it does not, like the idea of the unconscious, force us to imagine any literal and thus exclusive location, such as within us.

The Otherworld lies, as it were, all around us, at the points where our world ceases. It lies beyond the edge of maps where 'there be dragons', or below the threshold of consciousness where there be archetypes. It can be imagined as a subterranean Underworld or as a celestial Heaven, a past Arcadia or a future Utopia. For a child it can begin in the cupboard under the stairs.

The Otherworld exists precisely to define this world. We may locate it in another culture or class, in the city or in the country, in a book or in a drop of pond water under the microscope. In a sense, every person is an Otherworld to every other. And every Otherworld may be heavenly or horrible – but it must be utterly absorbing, wholly enchanting.

HOW THE UNCONSCIOUS BEGAN

The question of how the Otherworld became situated inside us – the question, that is, of how the unconscious arose – is one of central interest to this book. While the term 'unconscious' was unknown before Descartes,[8] the idea of the unconscious is at least as old as the first Neoplatonists.

Plotinus recognized that the psyche can be conscious at one level and unconscious at another, and that it has memories of which it is unconscious.[9] He was also 'the first to make the vital distinction between the total personality (*psyche*) and ego-consciousness (*emeis*)'.[10] Whatever was not attached to the ego was temporarily or permanently unconscious; but there was constant traffic between ego and unconscious.

At the beginning of the seventeenth century, however, there emerged a new kind of consciousness, which I shall be examining more thoroughly at a later stage. Its novelty lay in two extraordinary claims: firstly it asserted that it was entirely separate from the world, which henceforth was to be regarded as exclusively outside us – it was the subject in relation to which everything else was an object. Secondly, it claimed to be the whole of the psyche, effectively denying the existence of the unconscious.

If Descartes was not wholly responsible for this double act of polarization, he was its spokesman. He called the new subjective consciousness, Mind, and the objective world, Extension.[11] Instead of the old interaction of microcosm and macrocosm, of human psyche and world, where each reflected the other's oceanic richness with marvellous congruence, we are left with an inner world diminished to mere consciousness, and cut off from a stark and soulless outer world.

The new consciousness was centred around a subject, an *ego* as we now call it, which was so narrow, so focused, so bright, that it threw the rest of the psyche into deep shadow. All the twilight intercourse between consciousness and the unconscious ceased. From the ego's point of view, the unconscious did not exist. From its own point of view, of course, the unconscious existed more profoundly, more darkly, sealed off as it was from direct expression through consciousness. Its stifled cries were not heard for three hundred years, when they came to light in the psychologists' consulting-rooms. Indeed, psychology was founded specifically to disinter this buried part of the psyche; or we might say that the suppressed unconscious grew so importunate that we were compelled to invent psychology in order to contain it.

From the daimonic outlook, the situation could be simply put thus: banished from the outer world, soul and its daimons were forced to take refuge in the only place left to them – the human psyche. But this inner world had in turn been straitened to a brilliant but inhospitable consciousness, compelling them to hide in the darkness behind. The unconscious was filled with the outcast daimons – except that they did not so much fill it as form it. The modern unconscious was created by the new ego-consciousness's separation of itself from the rest of the psyche and from the world at large. Although I have described this separation as two different movements, they are really one because, as Jung noticed, psyche *is* the world. To cut oneself off from psyche, soul, the unconscious, is also to become estranged from Nature.

PISHOGUE AND GLAMOUR

Ever since the triumph of Cartesian dualism, Western philosophy has been preoccupied with the problem of the relationship between subject and object – how can I, as subject, know a thing, as object? Is my knowledge real? Is there an objective reality separate from my subjective perception? Valiant attempts have been made to solve the problem by the same philosophical tradition that created the problem in the first place (a combination of Kant and Wittgenstein might do the trick), but it may be easier to dissolve the problem altogether.

In the daimonic tradition subject and object are not placed in polar opposition. A subject can be distanced from an object while yet remaining connected to it. The subtle distinction between *pishogue* and *glamour* in Irish fairylore embodies a sophisticated epistemology.[12] Pishogue is an enchantment placed on us so that we see an object differently. Glamour is an enchantment placed on an object so that it appears differently to us. The locus of reality is shifted between subject and object as if, lying now more with us, now more with the world, it finally lies in-between.

But this is nothing other than the movement of the Romantic imagination. Wordsworth wanders lonely as a cloud and comes across a host of daffodils, 'tossing their heads in sprightly dance', which, later, 'flash upon that inward eye/Which is the bliss of solitude'.[13] Blake asks himself the question: 'When the Sun rises, do you not see a round disk of fire somewhat like a Guinea?' 'O no, no,' he replies, 'I see an Innumerable company of the Heavenly host crying "Holy, Holy, Holy is the Lord God Almighty." '[14]

For Wordsworth, Imagination is like pishogue: when he looks at his golden daffodils, it is as if he sees a host of fairy dancers concealed within. For Blake, it is like glamour: when he sees a heavenly host of angels, it is as if he is looking at the golden sun outwardly revealed.

PEER GYNT AND THE TROLLS

This Life's dim Windows of the Soul
Distorts the Heavens from Pole to Pole
And leads you to Believe a Lie
When you see with, not thro', the eye.[15]

These lines of Blake's pinpoint the fundamental shortcoming of the modern post-Cartesian consciousness: its literalism. To see with the eye alone is to see the world as if in single vision, as two-dimensional only, as literal. To see the world through the eye is to cultivate what Blake called 'double vision',[16] which perceives in greater depth, beyond the literal to the metaphorical. Single vision sees the sun only as the sun; double vision sees it also as a heavenly host. We need double vision to see daimons – to see that they are real, but not literally so. Unfortunately we have become so literal-minded that the only reality we recognize is literal reality which, by definition, rules out daimons.

Reality is far from being intrinsically literal. It is literalized by the peculiar perspective of our modern consciousness. It is peculiar because it is the only perspective which insists that it is not a perspective at all but a true vision of the actual world. It has in fact lost perspective because 'perspective' means 'seeing through', and it fails to see through itself. So forceful is the literalism of our world-view that it is almost impossible for us to grasp that it is exactly that – a view, and not the world. But it is this literalism, with all its claims to hard factuality, wherever its presence is least suspected, which I shall be attempting to dissolve throughout this book.

Moreover, literalism divides double vision into *polar* vision – it not only literalizes this world but also, as it were, the Otherworld. In Ibsen's play *Peer Gynt*, the eponymous hero – the very type of a poet – is captured by trolls and taken to their mountain lair. The king of the trolls extols the virtues of troll vision which, for example, sees beautiful maidens instead of cows. If Peer were to have a simple eye operation his eyesight too could be changed into troll vision. Peer indignantly refuses. 'He is perfectly willing, he says, to swear that a cow is a beautiful maiden, but to be reduced to a condition in which he could not tell one from the other – that he will never submit to.'[17]

Peer refuses to give up the double vision of the poet. For to see cows always as beautiful maidens is like being able to see only the heavenly host and not the sun. In both cases we are as much victims of single vision, of literalism, as we are when we see cows only as cows – devoid of meaning and metaphorical possibilities.

SALVATION THROUGH SCIENCE

We cannot see the world except through some perspective or imaginative framework – in short, some myth. Indeed, the world we see is the myth we are in. We have a choice of what myth we will look through but we do not have a choice of no myth at all. It is extremely difficult to become aware of the fact that the world is actually our map or picture of the world – difficult to see through our own perspective. But if we do not, we remain blindly in one version of the world. Literalism is a blindness of this kind.

And so, the early scientific ideal of a pure empiricism, an entirely neutral fact-gathering, was neither possible nor even desirable: science simply could not take place without some principle of selection among facts, some mental map. The scientists who ridiculed the notion of stones falling out of the sky or of continents moving about lacked a map of the world that could accommodate meteorites or the idea of continental drift. In such cases the maps are eventually altered. The danger arises when we refuse to alter the map.

James Lovelock recounts the scandal of how, despite the vast sums of money spent on satellites, balloons and aircraft measurement, scientists nevertheless failed to predict or find the hole in the ozone layer. Their instruments were actually programmed to 'reject data that was substantially different from model predictions. The instruments saw the hole, but those in charge of the experiment ignored it, saying in effect, "Don't bother us with facts; our model knows best." '[18] Here we see science becoming scientism, whose map of the world has become the world.

Scientism can be roughly described as a combination of logical positivism – which rejects metaphysical speculation and holds that no statement is meaningful that cannot be empirically verified; and materialism – by which I mean, of course, the philosophical doctrine that matter is the only reality.

Even so, these philosophies are not enough in themselves to constitute scientism because many ordinary scientists who make quite modest claims for science routinely subscribe to them. Rather it is the extension of these philosophies into areas which do not properly concern them which defines scientism. It is the idea, says Mary Midgley, of *'salvation through science alone'* (her italics).[19]

For example, now that we have modern biology, opines Richard Dawkins, 'we no longer have to resort to superstition when faced with the deep problems; Is there a meaning to life? What are we for?'[20] 'Our goal', writes Stephen Hawking, meaning the goal of science, 'is nothing less than a complete description of the universe we live in.'[21]

Scientists are not generally trained in, or good at, philosophical reflection, so perhaps we should be lenient towards these opinions, pausing only to remind Dawkins and Hawking that it is doubtful that there can ever be 'a complete description of the universe'; and if there can, even more doubtful that science alone can supply it – it certainly cannot supply 'the meaning of life' without ignoring most of life's complexity.

Ignoring complexity is a feature of ideologies in general, and indeed the main reason for their success. Their simple and literalistic perspective promises freedom from doubt, ambiguity, difficulty. They concentrate on a single image which embodies their partial side of the truth so strikingly that it numbs the disciple's imagination and closes it to other possibilities. 'Facts which will not fit simply are not digested', writes Mary Midgley. 'Examples of such hypnotic images are the class war in Marxism, the conditioned rat in behaviourism, the suppressed sexual desire in psychoanalysis, and the "selfish gene" in sociobiology.'[22]

Just as daimons were polarized into literal angels and devils, so literalism polarizes an imaginative and ambivalent view of the world into opposing ideologies, each of which believes it is on the side of the angels and demonizes the other. Communism demonizes Capitalism, and vice versa. Fundamentalist Christians demonize Neo-Darwinists, and vice versa. Even if an ideology believes that it has triumphed over its opponent it is still harried by daimons from within – the Capitalist fears 'reds under the bed', the Communist sees 'class traitors' everywhere, the Christian fundamentalist sees the hand of Satan in quite innocuous activities. Ideologies are prone to fanaticism because they are unconsciously charged by the daimons they have denied and the myths they have repudiated. They are in the grip of the shadow cast by their own certainty, like the notorious old puritans whose denial of sexuality caused them to see wantonness everywhere.

Even liberalism, which prides itself on its tolerance, can demonize beliefs which seem, for example, authoritarian. While acknowledging its ethical debt to Christianity, liberalism rejects its more challenging categories – sin should be treated with psychotherapy, spiritual despair with anti-depressants. That oxymoronic creature – the fanatical liberal – sees 'political incorrectness', like the work of Satan, everywhere; and can admit of no value outside its own secular humanism.

7

Matter and Spirits

THE VIOLATION OF DAME KIND

A good example of the polarizing, hence literalizing, effect of an ideology is rationalism – not reason, which has no problem with daimonic ambiguity, but that reason at all costs which has become one of the defining ideologies of Western culture. Indeed, I shall largely be characterizing the distinctively modern ego as the rational ego. Interestingly, it characterized itself as masculine in contradistinction to the feminine world, Nature, on the one hand, and to the feminine psyche, soul, on the other – both of which it had banished to an opposite pole. It had, in a double sense, distanced itself as far as possible from its own matrix, a word which implies 'mother': both Mother Nature, or Dame Kind as she was known in medieval times; and the feminine psyche out of which modern consciousness was born.

(Although it is historically true that the rational ego was mostly located in male scientists, we should not collude with its literalism by identifying it with *men*, any more than we should literalize 'feminine' Nature into a female.)

The literalization of Nature meant that its ambiguity was ruptured. For, to traditional cultures – no less than to the Romantic imagination – Nature is always double-edged, both friendly and dangerous, fertile and destructive, this-worldly and otherworldly. It is not only the traditional abode of daimons, it is itself daimonic. The moment it is divided by the scalpel of the rational ego, that half of its ambiguity, as it were, which has been suppressed returns in a demonized form. As far as the rationalists of the seventeenth century were aware, they had at last unsexed Nature and were perceiving her truly, as an objective world they could examine coldly and dispassionately.

But the language they use to describe this objective inquiry betrays another agenda. It depicts Nature as a wild and dangerous woman who must be fought, harried, tormented, uprooted, interrogated, tortured, held down and penetrated, pierced, vanquished – these metaphors of rape and violence are not exceptional. They are used over and over again. They are '*the common and constant idiom of the age*'.[1] Yet the scientists went on blithely believing in their rational detachment.

Here is a graphic demonstration of what Jung usefully called the work of the archetypal *shadow*: we cannot encounter directly what we have repressed, what we cannot face, because it is by definition unconscious; and so we encounter it indirectly, as if it were outside us, cast like a shadow out of the unconscious on to the world.

Rationalism's further determination to neutralize turbulent Nature led to the emphasis on another ideology: materialism. But although in one sense materialism represented the successful reduction of Dame Kind to the soulless machinery of matter, in another sense it was itself the successful ambush of rationalism by the 'mother' it had spurned – the etymological connection between the Latin *mater*, mother, and *materia*, matter, 'is neither a coincidence nor a joke'.[2] The rational ego had unconsciously fallen into the hands of an archetype, a goddess (perhaps, as James Hillman suggests, Hera, wife of Zeus)[3] whose single perspective imposes on everything a single reality. Everything is only matter.

If we follow this idea through, we find that this perspective cannot define reality for long. The ambiguity of Nature reasserts itself; she shape-changes, shaking off the grip of a single goddess and becoming an elusive nymph, dancing away in a mist of energetic particles. The more we try to pin her down, the faster she recedes into the Land of Quarks, leaving nothing behind but the shadow of materialism itself: an insubstantial, colourless nonentity.

Analogously, rationalism also eventually found its limits at the edge of the rational universe beyond which fantastic events occur, whether in the subatomic realm or in the astronomical. But if we understand rationalism as a perspective which constructs its own rational universe, then we can turn the whole thing on its head: it is rationalism itself which beyond a certain limit becomes irrational, reinfested with imagination, besieged by returning daimons in different shapes. It is not so much that the objects which rationalism reflects become irrational; it is more that the mirror of rationalism itself distorts, sending back weird images of astral enormities and bizarre quantum events.

I shall be looking at this world beyond the edge of rationalism later. Meanwhile, it should be noted that rationalism's polarizing tendency has meant that it is not only undermined by irrationality from within – it is also threatened by its opposite from without. It faced a challenge, for instance, from Romanticism which, while it had no objection to Enlightenment reason, reacted against the unreasonable extreme of rationalism with a promotion of imagination. Christianity was able to side with rationalism for a while, in an etiolated, deistic sort of way; but under attack from materialism and, later, evolutionism it was compelled by their literalism to retrench into a literalism of its own, asserting the literal truth of the Bible and thus leaving itself open to ridicule from the Darwinists.

Then, in the middle of the nineteenth century, the last thing expected by rationalists and Christians alike happened.

TURNING THE TABLES

Just as rationalism and materialism – scientism – seemed finally to have routed religion; just as the scientists were happily forming themselves into a professional body, the 'high priests' (as T. H. Huxley called them)[4] of the new orthodoxy; just as it was widely believed that the whole universe would be satisfactorily explained within a few short years – the daimons broke through.

Long banished from the natural world, they erupted in, of all places, the genteel Victorian drawing-room. Still banned by the rational ego from appearing as images in the mind, they were impelled to manifest literally – as disembodied spirits.

Few people were immune to the tide of Spiritualism which swept across America and Europe. It was all the rage; even Darwin attended a seance.[5] The spirits of the dead spoke to their living relations through a thousand mediums. But just as there has always been an overlap between the realm of the Dead and that of the daimons, so many of the spirits were unknown to the living. Often noisy, mischievous, fibbing, poltergeist-like pranksters, they were as much like fairies as deceased humans.

The striking feature of Victorian Spiritualism compared to its counterparts in other cultures – shamanism, say – was, paradoxically, its materialism. The spirits were pressed to prove their existence in tangible ways and they obliged with enthusiastic displays of banging, clattering, trumpet-blowing and table-turning. They arranged for 'apports' – ordinary objects came flying as if through solid walls; they left imprints of their hands and faces on hot wax; above all, they materialized themselves via the ectoplasm that flowed from the orifices of the entranced medium. The whole phenomenon was at once spectacular and leaden, a literalistic business which counterfeited rather then countered the literalism of both fundamentalist Christians and fundamentalist scientists.

Even when Spiritualist doctrines began to emerge, under the likes of Madame Blavatsky and Annie Besant, their 'theosophical' inclination was to deny the daimonic and, instead, to mirror the materialism they opposed: everything was spirit, not matter – which was only spirit vibrating, as it were, at a very low, very slow rate.

But the to-ing and fro-ing of literalisms did not stop here. As Spiritualism became more materialistic, so materialism was infiltrated by Spiritualism in another guise – the idea of unseen physical forces. Experiments with electricity and telegraphy were like the other side of psychic research into spirits and clairvoyance. A scientist like Sir William Crookes could spend years investigating Spiritualism and, having established the existence of the spirit world to his satisfaction, return to his laboratory work on radioactivity and X-rays.[6]

What Western culture claims as the increasing triumph of rationalism and the progress of science, the daimonic tradition reads as the perpetual striving of the daimons to restore the true ambiguity and equilibrium of reality, either by countering one ideology with a demonized opponent, or by subverting it from within.

THE ATOMS OF HADES

If I may recapitulate for a moment: daimons inhabit another, often subterranean, world which fleetingly interacts with ours. They are both material and immaterial, both there and not-there – often small, always elusive shape-shifters whose world is characterized by distortions of time and space and, above all, by an intrinsic uncertainty.

The point is: the words 'subatomic particles' could be substituted for 'daimons' in the paragraph above without any loss of accuracy. This is not a coincidence – the subatomic realm, like the unconscious, is where the daimons took refuge once they were outcast from their natural habitat.

Electrons, for example, are no more literally real than the Sidhe – and no more metaphorical either. We cannot even say whether they are waves or particles, only that it depends on the observer. Whatever experiment we conduct to observe either waves or particles observes only that aspect of the electron, as if the experiment – the act of observation – determines what we subsequently observe. (The Otherworld always mirrors whatever perspective we bring to bear on it.)

At the same time, we cannot know for sure what any electron will do. Identical electrons in identical experiments may do different things. Werner Heisenberg formulated his Uncertainty Principle to describe the subatomic world: everything we measure is subject to random fluctuations; we can either measure a particle's position or its speed, but not both. Worse still, a particle simply does not possess a definite position and momentum simultaneously – only by measuring one or the other does the fuzziness, as the physicists say, clear to a result.[7] There is an inherent uncertainty in the subatomic world which is variously characterized as murky, fuzzy, blurred, irrational – 'a maelstrom of fleeting ghostly images'.[8] Nowhere is empty; even the spaces in atoms are thought to be full of daimonic entities – 'virtual particles' which appear out of nowhere, interact and vanish.[9] Their presence is only inferred from their effects on other particles. Like the shades in Hades it is only their lack of energy that prevents them from taking on a real permanent life.[10] In one way we can perhaps see that the subatomic realm is the creation of the rational ego which is so substantial that, if it recognizes an Otherworld at all, it can only make the daimons seem correspondingly insubstantial – shades as grey and fleeting as those who fled the literalistic bludgeon of Heracles.

The idea of particles is being replaced as a model by the more versatile 'strings' which, when combined with ideas of supersymmetry, become superstrings inhabiting a ten-dimensional spacetime or (in another version of the theory) one with twenty-six dimensions.[11] Superstrings are said to be our best bet yet for a grand unified theory which, some theorists suggest, might necessitate a duplication of itself. This, in turn, suggests that there might be a second version of our universe. Here, we are back on familiar ground. Imagination goes on duplicating Otherworlds beyond whatever boundaries we ascribe to this world. Thus this 'second universe' is 'a shadow world inhabited by identical copies of the sorts of particles familiar in our own universe . . . but able to interact with our world only through gravity'.[12]

FUZZY PICTURES

When I try to picture atoms, I still think of them as composed of a tiny nucleus, made of protons and neutrons and orbited by a varying number of electrons, like a tiny solar system you can build out of billiard balls. I know that this bears no relation to what may be called the truth. It is a picture which became outdated a long time ago. But what image am I supposed to hold in my mind now?

All pictures of the subatomic realm, say the scientists, are models. But models – whether replicas, blueprints, maps or knitting patterns – are always models of something that we have already encountered in the actual world. Atomic models do not correspond to 'real' atoms in the same way because we know nothing about such 'real' atoms – except in terms of the models. On the other hand, we do know about atoms. We have masses of data. But they can only be expressed by a mathematical model, and this bears no relation to anything we can visualize. Indeed, the only way mathematics can correspond to the physical world is as measurement.

In the case of atoms, however, it is never clear what is being measured; or else we measure one thing at the expense of another. And, besides, we do need to visualize the atomic world, as we need to visualize every Otherworld. Mathematical models are not enough; they have to be translated, even if only into billiard balls. Even scientists constantly translate: their talk of patterns and symmetries is model-talk. So, too, are the words electron, proton, quark, etc. What do these signify? Real 'objects' of which we have no knowledge? Mathematical models? Or the model of the mathematical model we try to visualize?

The answer is, such words refer to all three – sometimes to a putative 'objective reality', sometimes to a purely subjective picture, and sometimes to an imagining, a fairy tale.[13] The distinction between model and reality is 'hopelessly blurred';[14] and the further down we get or the further away – the 'smaller' we get – the more blurred. In what sense do 'virtual particles' exist, coming out of nowhere and instantly disappearing again, leaving only the faintest of traces but never being directly observed?

Scientists are divided among themselves – even within themselves – over the question of subatomic reality. Influenced by the whole literalistic cast of scientific thought, most of them naturally believe that their models do approximate to an objective reality; that model and reality will fit more closely as we find out more; and that we will eventually end up with a set of equations which will describe the 'laws of nature'.

Other scientists, or even the same ones at different times, hesitate to believe that we can ever know reality because we can only know about models. 'Physics,' said Nils Bohr, 'tells us what we can *know* about the universe, not how it *is*.'[15] In fact there may be no such thing as an objective reality separate from what is revealed through our observations. Thus some physicists have said that the subatomic realm is primarily metaphorical.[16] In the 1970s Fritjof Capra's *Tao of Physics* compared the subatomic enterprise to Oriental religion. I will be suggesting that its root metaphors lie closer to home, in the Western esoteric tradition. Even a cursory glance at Neoplatonism, Gnosticism and alchemy will reveal a way of imagining that may begin to resolve the nuclear physicists' dilemma. For their stock-in-trade is a reality which may or may not be there; which is both subjective and objective (or perhaps both); which is both literal and metaphorical; which, if it is there, can only be imagined and, if it is not, is imagined as being there and is therefore in another sense there; which is elusive, ambiguous, fuzzy – which is, in short, a daimonic reality.

8

'How Natives Think'

No matter where we look – ancient Greece, Africa, China, South America – human beings have a universal tendency to divide the world in two. More precisely, they classify the world in pairs. Western culture favours, as we have seen, pairs of *opposites* produced by its fondness for polarizing. Other cultures recognize that the terms of a pair can relate to each other in many ways – an oppositional relationship is exceptional rather than the rule.

HARD WORLD, SOFT WORLD

In theory, there are countless pairs from which to form what the anthropologist Rodney Needham calls a dual symbolic classification.[1] Surprisingly, in practice, the same limited number of pairs crops up again and again all over the world.[2] For example:

Right	Left
Sun	Moon
Light	Dark
North	South
Even	Odd
Male	Female
Dry	Wet
Hot	Cold
Hard	Soft
Politics	Religion

Not all cultures use these pairs, but most – if not all – use some of them. According to the rules which govern this system of classifying the world, the terms in each column need not hold any property in common. They are not synonymous but homologous. We cannot say 'Sun equals Male' or 'Sun symbolizes Male' or 'Moon is synonymous with Female' – we have to say 'Sun is to Moon as Male is to Female, as Even is to Odd', and so on. This is written in abbreviated form as – Sun: Moon:: Male: Female:: Even: Odd. In other words, the terms relate to each other by analogy.

When therefore an African tribesman says that a witch-doctor is dark and soft, we will be confused if we take him literally. We have to understand that he is implicitly referring to a system of analogy. Witch-doctors: chiefs:: dark: light:: soft: hard:: religious authority: political power.

Just as confusing to an outsider might be the analogies which define English political life. Tory: socialist:: right: left. But 'left' socialist: 'right' socialist:: hard: soft; while 'left' Tory: 'right' Tory:: wet: dry. (Actually there are no Tory 'drys' as opposed to Tory 'wets' because wet in this context is drawn from another set of analogies.)

The lesson of analogical thinking is that the symbolic value we attach to things is not fixed and absolute. In Christian dress codes, for instance, we think of white as symbolizing purity. But we must recognize that the meaning of white cannot be divorced from its analogical underpinnings. White: black:: wedding dress: mourning dress:: bride: widow. For nuns, white: black:: novice: bride (of Christ). For priests, white: black:: surplice: cassock:: sacred: profane. Black can signify anything from death to marriage, depending on its context – the analogical system it is in.

Analogical thought seeks to resolve contradictions by transposing them to different metaphorical levels. In many tribal cultures a woman can be both 'wet' and 'dry'. This seems contradictory until we grasp the implicit analogy – a woman is to a man as wet is to dry; but a woman is to a menstruating woman as dry is to wet. We do this sort of level-changing ourselves. A man is sometimes said to be hard in relation to a woman who is 'soft'; but the same man can be 'soft' in relation to a 'hard' woman. The first analogy expresses a metaphorical contrast on the physical level – man: woman:: hard: soft:: (physically) strong: weak. The second uses the same terms but shifted to the emotional level – man: woman:: soft: hard:: sensitive: unfeeling. If a young African male is described as 'soft', a different system is usually implied – soft: hard:: uncircumcised: circumcised:: boy: man. It takes an age to unpack the analogies implicit in a metaphorical system of any complexity, yet we talk in this kind of shorthand all the time. It lies at the root of our thought. Consider a few more senses of hard/soft (I have put in brackets the area to which the sense refers) –

Hard: soft:: difficult: easy (jobs, work)
Hard: soft:: strong: weak (drugs, drink, pornography)
Hard: soft:: stern: lenient (judgement)
Hard: soft:: angry: gentle (words)
Hard: soft:: dazzling: dim (light)
Hard: soft:: sciences: arts (academic disciplines)
Hard: soft:: extreme: temperate (climate)
Hard: soft:: machines: programs (computer ware)

LIFE AS A TIGER

Understanding the principle of analogical thought helped to solve the problem of totemism which had exercised anthropologists for so long. The tribes they studied were divided into clans, each of which was represented by a totem animal or object. Clan members seemed to identify with their totem. 'I am a bear,' they might say, or 'I am an eaglehawk.' They even claimed descent from their totem animals. So although the anthropologists came up with many theories to explain totemism – in 1920, Arnold van Gennep reviewed forty-one[3] – they could not shake off the feeling that tribal peoples not only thought differently from Westerners, but also thought in a way that was distinctly credulous, childish, primitive. How could anyone believe they were a bear?

I do not share the anthropological puzzlement because, as a boy, I grew up in a tribe whose clans were tigers, lions and leopards. I was a tiger. As well as the tripartite division, the tribe was also divided into two 'streams'. The A stream contained those who were 'clever' and the

63

B, those who were less 'clever'. Contrary to appearance it was not better to be in the A stream because it was not socially valuable to be 'clever'. It was, however, highly valuable to be good at sports, and more people who were good at sports inhabited the B stream than the A. The B stream called the A stream 'soft' and itself 'hard'.

Competition was fierce, but it did not take place between the A stream and the B. It took place on the sports field between the clans, or 'houses' as we called them. Tigers were better at games than lions, while leopards were unpredictable. Tigers called lions 'soft' and themselves 'hard'. I felt a greater affinity with my fellow tigers in the B stream than with my academic colleagues in the A stream.

In *How Natives Think*,[4] Lucien Lévy-Bruhl proposed that tribal peoples lived in a state of 'mystical participation' in the world. It was an idea that Jung eagerly took up to describe the lack of distinction in the tribal mind between subject and object – 'What happens outside also happens in him, and what happens in him also happens outside.'[5] No wonder, then, that the tribesman felt a 'mystical identity' not only with his fellows but also with his totem animal.[6]

However, the 'supernatural' orientation of Lévy-Bruhl's thinking about so-called primitive mentality fell into disrepute, mostly because he was thought to have made too strong a contrast between 'primitive' and 'civilized' thought. It was a French anthropologist, Claude Lévi-Strauss, who, drawing on the work of his English predecessors, A. R. Radcliffe-Brown and E. E. Evans-Pritchard, solved – or, rather, dissolved – the problem of totemism.

Lévi-Strauss showed that the way of thinking embodied in totemism was only a particular instance of traditional thought as a whole. When the tribesman says 'I am an eaglehawk', he is really saying 'I am in the same relation to a member of the crow clan as eaglehawks are to crows.' He is using a species of animal to distinguish himself from members of another group. This can even be reflected in social life when, for instance, the eaglehawk clan, like their namesake, does the hunting and has first pick of the prey, while the crow clan (like crows) take what remains.[7]

Lévi-Strauss asserted that these kind of distinctions are used to form a whole network of logical relations which are primarily addressed to the intellect and only secondarily to the '*sentiments*'. His analysis was a salutary corrective to the old prejudices which characterized 'primitives' as illogical and childish; but, at the same time, he undervalued the extent to which a traditional culture hangs together because each member feels himself to be intimately connected to every part of that culture.

When I was a tiger, I would have found it impossible to explain to an anthropologist the subtle but very strong affinity I felt with other tigers, as well as the different but equally strong – often hostile and competitive – affinity I felt with my A stream classmates. How much more powerful, then, must be the affinity tribal peoples experience, both with their totems and with the entire network of relationships which simultaneously differentiate and unite the clans. No part of their lives is left undefined by one relationship or another. If Lévy-Bruhl's word 'mystical' is inappropriate for a relationship which is also perfectly normal, the word 'participation' seems apt.

It especially applies, for example, to that awe which accompanies encounters with daimons, whether as a dead relative, a tree *numen*, a *genius loci*, etc.[8] Many have seen such things and all believe in them. They are in one way mystical – they are held to be supernatural – but at the same time they are entirely commonplace and natural. It is as if their function was also structural, in Lévi-Strauss's sense, helping the tribe to define itself by analogy with the Other – Us: Them:: humans: daimons:: this world: the Otherworld. Lévi-Strauss emphasizes the natural side of daimonic events while Lévy-Bruhl is struck by the supernatural side. But it does no good when considering daimons to take sides.

In fact, Lévi-Strauss tempered his insistence on the intellectual side of tribal life. Its thought, he realized, is not logical but analogical.[9] And the analogical relations between things (such as eaglehawks and crows and their two clans) are not consciously constructed any more than tribal myths are consciously invented. Here he moves back towards Lévy-Bruhl – who also modified his position.

His description of tribal thought as 'pre-logical' did not imply 'illogical'. It meant that traditional cultures are untroubled by logical contradictions.[10] He also thought that the debate about 'primitive' versus 'civilized' thought was a red herring, since there is a substrate of 'primitive' thought even in 'civilized' people.[11] Indeed it may well be that rigorous logical intellection is rarely found outside French intellectuals. Certainly, without Lévy-Bruhl's sense of passionate participation, valuable structural analysis can become an arid post-structuralist system of 'signs' manipulated by the intellect and lacking the transformative power of analogical relations that are lived and felt.

THE GREAT CHAIN OF BEING

It may be instructive to compare the world-view of traditional cultures to that of our own pre-modern society. The medieval world-picture was formed in all its essentials by the ancient Greeks and despite serious changes of emphasis at the Renaissance, and serious reversals during the seventeenth century, remained the dominant world-view until the early eighteenth century.[12]

It was a multi-levelled picture, consisting of three interwoven models. The first of these was the Great Chain of Being in which everything in the universe stretched in descending order down from God, through the classes of angels to mankind, the animals, plants, metals and stones. As well as a chain, it was thought of as a ladder by which everything could strive upwards to the class above, as mankind strives towards God. And this sense of ascent carries the seed of our modern theory of evolution.

Pre-literate, tribal cultures – which I am calling 'traditional' – lack strict hierarchical world-views, which seem to be the result of monotheism and its concomitant theocentrism. Their 'chains of being' are not vertical but horizontal. They stretch back in time to the gods and ancestors through genealogy; or sideways in space through series of corresponding realms such as the animal world, the sky-world or the underworld. At the same time their sense of participation in the universe is much the same as for the pre-modern Westerner whose chain of being 'made vivid the idea of a related universe where no part was superfluous; it enhanced the dignity of all creation, even the meanest part of it . . . Here was ultimate unity in almost infinite diversity . . .'[13]

The second model within the medieval world-picture was the doctrine of correspondences; and this was the same as tribal systems of dual classification. Two pairs of qualities dominated: hot/cold, moist/dry. These generated the four elements out of which everything was made:

earth (cold and dry), air (hot and moist), fire (hot and dry) and water (cold and moist). The elements of the macrocosm were reflected by the humours of the microcosm: man was melancholy, sanguine, choleric or phlegmatic depending on the preponderance of black bile (cold and dry), blood (hot and moist), yellow bile (hot and dry) or phlegm (cold and moist) respectively in his 'complexion'. Melancholy: choleric:: earth: fire.

The correspondence between macrocosm and microcosm was the most common. Each provided a metaphor for the other. The larger world of the heavens above provided a metaphor for the smaller 'world' of man on earth below, which can be expressed as – world: man:: big: little:: above: below:: heaven: earth. In addition, the divine realm (including the angels), the commonwealth (the body politic), the animal and plant kingdoms were all imagined as superposed planes 'connected by an immense network of correspondences'.[14] Thus any disorder among the stars, for example, reflected or presaged disorder in the State.

Humans sum up the universe in themselves. Every part of our bodies corresponds to some heavenly body or constellation – or simply to the lower heavens whose storms for instance correspond to our passions, just as King Lear on the blasted heath strove 'in his little world of man to outscorn the to-and-fro conflicting wind and rain'.[15] We were linked to the stars spiritually as well as physically. They influenced, but did not determine, our lives. They were seen as astronomical bodies and astrological powers simultaneously. An alchemist was not in any way exceptional in using a word such as 'Mars' to imply all at once a planet, a metal (iron), a god and a psychological dominant. Perhaps it is only by imagining the medieval idea of 'the stars' in this latter way, as inner archetypal images, that we can nowadays begin to recapture the old sense of participation in a network of intimate connections.

We express this participation in terms of metaphor; medieval man called it *sympathy*. Shakespeare could use metaphors of the sun and gold to express the concept of kingship because there was sympathy between these disparate objects owing to the implicit system of correspondences – king: queen:: sun: moon:: gold: silver. Sympathy captures the idea of a living relationship in the way that our word 'metaphor' rarely does. We might say that Lévy-Bruhl's participation emphasized the sympathetic nature of traditional thought, while Lévi-Strauss's grasp of analogy emphasized its doctrine of correspondences.

Finally, I should add that apart from the Great Chain of Being and the doctrine of correspondences, the third model of the medieval world – which interpenetrated these other two and prevented them from rigidifying – was the model of the *dance*. The cosmic hierarchies were animated by harmonious motion. Most famously, the stars danced to the music of the spheres. Every rustic measure, round dance and maypole ceremony was a ritual echo of the universal circular dance to promote harmony, fertility and good fortune.

(Although there is plenty of evidence that a belief in fairies was not only commonplace but probably more widespread than any knowledge of the official theological cosmos, they were not given a place in it. C. S. Lewis grappled with this anomaly by suggesting that it is of the very nature of daimons as 'marginal, fugitive creatures'[16] to resist being pressed into any official model of the cosmos, the medieval one no less than our own. They are always unofficial and beyond the pale. 'Herein lies their imaginative value', Lewis continues. 'They introduce a welcome hint of wildness and uncertainty into the universe that is in danger of being a little too self-explanatory . . .')[17]

GOOD TO EAT, GOOD TO THINK

Classifying the world according to pairs related by analogy is a universal characteristic of thought. It underpins the thought of Western culture which, however, polarizes analogical thought into logical thought. Logic is oppositional, asserting that a thing cannot be A and not-A. Analogy shows us that a thing can very well be both A and not-A, just as an African woman can be both 'wet' and 'not-wet' (dry). Analogy preserves ambiguity by simultaneously embodying similarity and difference. But unlike the conscious operation of logic, we are scarcely more aware of our analogical thinking than a tribal culture. We rarely recognize for instance that the way we think about and describe people is often in terms of concrete qualities analogically related. Consider the pairs hot/cold, warm/cool, heart/head in such expressions as hot-headed, cold-hearted, cool-headed, warm-hearted (but, interestingly, not cold-headed or hot-hearted). We take the things that lie around us, whether sensory experiences like hot and cold, or everyday objects like crows and eagle-hawks, and we use them to order the world and to think with.

At least, this is the sort of view held by Lévi-Strauss when he dismisses the functional explanation of totemism: animals are not so much *bonnes à manger*, good to eat, he says, as *bonnes à penser*, good to *think*.[18] But, as we have seen, the word 'thinking' does not express at all well the elaborate systems of metaphor and analogy which arise spontaneously in all societies, it seems, and which operate unconsciously. Animals, I suggest, are good to *imagine*.

Analogical 'thinking' is the way in which imagination chooses to structure itself. It is also a fundamental characteristic of imagination's primary products: myths. By understanding something of how myths work, and according to what rules, we shall understand better how imagination works and therefore what the human soul is like.

9

The Daimons' Tales

'The Greeks, a certain scholar has told me, considered that myths are the activities of the Daimons, and the Daimons shape our characters and our lives. I have often had the fancy that there is some one myth for every man, which, if we but knew it, would make us understand all he did and thought.'[1]

The idea that the daimons who inhabit myths also invented them is an outstanding metaphor for the way myths generate themselves out of Imagination. When Lévi-Strauss tells us that he is seeking to show *'comment les mythes se pensent dans les hommes et à leur insu'* – 'how myths think themselves out in men and without men's knowledge'[2] – he is pointing to exactly this autonomous and unconscious creative process.

Depth psychology has taught us that myths are the stories of the soul. If we want to understand the Western psyche we have to study its myths. Mostly – and especially since the Renaissance – this means Greek and Roman mythology. However, there is also a case to be made for Norse and Anglo-Saxon mythology, particularly as it underlies northern European culture which, in turn, produced such key Western movements as Protestantism, without which modern rationalism could not have arisen. Ted Hughes thinks that Norse myth is 'the better part of our patrimony still locked up';[3] and that we have neglected it in favour of Greek myth. He may be right; and, in *Daimonic Reality*, I indicated the key role played by the Norse hero Sigurd (which I am going to recapitulate) in the psychological background to the modern rational ego.[4]

It is difficult for us to believe in the reality of the gods, daimons, heroes and heroines of myth because we give so little credence to metaphorical reality. In calling the gods 'archetypes', Jung hoped to make them acceptable again to a scientific age. In doing so he ran the risk of making us forget that the gods and daimons do not manifest themselves in abstractions. They come to us in concrete images within dreams and imaginings – as persons, or personified images.

This does not mean that we have to believe in them as literal persons. Each god 'is a manner of existence, an attitude towards existence and a set of ideas . . . A God forms our subjective vision so that we see the world according to its ideas.'⁵ Thus it is not true that we have ideas – ideas have us. And it is as well to know what ideas, what gods, govern us lest they run our lives without our being aware of the fact. The god behind this book, for example, is probably – it is only fair to warn you – Hermes.

APOLLO AND HIS BROTHER

The world of 'far-seeing' solar Apollo is one of light, clarity, order, formal beauty, detachment, far-sighted goals.⁶ It is easy to identify him as the god behind science. Nietzsche placed Apollo at one pole of the psychic spectrum; at the other he put Dionysus, god of wine, of nocturnal rites of ecstasy and communal abandon. From Apollo's viewpoint Dionysus is irrational, chaotic, riotous and shady; from where Dionysus stands Apollo looks too cold, dispassionate, intellectual, rigid and individualistic.⁷

Apollo has a younger brother, Hermes, one of whose very first acts is to steal Apollo's cattle. He also twists the cattle's hoofs around and makes himself a pair of sandals which he wears back to front in order that his tracks will mislead his pursuers into thinking he has gone the opposite way. From Apollo's outlook, he is a tricky, thieving thorn in the side; from Hermes' point of view his elder brother is pompous, moralizing, high-minded, superior and lamentably lacking in duplicity.

When he is not in relation to Apollo, however, Hermes – whom Jung called the archetype of the unconscious – is the god of communication, of trade and commerce, of crossroads and boundaries, of deceit and thievery, of herds and fertility, of magic, oracles and dreams. He is the messenger of the gods, the only one who can travel freely between the realms of the gods, of mankind, and of the Dead. As Hermes *psycho-pompos*, he guides souls into Hades.[8] He brings us dreams. To the Hermetic philosophers of the Hellenistic era he was Hermes Trismegistus, 'thrice-great'; to the alchemists he was Mercurius – instigator, operator and very goal of the Art.

As god of boundaries, Hermes presides over the twilight realm of daimonic reality. He enables commerce to take place between this world and the Otherworld. His theft from his shining clear-eyed brother is like the thieving which the unconscious is always performing on consciousness, snatching away words, ideas, images, just when we most need them. If we wish to retrieve them we cannot follow the literal tracks – we have to twist them round and go in the opposite direction to the one they seem to be pointing to. To gain access to the Hermetic depths of the unconscious, we are guided backwards, downwards, by Hermes who also and paradoxically connects us to the skyworld of the gods above.

Hermes connects us to ourselves, and ourselves to the world. He alienates Apollo, but also reconciles him: he gives Apollo the lyre he has made out of a tortoise and his brother is so delighted that he makes Hermes Lord of the Herds – Hermes knows how important barter and reciprocity is in the psychic realm, no less than in the mercantile. Hermes bridges worlds and acts as a nexus of exchange.

Because he is brother to Apollo and also the first to carry the child Dionysus – standing in for the Dionysian perspective while it matures – Hermes maintains the connection between Apollo and Dionysus by participating in both their natures and preventing them from splitting irretrievably apart.

THE STRUCTURE OF MYTH

As Rodney Needham reminds us, myth 'reflects history, provides a social charter, embodies a metaphysics, responds to natural phenomena, expresses perennial verities, copes with historical change, and so on almost endlessly . . .';[9] but no theory of myth comes close to explaining all myths.[10] The reason for this is simple: theories about myth are themselves further variants of the myth, re-tellings in the language of the day, even if it is unpalatable psychological jargon. Myth, like Nature, kindly provides 'evidence' for the truth of any theory we care to hold; but that theory will in the end flow back into the source stories that circle the earth like great ocean streams.

What myths most resemble, I suppose, are dreams. At least, the natives of south-west America say that they are either dreams or created out of dreams, while the Dreamtime of the Australian Aboriginals suggests that 'myths and dream evince a similar insight into reality'.[11] Freud thought that myths were, like dreams, 'wish-fulfilment fantasies'. Jung thought that they were revelations of the collective unconscious. Lévi-Strauss averted attention from the content of myths to their underlying structure. He noticed that while a myth may apparently change over time and space, its structure remains constant.

For example, the story of Oedipus, who unwittingly kills his father, sleeps with his mother (who kills herself) and blinds himself out of horror and remorse, is structurally echoed by the story of Phaidra who wants to sleep with her stepson and, when he refuses, finally accuses him of doing so – whereupon he is killed by Theseus, his father and the husband of Phaidra (who kills herself). In other words, the father kills the son instead of the son killing the father; the son does not sleep with his (step)mother, although he is accused of it; both mothers kill themselves; both the surviving son/father suffer profound remorse.

Although I am far from indifferent to the content of myth – later on I will be looking closely at heroes – for the moment I want to concentrate on this structural aspect. To take two myths at random from Greek mythology:

The first tells us how Zeus the sky-god takes the form of a bull in order to carry off a human girl, Europa.[12] Her brother Cadmus searches for her. He is told to follow a cow and, when it stops, to found the city of Thebes, having first sacrificed the cow to Athena. Looking for water, Cadmus slays a dragon guarding a sacred pool. He sows its teeth and the crop is a troop of men, the Spartoi. They kill one another, but the survivors co-operate with Cadmus to found Thebes. Cadmus marries Harmonia, daughter of Ares, god of war. Cadmus and Harmonia are turned into dragons.

The second myth tells us how, meanwhile, Europa has a son by Zeus.

He is Minos, who marries Pasiphae. Zeus' brother, the sea-god Poseidon, sends Minos a beautiful bull to be sacrificed. But Minos keeps the bull and, in punishment, Poseidon causes Pasiphae to lust after the bull. Through the ingenuity of Daedalus, Pasiphae is changed into a cow, has sex with the bull and gives birth to a monster, the Minotaur.

This second story which seems consecutive to the first, and entirely different, is actually symmetrical with the first myth, but turned upside down.

In the first a bull (= Zeus) carries off Europa who has a human child, Minos; in the second, a bull (= Poseidon) cohabits with Pasiphae who has a monster child, the Minotaur.

In the first, Europa has a human brother, Cadmus, who is required to sacrifice a cow sent by the gods; in the second, Pasiphae has a human husband, Minos, who is required to sacrifice a bull sent by the gods (which he fails to do).

In the first, Cadmus kills a monster whose remains generate live humans; in the second, the bull is replaced by a monster (the Minotaur) who kills humans.

But, in the first, Cadmus is himself (turned into) the monster while, in the second, the monster is himself Minos (because the word Minotaur means Minos-bull).

We see how the two myths are structured in the same way, but also how the first is converted into the second by, as it were, changing all the signs – bulls become cows, brothers become husbands, sky-gods become sea-gods, and so on. We are presented with a series of contradictions which are analogous to each other:

Nature: Culture:: gods: men:: wild: tame:: monsters: domestic animals. (The ambiguous bull – tame but wild – is the mediator between both sides.)

Lévi-Strauss's method of structural analysis shows that each myth within a mythology, if taken separately, seems to be part of a larger pattern which only becomes apparent when several myths – and the way they are transformed into each other – are analysed.[13] It is not that all myths say the same thing; rather, that the sum of what all the myths say is not expressly said by any of them. Together, however, they publicly express, but in disguise, those contradictions which define human existence.

FEMININE SUN, MASCULINE MOON

In his four-volume work *Mythologiques*, Lévi-Strauss traces hundreds of such transformations of myths up through South America, into North America and back again. He shows how each myth is a variant of the next, according to rules of symmetry and inversion, so that we are led across continents in a great mythological loop. The countless variants are nevertheless generated, like the limited number of pairs in binary classification, by a limited number of elements. Even a mythology as incomparably rich as the Greeks' has a finite number of deities and heroes, suggesting that there is a finite number of perspectives through which the world can be imagined.

Myths are imaginative templates which, when laid over the world, make sense of it. We cannot think without them, because they provide the structures which determine the way we think in the first instance. The uncanny similarity of myths from all over the world, 'as alike as the lines on the palm of the hand',[14] tells us that each culture is ultimately intelligible to another because they share a common human imagination.

Lévi-Strauss emphasized the archetypal nature of structure.[15] He did not subscribe to Jung's emphasis on the archetypal nature of mythic contents. This was partly Jung's fault. He tended to assign fixed values to gods and goddesses, and did not always appreciate that their value can change according to context, just as Hermes has a different meaning in relation to Apollo than in relation to Dionysus. He lacked the principle of analogy.

To give a simple example, Jung was inclined to say that the sun always symbolized consciousness and the masculine principle, whereas the moon symbolized the unconscious and the feminine. However sun, consciousness, masculine are not synonymous but homologous terms; they are related analogously – sun: moon:: consciousness: the unconscious:: masculine: feminine. Thus, when his symbolism did not work, when some mythologies – Norse, for instance – seemed to assign a feminine value to the sun, Jung was forced to conclude that every archetype 'contains its own opposite'. But it is not a question of opposition. Norse mythology simply uses a system of analogy in which the terms are reversed. Sun: moon:: feminine: masculine.

Archetypes are, like soul itself, 'empty' in themselves. They can only be known through the many images they adopt. They shape-shift, taking on different values, different masks, according to the relationship they are in. An archetype such as Jung's *anima* takes on the image of a daughter in relation to the wise old man (for example, Antigone and Oedipus); of a mother in relation to the hero–son (Thetis and Achilles); of a wife in relation to a hero–husband (Andromeda and Perseus).

At the same time, the archetypes should not be dissolved into an empty system of signs, as structuralism is prone to do. They embody a unity of perspective throughout their multiplicity of masks. Like Lévy-Bruhl, whose principle of 'mystical participation' he seized on, Jung was right to stress the extent to which gods and their stories live and move and have their being within us.

DREAMTIME

The appearance of goddesses and heroes in our dreams – or personages who are rooted in these archetypes – tells us that we are living in the midst of myth. Moreover, the rules of mythic transformation, of which symmetry and inversion are the main ones (there are others such as alternation) apply as much to the individual psyche as to the collective.

According to analytical psychology, the images in a series of dreams will refer to a kind of nucleus, a central image which Jung called the self, such that 'by means of analogy the images appear as it were to revolve around it, gradually concentrating more and more upon its essential nature. Thus the material referring to the central image amplifies the central content, or throws now one, now another of its aspects into relief until a complete picture is built up and crystallizes out.'[16]

The idea is that the dreams are converging on the single unifying image of the self; or, conversely, that each dream is a different aspect of the self. However, Jung thought that the self was never arrived at, even though it was present as a kind of 'virtual point', an imaginative centre which organized the psyche's imagining around itself. By the same token, the multiple variants of American myths that Lévi-Strauss analysed could be described as striving to reconcile the contradictions they embody in some grand synthesizing myth. But there is no such actual meta-myth any more than there is an actual Self. There is only a hypothetical source of light, as it were, which is diffracted by the stained glass of mythology into a myriad colourful myths and dreams.

All this is an abstract way of describing what all dreamers know – that their dreams enact variants of their conscious lives. The brokenhearted woman dreams for years that her faithless lover: has returned, has rejected her again, is tender and loving, is cruel and mocking, has married another, is married to her and they have four children . . . Jung talks about the compensatory role of the unconscious in relation to consciousness; but, once again, this is too oppositional. Dreams enact the unrealized possibilities of our actual lives. As they unfold, the heartbroken woman begins to see that the variant of the 'myth' she actually lived was not the only one, or even the real one – it was simply the literal one. And all the different roles she played in dreams, and all the different feelings she experienced, are equally 'her' within the totality of a psyche which treats our lives impersonally as if they were myths.

THE SELF-TRANSCENDING HUMAN

So, at the close of his *Mythologiques*, after he has structurally related hundreds of myths to each other, Lévi-Strauss cannot say with any certainty what Imagination is doing. It is generating myths which apparently go on embodying and striving to resolve contradictions, until all the permutations are exhausted – but to no purpose, it seems, beyond the process itself.

The labyrinthine shape-changing of myths mirrors the pathways of soul which 'seems more interested in the movement of its ideas than in the resolution of problems. Therefore no classical psychological problem can ever be solved . . .'[17] It is as if we recognize the contradictions of our human existence and are intensely preoccupied with them. We are self-transcending, paradoxical beings – both part of Nature, for example, and yet outside of it. We use abstractions to express our contradictions where traditional cultures use concrete images. The problems of mind/matter or consciousness/unconscious about which we philosophize are only re-statements of the problems of this world/ Otherworld or Skyworld/Underworld about which we mythologize. However in neither case can the problems be solved because they are not problems, but mysteries. Myths tell us to live without resolutions in a state of creative tension with our two-foldness.

Myths do not, so to speak, get us anywhere. While there are myths about progress, myths do not themselves progress. Indeed, Lévi-Strauss even saw literal scientific 'progress' as, in reality, a system of myths which 'will never consist in anything other than proceeding towards re-groupings, in the midst of a totality that is closed and complementary with itself'. In fact, '. . . mythological thought is not prescientific; it should be seen rather as an anticipation of the future state of science . . .'[18]

Finally, and incidentally, if there is one classificatory pair, one contradiction, which acts as a kind of rubric for all the others (says Lévi-Strauss at the end of *Mythologiques*), it is heaven (sky)/earth. It is their primordial separation which brought on all our woe; and it is their impossible, longed-for reunion wherein all our happiness lies.

IO

The Hero and the Virgin

The Christian myth is straightforward in its basic outline.

A young hero is fathered by a god on a mortal woman. However, when he grows up he makes a claim unknown in pagan mythology and unusual for heroes. He claims to be identical with his father, which is to say, a god. In some sense, then, he is the father of his own mother. He is killed, or sacrificed, as many heroes and gods have been before him; but he uniquely rises from the dead.

The relation to his mother, Mary, might be put like this – Christ: Mary:: god: woman:: father: daughter:: immortal (bodily Resurrection): mortal.

We might call this set of analogies the Protestant version of the Christ myth. But there is another version of this myth which is exactly symmetrical but inverted. It is, so to speak, the Catholic version. It tells of a goddess who has a hero son. (It should be by a mortal man, Joseph; but the myth prefers parthenogenesis – virgin birth.) Although her son dies, she returns to her abode in Heaven by being bodily lifted up there, or 'assumed'. Now, this myth does not contradict the first in any way; it merely changes the emphasis by reversing all the terms – Jesus: the Blessed Virgin:: man: goddess:: son: mother:: mortal (crucified): immortal (bodily Assumption).

This second way of structuring the Christian myth was for centuries unofficial. It was a movement from below, from the people, which forced the papacy to create two articles of dogma which have no biblical justification. The first was the Immaculate Conception which effectively makes Mary a goddess by asserting that she was born without sin; the second, made about a hundred years later, in 1950, was the Assumption

– which asserts that Mary did not die but was lifted bodily up into Heaven. Roman Catholic orthodoxy ratified the myth thrown up by the popular imagination.

The myths are clearly expressions of the traditional tension between human and divine, mortal and immortal, masculine and feminine. In a pagan society variants of the Christ story would go on proliferating, as if attempting to resolve these contradictions by constantly transposing them into other terms and on other levels. But Christianity does not do this. It does not offer us a mythology. Potentially it did, because there were powerful variants which said that Jesus could not have been crucified – as God, he was pure spirit and therefore only his apparition hung on the cross. Conversely, there was a variant which held that Jesus was not God, but only a man – albeit an outstandingly good man. But these myths were called heresies and banned. However, their spontaneous appearance meant that the main body of the Church had to sit down and define what exactly Jesus was. At the Council of Nicaea, they came up with the official myth: that a man, Jesus of Nazareth, was also the Christ, meaning the Anointed One. He was both man and God. The only myth he was officially permitted to mirror was the myth of Adam. Just as Adam was a god-like man who, through a sin, 'fell' from an earthly paradise into the human condition, so Jesus was a man-like God who, through a sacrifice, 'raised' mankind up to a heavenly paradise.

The reduction of Christian mythology to a single story meant that the intolerable tension between man and God could not strive through many versions to resolve itself – which seems to be the natural inclination of the mythopoeic Imagination. Instead, the God-Man of the Gospels remained as a paradox which, deprived of imaginative elaboration, could only be met with that equally paradoxical state of mind called faith. 'I believe because it is impossible,' said Tertullian (or words to that effect).[1]

The paradox at the heart of Christianity is what made it so offensive to the Jews, so ridiculous to the Greeks and so awe-inspiring to the Christians. Nevertheless, unofficial variants were never wholly expunged. It is clear that those systems of thought labelled 'Gnostic' tend to mirror Christian orthodoxy; alchemy, for example. What is less obvious, as I hope to show, is that whole areas of modern thought, such as philosophical materialism or Darwinism, which seem so opposed to Christianity, are disguised variants of the 'myths' that Christianity excluded when it became institutionalized.

While the story of Christ was in many ways a typical hero myth – the virgin birth, the supernatural acts (miracles), the rebirth into immortality – in one respect it was unique: it claimed not to be a myth at all. It claimed to be history. Traditional societies do not distinguish between myth and history in the way that we do. Mythical events were not thought to have literally happened; yet in another sense they were true, as if they had. 'These things never happened; they are always',[2] wrote Sallust sublimely (86–34 BC). Conversely, historical events are always mythologized (the Trojan war, for example). It is as if what literally happened is less important than what metaphorically happened. But the two are combined to create what 'really' happened.

When the story of Christ was held to be history, its events literally true, myth suffered a blow. It began to acquire its modern meaning of something unreal, imaginary (as opposed to imaginative) and merely fictional. At the same time, truth and reality began to be measured by their literal truth and reality. Literalism began with Christianity.

HISTORY AND MYTH

Thus it is difficult for us to allow the intermingling of myth and history. We are surprised by the way traditional genealogies slip seamlessly from history back into pre-history. When tracing the lineage of the kings of Ireland, for example, we suddenly find ourselves out of history and into myth as the ancestors become members of the mythical Tuatha de Dannan. Even more striking are those cultures whose chiefs trace their ancestry back to the totem animals. History, the past, is also an Otherworld which provides us with the myths of How It All Began.

Attempts to turn myths into history generally end in absurdity. (There are exceptions: archaeologists were shaken when Heinrich Schliemann dug up the place where he thought the city of Troy had been, based solely on 'information' in *The Iliad* – and unearthed several superimposed cities.) But the converse is the rule: we can agree only on the barest

of facts – a date or a death, say – before we diverge in different readings
and interpretations. In other words, we always mythologize. The Yugo-
slavian hero, Marko Kraljevic, died in 1394.[3] Like a Greek hero he
was parented by a supernatural being – a vila, a fairy. Like Heracles, he
killed a three-headed dragon. But these sorts of beliefs about Marko did
not evolve over centuries; they were current within a few years of his
death.

A hero does not survive in the collective memory unless he is to some
extent mythologized – brought into line by the popular imagination with
an archetypal pattern. Imagination always exerts a gravitational pull
on historical events, bending them into confabulations, fictions, myths.
For instance we cannot help believing, it seems, that our heroes have not
really died but are only sleeping, waiting for the time when we are in
danger – when they will wake and rise to save us. This was not only
believed of mythical heroes such as King Arthur, but also of historical
ones such as Charlemagne, Barbarossa and Frederick the Great.[4]

Myths are naturally conservative, seeking out the archetypal pattern,
so that whatever elaboration we make on a myth will, if it is not from the
mythopoeic imagination, be forgotten. On the other hand, a comparatively trivial tale will always be remembered if it has come from there.
'If a tale can last, in oral tradition, for two or three generations, then it
has either come from the real place, or it has found its way there.'[5]

Structural analysis tells us that we can go further still with myth and
history, and say: history is that mythical variant which we have chosen
to take literally. History is therefore shadowed by other symmetrical and
inverted versions of itself, just as our personal lives are shadowed by the
other lives we live in dreams and imagination.

We tell ourselves that modern Western culture developed historically
out of the Middle Ages via the Renaissance; but this whole movement
might be read less as a development than a symmetrical inversion of
the old world – a movement 'from God to man, from dependence to
independence, from otherworldliness to this world, from the transcendent to the empirical, from myth and belief to reason and fact . . . from
a supernaturally static cosmos to a naturally determined evolving cosmos,
and from a fallen humanity to an advancing one'.[6] It is likely, therefore,
that our culture will, in turn, not so much 'advance' as symmetrically

invert once again, returning to the old outlook but in another guise. Indeed, as the scientific world-view approaches its limits, this may already be happening.

THE METAPHORICAL AND THE LITERAL

The distinction between historical and mythical is analogous to that between literal and metaphorical. In both cases it is a distinction that disappears in the daimonic world-view of traditional cultures, which is both metaphorical and literal. More accurately, it is a world-view which precedes any distinction between metaphorical and literal. It is literalism which has polarized them, just as it has proclaimed this world real and the Otherworld unreal. But to traditional cultures, this world is as metaphorical as the Otherworld is literal. Their use of language confirms this: where the literal meaning of words is absent, so too is the metaphorical. 'Statements made by primitive people cannot really be said to be of one sort or of the other. They lie between these [literal and metaphorical] categories of ours. They do not properly fit.'[7]

The American thinker, Owen Barfield, infers the same daimonic vision from medieval art which, he says, combined a literal view of the world with a metaphorical. It does not hesitate to represent invisible or spiritual events by material means – a farm cart does for Elijah's chariot of fire, angels (with or without wings) are dressed in ordinary clothes and so on.[8] Nothing was literal to the medieval mind. Everyday things carried the sort of multiple significances which today we attribute only to symbols. Before the scientific revolution, 'it is the concept of "merely literal" that was difficult'.[9]

PAINTING DRYADS

The distinction between literal and metaphorical was another product of the rise in the seventeenth century of the single, towering, sealed-off, rational ego which places itself at the centre of a world compelled, in turn, to dispose itself all around us and outside us and in a literal fashion. Traditional consciousness is more fluid and, so to speak, poly-centric: the ego still provides the same sense of identity but it can place itself as a matter of course in things which modern consciousness would call 'outer'.

For us to recapture this sort of identity requires an act of imagination, as, for example, when we put ourselves in another's place (the essential movement of compassion). Daimonic shape-shifting is precisely a meta-phor for the transformation of self that begins with such acts. These metamorphoses are sufficiently unusual in Western culture for us to call 'mystical' the experience – less unusual among children, and adults like Keats and Wordsworth – of an at-one-ness with Nature.[10] But this experience is the same in kind, if not in degree, as any experience of deep absorption in, or enchantment by, another person, object or activity – most commonly, perhaps, when we are 'lost' in music, transported by a story, entranced by a play and the like. Completely self-forgetful, we merge imaginatively with the object of attention. (Love may be nothing other than this degree of attention.) The same is true for making art. Although we cannot return to the daimonic condition of traditional vision, we can recreate it through the 'high-temperature fusing power of the creative imagination'.[11]

A painting of a tree is a bad painting (we say) if it is merely a copy of a tree, recording the surface only. Plato objected to art on these grounds. Because reality lies in the eternal world of Forms, from which everything in this world derives, then everything we see is already a copy of an Original. To then make a copy of this copy, said Plato, is a further retreat from reality and therefore misleading and pernicious.

Plotinus refutes Plato's notion by pointing out that 'if anyone dispar-ages the arts on the grounds that they imitate Nature, we remind him that natural objects are themselves only imitations, and that the arts do not simply imitate what they see but re-ascend to those principles (*logoi*) from which Nature herself is derived'.[12]

Through imagination, then, we can envisage the Form of the Tree, the treeness of a tree, which makes our re-creation of the tree more real even than the natural tree. The tree is no longer a literal tree – but neither is it purely metaphorical, as if we were painting the dryad of the tree instead of the tree. The painting, in other words – like all works of art – fulfils the criteria of the daimonic. It is both literal and metaphorical (or, rather, a creation that makes the distinction redundant). It is both universal, its treeness, and particular, an oak. It exists between the artist and the world in a representation which draws on both; and, as such, is both personal and subjective (the artist's perception) and impersonal and objective (the archetypal image of the tree). The work of art instructs us in that very Blakean double vision which is required to view it.

I I

Rites of Passage

PUBERTY RITES

There is no society which does not, or did not originally, practise initiation – a set of rites and a body of teaching which transform the individual from a child to an adult, or even from someone regarded as not fully human to a person. The most important initiation rites take place at puberty. Boys tend to be initiated in a group whereas girls are more likely to be initiated individually, at the time of their first menstruation. Both are required to 'die' and to be reborn.

A female candidate for initiation is, typically, shut up in a windowless hut or dark cave which is both the tomb of her girlhood and the womb out of which steps the woman she has become. She is not allowed to care for herself but is fed like a baby by the older women who also instruct her in tribal lore. From this infantile condition, she is born again. Dressed in new clothes and robed in her new knowledge, she comes out of seclusion to be hailed by the whole tribe.[1]

A boy of the Sioux tribe is prepared in a sweat lodge built of bent willow branches and covered in blankets to retain the heat and the steam generated by water poured over red-hot stones. From here, he is taken straight to a hilltop and installed in a cramped 'vision pit' for days without food and water. At the end of this time he will, with luck, have acquired a vision, and have been changed from a boy to a man.[2]

Australian Aboriginal boys are usually, like old Christian ascetics, deprived of all sensory experience, having to fast in silence and darkness. They may not speak and may only look at the ground. If they eat, they are not allowed to use their hands, as if they were babies or animals, or

86

even the Dead who are supposed to be similarly handicapped.[3] African boys are commonly carried off into the bush by tribal elders disguised as daimons or ancestors, and 'buried' in shallow graves without food or drink. (Daimons are always present at rites of passage, whether in the masks of the elders or, so to speak, in person. They are the genii of the thresholds who preside over all transitions.) After a period of intense privation, the boys usually suffer circumcision or scarring known as scarification.

The 'death' of initiates therefore involves, either singly or in combination, a regression to babyhood, a symbolic burial, an assimilation to the realm of the Dead.[4] It always entails, through the portal of a cave, pit or grave out in the wild bush, contact with the Otherworld and its denizens.

There is no sense in which initiation rites are invented. They were laid down, like myths, in the Beginning, by the daimons, gods, or ancestors. Indeed, they usually recapitulate and reaffirm cosmogony.[5] The rites imitate the pattern by which the cosmos came into being and established all subsequent patterns of tribal organization, village lay-out, hut-building, pottery-making, and so on. Every social structure and activity is meaningful because it is related to every other, and ultimately reflects the order of the universe.[6]

All this is revealed to the initiate as part of his 'rebirth'. But we should not underestimate the genuine hardship of the 'death' experience. In one sense he knows that he will not literally be killed; in another, he is not at all sure. The men who come for him, often to drag him away from his family and forcibly abduct him into the bush, are no longer men he knows. They may be masked and painted – at any rate they are transformed into terrifying, knife-wielding daimons who give him no comfort during the lonely, fearful, hungry, painful vigil. The severity of the ordeal makes all the more impressive the revelation he is granted, either through visions or through education in the tribal lore. All of a sudden he is transported into the vast new world of the tribal imagination. As the great myths and rituals are unfurled one by one in front of him, a dazzling meaning opens out like a fabulous carpet along which he processes into manhood.

As well as puberty, the other main biological events of life – birth, sex and marriage, death – are marked by what Arnold van Gennep called rites of passage.[7] These are the liminal ('threshold') times, the daimonic moments, when we are in transition between one state and another, and therefore (as folklore affirms) vulnerable to otherworldly intervention. The Sidhe will snatch an unbaptized baby, an unchurched mother, a maiden on her wedding night – all of whom are between worlds, as if still fluid and unfixed by Christian rites of passage. If our own elders do not abduct us into the Otherworld, then other daimons might.

Rites of passage can be mapped on to other areas in order to structure the whole of tribal life. For example, the Dowayos of Cameroon classify the world according to a system using the terms soft/hard, wet/dry.[8] At birth humans have 'soft' heads which are vulnerable to 'hot' objects. At puberty a boy is 'wet' until circumcised, and at his 'wettest' during circumcision when he kneels in a stream, bleeding into the water. The ceremony is also analogous to the seasons: it takes place at the end of the wet season and, as the dry season sets in, so the boy is 'dried', both by circumcision and by the symbolic application of fire. The culmination of the process takes place when his head is 'baked' by firing branches above it. From now on he is held to have a 'hard' head, while the head (glans) of his penis is held to be 'dry' and 'properly made'. At death, the head is 'wet' and has to be 'dried' by storing it in a skull house until it is purged of soft flesh and becomes hard bone.[9]

Even when the anthropologist has cracked this complicated code, he might not realize that the whole analogical system is also an elaborate metaphor – the model from which all the hard/soft, wet/dry analogies are drawn is the process of making pottery. The heads of the boys, of their penises, of the dead are dried, baked, hardened, fired, etc., as if they were pots. (As so often, technology has provided a fertile model for thinking about ourselves.) Yet, when the whole system was studied more deeply by the anthropologist Nigel Barley, he decided that it was not possible to say for certain whether the rites of passage were structured by pottery-making, or whether it was the other way round. Each activity presupposed and reflected the other.[10]

WHY WE COOK CHILDREN

According to Lévi-Strauss, the uniquely human art of transforming raw stuff by fire into cooked food provides a metaphor for the relationship between Nature and Culture. Initiation rites structured in terms of cooking are extremely widespread. Both newborn babies and mothers who have just given birth often have to be 'cooked'. Pueblo women, for example, give birth over hot sand to 'cook' the baby; new mothers among many Californian tribes are placed in 'ovens' hollowed out of the ground; and so are pubescent girls.[11] 'Cooking' is essential if someone falls too deeply into biology and becomes, as it were, too saturated with themselves and in danger of 'rotting' – a transformation, without fire, back to a state of Nature.

Sweat lodges are found among the native Americans and in parts of central Asia (there is evidence too of something similar among the ancient Celts). At least part of their purpose is to cook initiation candidates, not by roasting, but by steaming. Turkish baths and saunas are relics of this initiatory practice which has been – like circumcision itself – debased by modernity into a matter of mere hygiene. That it is not is made explicit by the Japanese who are obliged to wash thoroughly before boiling themselves in searingly hot communal baths. Native Americans such as the Sioux add smoking to steaming: their apprentice shamans are brought to a state of vision by smoking tobacco in the sweat lodge.

We cook ourselves, then, at moments of biological crisis in order to transform ourselves from natural beings into social beings. At death, we are roasted or rotted (cremated or buried). In this case, rotting has the opposite meaning to that of childbirth and puberty. It signifies the assimilation of the individual back to a Nature transformed into super-Nature, or the Otherworld. We can be sure of this because rotting usually signifies removal of the flesh from the bones which are exhumed; the same result is achieved by exposing corpses to the air and allowing birds to pick off the flesh. A system of analogy is implied – flesh: bones:: soft: hard:: mortal: immortal:: body: soul.

It is axiomatic that contact with the Otherworld is initiatory. It is a kind of death, not of the body, but of the ego. Because the ego of its nature clings violently to life – to the reality it imagines is the only reality – it can only be uprooted by external force, by a kind of near-death experience. The pattern of initiation, laid down by the gods or ancestors, is embodied most fully in the initiation of those special individuals who become the tribe's witch-doctor, medicine-man or shaman. It is they who, in trance or ecstasy, travel into the Otherworld to be killed, raised up and instructed by daimons (who are sometimes said to be the souls of dead shamans). Puberty rites are often a concrete replication of this operation, with the daimons played by the men of the tribe.

But there is a crucial sense in which shamanic and puberty rites are reversals of each other. Puberty rites represent the death of the childish self and a rebirth into adulthood – which is also the birth of the ego, of individuality, of full humanity. Shamanic initiation represents the destuction of the ego, the birth of the 'twice-born' man with superhuman powers. It is a return to Nature from Culture, where Nature now signifies super-Nature, the realm of the daimons and gods.

During their initiation in the Otherworld, Siberian shamans are frequently boiled so that their flesh can be removed fron their bones, which are forged anew out of iron by daimonic smiths.[12] Boiling is the cultural equivalent of natural rotting. Whereas a raw child is transformed by fire (roasted) to become a man (Nature transformed into Culture), a cooked adult is transformed by water (boiled) to become a 'superman' or shaman (Culture transformed into Nature).

THE CRAVING FOR INITIATION

If puberty rites are delayed for any reason, young people can reach their late teens or early twenties but still remain children. No initiation, no adulthood. Ritual transformation – imaginative transformation – takes precedence over merely biological, only literal, change. The universal incidence of puberty rites suggests that they are archetypal – a fundamental requirement of the soul. It is little wonder, then, that adolescents in secular Western society, who are deprived of official rites, unconsciously seek authentic initiation through drink, drugs, sex, rock 'n' roll. They long to get out of themselves, get out of their heads; they positively need fear and pain and privation to know if they can stand it, to know if they are men and women, know who they are. They want scarification – scars, tattoos, piercings – to show off. Some even commit crimes specifically to incur punishment – the initiation of prison – only to be given 'counselling' instead.

For all its admirable compassion and humaneness, modern Western liberalism has a horror of that fear and pain which seem to be essential components of initiation. Still, happily or unhappily, there is always enough fear and pain to go round. Whether we like it or not, we suffer sickness, bereavement, betrayal and anguish enough. The secret is to use these experiences for self-initiation. Instead, we are usually encouraged to seek a cure for them, rather than to take advantage of them for self-transformation. It is, on the whole, a mistake to medicalize suffering and even death because they are primarily matters of soul and only secondarily of the body.

Our lack of formal initiation rites may mean that our boys are driven to all kinds of excessive behaviour in order to feel that they are men; and yet they will never be sure of it as long as their manhood is unsanctioned – and so extreme, even criminal, behaviour is more likely. Meanwhile, girls whose biological womanhood is not recognized and admired by the tribe may feel undervalued. 'Hidden behind many current afflictions of the feminine – anorexia, bulimia and obsession with surface beauty – is a ritual emptiness, a lack of being seen, a spiritual omission.'[13] Without initiation we are all in danger of remaining childish, dependent, self-centred and uncertain of who we are.

Once we begin to understand the human craving for initiation, we begin to see it everywhere. For instance, during a special sacred time of about two weeks in summer, young European initiates fly to the Otherworld where they inhabit a liminal zone between land and sea. By day they are 'cooked' by a process of frying under a scorching sun, and periodically plunged into cold water; by night, they undergo an elaborate Dionysian ritual involving an orgy of wine, dancing and sex. They call this a 'Mediterranean holiday'.

POSTSCRIPT: NATURE AS DAIMONIC

Nowhere is the ambiguity of Nature more apparent than in initiation. The boundaries where this world ends and the Otherworld begins are always shifting – but Nature contains them both. A tribal village constitutes this world, what anthropologists call 'habitat' as opposed to the 'wilderness' which hedges us about. But wilderness is not only something to be feared and avoided at all costs, like chaos; it is also the location of burial sites, of ancestral mountains, of rocks and streams with helpful daimons – all places which must be visited at sacred times, for sacred reasons such as initiation, just as they must be eschewed at other profane times.

Nature is often personified as a powerful, shape-changing goddess, potentially benign or menacing, tame or wild, helping or dangerous, depending on where or when or how we approach her. Christianity polarized her of course, making of her an obstacle to the freedom of the spirit on the one hand; and, on the other, God's creation and the manifestation of His love. Modern literalism polarized her further, as we have seen: rationalism demonized her while sentimental Romantics divinized her (the authentic Romantic is always mindful of her traditional ambivalence).

In the next chapter I shall be describing Charles Darwin's ambivalent response to Nature. I am not concerned to attack Darwin, but I do want to test a hypothesis: if daimons and the Otherworld, myth and initiation, are universal realities, then they must still be present in a culture such as ours which pretty much rules them out. But what form would they adopt? Would I be able to recognize them? Could they be lurking in the shadows of such central beliefs of ours as Darwinism and its successor, neo–Darwinism, which claims to have superseded myth in its account of who we are and where we come from? Would it be possible to apply the same sort of sceptical inquiry to the Darwinists' story of our origins as they apply to myths, such as the Garden of Eden? Not that I want to espouse the Biblical creation myth, or Creationism. Rather, I would just like to pursue a *jeu d'esprit*, to see where it leads, and perhaps to question the literalism in whatever belief about our beginnings we hold fast to.

12

The Animals Who Stared Darwin in the Face

When Charles Darwin embarked at the end of 1831 on his five-year journey to the New World aboard the *Beagle*, he was a budding scientist who held the Enlightenment rationalist view of Nature – that it was a machine, like clockwork, which a transcendent God had set in motion and left to run its own course. At the same time he was by no means oblivious to the Romantic reaction which viewed Nature more poetically, sometimes pantheistically, as a realm of divine manifestation.

Darwin was an imaginative man who loved poetry (Milton's *Paradise Lost* was his constant companion), and his first encounter with tropical Nature is nothing if not Romantic. It is like an epiphany. The 'wild luxuriance' of the jungle, he says, is like 'the glories of another world';[1] the sight of it is a new overwhelming vision, 'like giving a blind man eyes'.[2] A walk into the Brazilian rain forest is entrancing and profoundly moving. He feels a 'sublime devotion' to 'Nature's God'.[3] How was he to express such enchantment?

He might have responded to his vision poetically and become a sort of Wordsworth, except that he hated writing. He might have spent his days praising the Creator of all this beauty, had he been the clergyman he was earmarked to become. But he was, and remained, a scientist. His job was not to lay himself open to Nature imaginatively, but to break it down into individual facts. He finds it difficult to do this because he does not really subscribe to the Enlightenment view of Nature as a machine designed by a Protestant God. He thinks of it as a creative power and the source of all forms of life – 'through her prodigious fertility, her powers of spontaneous variation, and her powers of selection, she could do everything' that God did.[4] In other words, Darwin imagines Nature as a kind of Goddess. He is barely conscious of this, of course, but he has an inkling because in his writings he apologizes to his readers for so often speaking of natural selection as an intelligent power: 'I have also personified the word Nature; for I have found it difficult to avoid this ambiguity.'[5]

The disparity between his initial ecstasy and his professional duty begins to tell. His journal changes tone. The constant beauty begins to 'bewilder the mind'; the barrage of images, the 'chaos of delight', becomes 'wearisome';[6] like 'a sultan in a seraglio' he grows 'hardened to beauty'.[7] Worse, he becomes increasingly giddy and then panic-stricken: 'animals are staring me in the face, without labels and scientific epitaphs'. It is a decisive moment – the moment when Darwin gives up the attempt to embrace Nature in all her wholeness, wonder and fecundity; and, from fear of 'chaos', begins to armour himself against her with labelling and facts.

This, we recall, is the trouble with Mother Nature. She is not the fixed entity that scientists, who view her through literalistic spectacles, would have us believe. She is a sea of metaphors which reflect back at us the face we show her. We characterize her by whatever perspective we look at her through – as an implacable enemy, for instance, or as a vast harmonious rhythm; as a wild creature who must be tamed, or as a nymph who must be left unspoilt or as a violent animal, red in tooth and claw. As Darwin quails in the face of a dizzying Nature, and fends her off, so she comes back at him, hostile and sickening. By the time he is fifty he will write, shockingly: 'the sight of a feather in a peacock's tail, whenever I gaze at it, makes me sick'.[8]

DARWIN'S NAUSEA

Darwin's first encounter with sickness was aboard the *Beagle*. He was horribly, miserably seasick for five years. He never adapted, never found his sea legs but, heroically, neither did he give up and go home. He longed to, because he also suffered from a crippling homesickness which blighted the richness and variety of all his later ports of call, from Tahiti to Mauritius. He fought off nausea by doing his naturalist's duty, doggedly collecting and cataloguing samples, longing to be home and cursing the sea – that 'raging monster' which all his life he 'loathed and abhorred'.[9]

Darwin's physical sickness is clearly a symptom of some more existential nausea. He hated the sea because it never stopped flowing, moving, rocking him to the foundations. It can be seen as a metaphor for his own unconscious life and especially its movements, the emotions. We know this because as soon as he reached home, he settled in the Kent countryside and hardly moved again. Any journey, even a day trip to London, caused him to become giddy merely at the thought, to retch violently and to put it off as long as he could.[10] But physical movement did not affect him as much as emotional movement. A trivial disagreement with a colleague prostrated him with nausea; the thought of what the critics might say about his books left him vomiting for hours. His sickness, never satisfactorily diagnosed, flaring up whenever he moved or was moved, made his life at times unendurable. 'A third of his working life was spent doubled up, trembling, vomiting, and dowsing himself in icy water.'[11] No wonder, then, that Nature, turbulent and chaotic as the abhorred sea, made him queasy. The more beautiful it was – a peacock's feather – the more moving and the more sickening.

THE IMBECILE STEPMOTHER

In the presence of the primeval forest, 'temples filled with the varied productions of the God of Nature', young Charles could not help but feel 'that there is more in man than the mere breath of his body'.[12] These were the temples he looked forward to worshipping scientifically in. But less than three years after his return to England, he had become a closet materialist. He had to hide his belief because, although materialism was current in the more radical medical schools and among self-proclaimed atheists, it was still anathema to the prevailing Anglican orthodoxy – and therefore to the respectability which Darwin dreaded losing.[13]

Not that he embraced atheism, either then or later. He was ambivalent on the question of God, agnostic, although one can see how in the course of his life the religious sense of his youth simply withered away. It was as if he just was not interested. Whenever he was badgered about his religious beliefs, he would prevaricate or contradict himself.[14] Meanwhile, his materialism was telling him that there was nothing 'more in man': mind could be reduced to matter, living atoms organizing themselves; and thought was merely a secretion of the brain, as the liver secretes bile.[15] As I have tried to indicate, it is the great attraction of the 'mother' hidden in materialism that she connects all psychic events to material ones, and makes all metaphors into matter alone. By taking the metaphor of 'only matter' literally, Darwin hoped to neutralize the disturbing power of Mother Nature, and fix her in a singleness of meaning which would give him the stability he longed for – which would settle the matter.

But Nature will neither settle nor run smoothly like the machine she is supposed to be. Whenever Darwin contemplates her she makes him shudder. He thinks of her as a kind of wicked yet imbecile stepmother – 'clumsy, wasteful, blundering, low and horridly cruel'.[16] He cannot endure life, he says, without science, his only bulwark against sickness and disgust. He strives to attain proper scientific detachment, but he cannot look out of his study window without being reminded of 'the dreadful but quiet war of organic beings going on in the peaceful woods and smiling fields'.[17]

But really the war is going on elsewhere. Behind Charles's smiling public face, beneath the peaceful domestic routine, the rational materialist is undermined by acute angst and racked by the nauseating feelings of the poetry-lover. Swallow them down as he may, they are thrown back up at him in a demonized Nature who is all the more vengeful for being denied conscious recognition. He knows she is pitiless because she killed with one of her diseases his little daughter Annie, whom he mourned every day of his life. Anyone else might have turned to, or blamed, God. But, for Darwin, God is too remote; Nature's random acts of brutality are immediate. His only way of coming to terms with her is to define and confine her scientifically, in a law. He calls the law 'natural selection', and it will be hailed as *the* mechanism of evolution. But there is more than a little of Darwin's own distorted vision in this 'law' which he and his successors claimed as an objective truth.

THE SURVIVAL OF THE FITTEST

The modern theory of evolution asserts that species evolve into other species by natural selection. Very occasionally a random mutation in the genetic make-up of one member of a species will favour its survival. It and its offspring are thereby naturally selected to prosper over the other members of its species.

The example of natural selection which convinced me of its truth is the case of the Manchester moths. In the nineteenth century, factory chimneys around Manchester were belching out so much smoke that the trees were turning black. A light-grey moth (*Biston Betularia*) rested on the bark of these trees and relied on camouflage to avoid being eaten by predators. As the trees became darker, so the moths 'evolved' a progressively darker coloration.[18]

Imagine my disappointment when I discovered that this is not a proof of natural selection. What really happened was this: there were originally a lot of grey moths and a few darker ones of the same species. The lighter ones tended to get eaten as their camouflage no longer worked, while the darker ones flourished. There was no evolutionary change, not even any natural selection, only a shift in population – rather as if some disease killed off white people but left black people untouched. Even if the evolutionist story were true it would only represent a tiny alteration in one species; there would still be nothing remotely approaching the change of one species into another.[19]

Darwinists may well protest that they would never claim the business of the moths to be evidence of natural selection. Yet the story is still in text books and encyclopaedias; and, even if it was not, the moth tale is still recounted proudly by the ordinary Darwinist-in-the-street. It is a sort of legend which those who know better are not assiduous in correcting. More than legend even: it was official theory at least as late as 1970 when the British Museum of Natural History's *A Handbook of Evolution*[20] described the 'industrial melanism' of the moths as 'the most striking evolutionary change actually witnessed' and as 'demonstrating natural selection'.[21] My point is: a lot of Darwinist 'proof' seems to operate at this level – seems in other words to be a sort of folklore.

Darwin altered the emphasis of 'natural selection' when he adopted the expression 'survival of the fittest' from Herbert Spencer (who also coined the term 'evolution'). It better suited his idea of life as a bitter struggle. For what happens, said Darwin, is that those animals which are best fitted to their environment are the most successful and have the most offspring. How do we measure the fitness of any animal? By its capacity to survive, say the Darwinists. So, the fit survive and those who survive are the fittest. It is doubtful that a simple tautology – that survivors survive – can ever be a meaningful law.

Even if it were not tautological, the survival of the fittest would still be dubious. It is a highly individualistic notion which rules out the co-operation, love and altruism which characterize many extremely successful species, including our own. The cut-throat competition that Darwin imagined as the distinguishing feature of Nature is not in fact much found. The overwhelming majority of the 22,000-odd species of fish, reptiles, amphibians, birds and mammals do not fight, kill for food or compete aggressively for space.[22] Besides, a whole host of factors influence success, not least luck; and, indeed, the idea that a competitive environment weeds out weaklings and ensures the survival of the fittest is, to be fair to the Darwinists, no longer widely subscribed to. 'Fittest' has tended to be quietly replaced by 'adapted'.

The 'survival of the fittest' or natural selection theories throw no light on how creatures evolve. It is just another way of saying that some animals live and breed, while others die out. It is neither a 'law' nor even a particularly accurate description of Nature. It is, if anything, more like a symptom of Darwin's sickened vision, his refusal to recognize the many faces of Nature and his insistence on a single face – which stared back at him as a cruel mask.

As Nature assailed him with waves of nausea, Charles frantically built sea-walls of habit and 'clockwork routine, his days alike as "two peas" '[23] in the effort to sand-bag his emotional life. But of course the walls he raised to keep Nature at bay became his prison. 'I have lost, to my great regret, all interest in poetry of any kind', he wrote sadly. Gone was the beloved Milton of his youth; lost his Paradise. Desperately he tried stronger meat still – Shakespeare whom he had always loved. But 'I found it so totally dull that it nauseated me.'[24] Something more than dullness here, we suspect. His only pleasure lay in little experiments with his cherished earthworms and the tiny flowers he would chide and praise;[25] and even this was allowable only because it could be smuggled in under the cloak of science. The worms could not save him, however. 'My mind has become a kind of machine for grinding laws out of large collections of facts.'[26] Poor Charles, a good and kindly man, has spent his life denying Nature her soul, and as a result has lost his own; the machine he would make her, he became.

13

The Transmutation of Species

THE FACTS OF LIFE

A surprising number of people believe that humans are descended from spacemen who have landed on Earth and, like the mysterious Nephilim in *Genesis*, 'mated with the daughters of men'. We may smile at this myth but it is not especially disreputable. All traditional cultures believe that they are descended from gods, god-like humans such as the ancestors or divine animals – many of whom came from the sky. Naturally we do not understand the clans who claim descent from a leopard or a bear because we think that they believe in a literal biological descent, which they do not. It is Westerners who take their myths of descent literally so that, when we ceased to believe that we were literally descended from Adam and Eve, who were created according to Archbishop Ussher of Armagh in 4004 BC, we were only too ready to believe we were descended from apes. Tribespeople would understand divine ape-ancestors at once, but *actual* apes . . . It would be their turn to smile. The last superior laugh is ours, of course, because unlike the naive tribespeople and the barmy extraterrestrialists we have a scientific theory of descent: evolution.

In 1992 a science writer called Richard Milton published a book, *The Facts of Life*, which questioned the scientific validity of the theory of evolution. When I read a review of it by Richard Dawkins, describing the book as 'loony', 'stupid', 'drivel', and its author as somone who 'needs psychiatric help',[1] I was naturally grateful to Dawkins for drawing my attention, through this closely reasoned critique, to a work I might otherwise have missed. Mr Milton turned out to be disconcertingly sane.

He wrote his book as a concerned father who was nervous about his young daughter being taught a theory as if it were Gospel truth.[2] There is, he says, not enough evidence to establish the theory of evolution as fact.

The theory, as everyone knows, is that all the organisms on the planet have evolved by 'random mutation'. Every now and then a member of a species is by accident born with some feature which gives it an advantage over its neighbours, such as a slightly longer neck to enable it to eat foliage from higher up the tree. Natural selection does the rest – and a giraffe evolves. So, in the course of millions of years there is what was called in Darwin's day a gradual 'transmutation of species'[3] whereby everything that is now alive evolved out of some common ancestor such as a simple organism in the sea. A lot of species did not make it, but were weeded out by natural selection (so the story goes); and we have fossils of them – all the dinosaurs, for instance – to prove it.

More crucially, the theory predicts vast numbers of fossils, such as invertebrates with rudimentary backbones, fish with legs, reptiles with half-formed wings – fossils of all those transitional species which link fishes to reptiles, reptiles to birds and to mammals. It predicts even more fossils of all the species intermediate between the earliest-known mammal (possibly a small rodent) and ourselves. It predicts yet more fossils of all those in-between species which did not make it – the monsters that randomly mutated into a dead end. In fact, we have not got a fossil of a single one (well, possibly *one* – I will come to that).

The lack of fossils puzzled Darwin and his colleagues, but they assumed the evidence would turn up eventually. We have been looking now in all the likely spots for more than a hundred years and have still found no fossils of transitional species (except, maybe, one). Nor are there any known transitional species of animal alive today. When are we going to cease promulgating evolution as a proven fact? wonders Mr Milton – who also rightly objects to the religious fervour with which it is promoted, and to the way any dissenters are shouted down or denied access to the scientific journals. He himself does not claim to know how life as we know it came to be. He is emphatically not a Creationist (a believer in the literal truth of the Biblical account of Creation). He would doubtless be dismayed by my own gloss on evolutionism. He simply deplores 'the extent to which ideological Darwinism has replaced scientific Darwinism in our educational system'.[4]

The fervour of an ideology can sometimes lead its devotees to be a little economical with the truth, and even to try a little sleight of hand with the evidence. The evolutionists are naturally eager to show us an 'evolutionary sequence'. But the only one with a decent number of 'steps' – it is the standard one – shows horses evolving in a straight line. It was constructed in a hurry and, as more fossils came to light, it turned out that evolution had not been linear and upward at all, but that (to consider size alone) the horses had been taller at first, then shorter again with the passage of time. Besides, although there are similarities between, say, the first two horses in the 'sequence', *Eohippus* and *Mesohippus*, the differences are still greater; and there is no evidence of any species connecting them. The suggestion that they form an evolutionary chain 'is not a scientific theory – it is an act of faith'.[5] Luckily there is *one* extant 'missing link' on which the theory of evolution largely rests: *Archaeopteryx*.

In 1861 quarry men at Solnhofen, Bavaria – an area famous for providing fossils – split a stone which contained a petrified *Compsognathus*, a dinosaur about the size of a pigeon. Amazingly, it had feathers. Or, at least, it had feathers by the time it was sold to the British Museum . . .

Called *Archaeopteryx*, the fossil was perhaps evidence not only of a transitional species, but also the moment when reptiles turned into birds. Its reptilian features included 'vestigial' claws, teeth and a bony tail. Its avian features were the 'true feathers and wings', and possibly its wishbone, analogous to the mammalian collar-bone, which dinosaurs do not have. It did not, however, possess the large pectoral muscles required for flight, so it must have been a glider or else a bit like a chicken.[6] In short, it could be a feathered dinosaur or a toothed and bony-tailed bird, depending on how we look at it – although the bird it was supposed to be evolving into (*Protoavis*) has been found in beds in Texas said to be seventy-five million years older than those in which *Archaeopteryx* was found.[7] Lastly, it must be remembered that *Archaeopteryx* is only conjecturally a 'missing link'. Like all other species it is isolated in the fossil record, with no trace of any immediate ancestor or descendant.

Archaeopteryx is ambiguous, eluding interpretation, shifting shape between reptile and bird according to the observer. To the eye of neo–Darwinist faith, it is intermediate between both bird and reptile. It fulfils, in other words, all the functions of a daimon, just as all missing links do. They are intrinsically fuzzy, open to different imaginative readings. They are even shady, like the missing link between humans and apes found in a Sussex gravel pit in 1912. A fragment of human braincase and an ape's jawbone provided the basis for a 'reconstruction' of Piltdown Man. When he was exposed as a hoax over forty years later, it was clear that scientists can be just as credulous as anyone else. When it comes to evidence for their ideologies, they see what they expect, and long, to see.

If, for instance, you look at *Archaeopteryx* through the eyes of the anti-Darwinist professors Fred Hoyle and Chandra Wickramasinghe, you see at once that it is a hoax.[8] The feathers are completely modern, lying unruffled on one plane while the rock in which the fossil lies has been split with such implausible precision through the centre of the feathers that the pattern of dendrites in the natural rock is uniquely absent in the feathered areas. The feathers are not even rooted in the tail, but merely lie around it. *Archaeopteryx* is a genuine *Compsognathus* fossil, claim the professors, but with the marks of feathers added, quite easily, by imprinting a bit of paste and powdered stone.[9]

The first *Archaeopteryx* was procured by Karl Haberlein and sold to the British Museum for a very large sum of money a year after the publication of Darwin's *The Origin of Species*. It was extremely fortuitous because Darwin's chief propagandist, T. H. Huxley, had just been musing that birds must be descended from reptiles and that one day a feathered reptile would turn up. Turn up it did, almost to Huxley's blueprint. Unfortunately, the head of this first *Archaeopteryx* was smashed so that the crucial question of the presence or absence of teeth was impossible to determine. Luckily, as if to settle the matter decisively in favour of the Darwinists, another *Archaeopteryx* turned up sixteen years later. It was found by Ernst Haberlein, the son of Karl, who also made a lot of cash from it. Luck? Coincidence? Or a case of the father passing on his skills, some of them archaeological, to the son?

There are a few other *Archaeopteryxes*, but they are either 're-classifications' of *Compsognathus* fossils or meagre remains similarly interpreted by the eye of faith.[10] Recent discoveries in China in the 1990s of two turkey-sized, flightless feathered replies called *Protoarchaeopteryx robusta* (because it is believed to be an ancestor of *Archaeopteryx*) and *Caudipteryx* (because of its tail feathers) are being hailed as more evidence that birds are descended from dinosaurs. But actually they are evidence only that some small dinosaurs, including *Archaeopteryx* perhaps, were feathered, not for flight, possibly for insulation, for camouflage or for fun – and not necessarily related to birds at all.[11]

EVOLUTION AND DEVOLUTION

Why do evolutionists believe in evolution against all the evidence? Partly, I suppose, because there is no credible alternative story; mostly, because it is a powerful creation myth which demands to be implicitly believed.

Structural analysis has already shown how myths which may look very different on the surface are in fact variants of the same myth. They are simply transformed by certain archetypal rules. This is true of myths of devolution and of evolution.

Traditionally, creation myths are devolutionary. They describe how we are descended from gods or god-like ancestors, and our present state is fallen, a regression from the perfection of the past. We are inferior to our forebears. Our task is to recreate the conditions of Eden or Arcadia, the state of past harmony.

Only our Western scientific myth is evolutionary. It describes how we have ascended from animals and our present state is advanced, a progress from the imperfection of the past. We are superior to our forebears. Our task is to create the conditions of the New Jerusalem or Utopia, the state of future harmony.

We notice that the two myths are, as so often, symmetrical but inverted. So, while the evolutionary myth claims that it is not a myth at all, but history, superseding all other myths, we see that really it is a variant of the devolutionary myth – an eccentric variant that wants to take itself literally.

Evolutionism places humans at the top of the tree, the position formerly occupied by the gods. It also endows us with god-like powers of reason etc. But it claims, too, that we are only animals, a product of mere biology. In other words, we have 'ascended' to become the 'divine animals' from whom so many traditional cultures claim descent.

The place where 'transmutation of species' really occurs is not in Nature but in myth. Species of gods and daimons are always appearing to humans in animal form. Witches and shamans take on the shapes of animals, and certain animals shed their skins to assume human form. The interchanging of humans and animals is a metaphor for the reciprocal relationship betweed this world and the Otherworld, the way each flows into the other. In the old days we believed in werewolves; African tribes still routinely believe in were-leopards or were-crocodiles. Nowadays we believe in were-apes. Myth has no objection to the changing of an ape into a man, or vice versa; but only evolutionists would dream of taking this literally: transmutation of species is a literalization of daimonic shape-shifting.

Transitional species are abundant in myth, where we not only have were-animals but also centaurs, satyrs, fauns, mermaids, etc.; but they are absent in fact. Evolution works imaginatively but not literally. The search for the magical were-ape, or 'missing link', which will transform the myth into history tends to follow the same sequence of events: a tooth or bone is found and excitedly hailed as evidence for the missing link. Time passes – and it is reluctantly re-classified as either man-like or ape-like.

MISSING LINKS

The search for 'missing links' in the evolutionary chain can be traced back to the Scholastic doctrine – axiomatic for over a thousand years – that 'Nature makes no leaps'. This in turn echoed the philosophical principle of continuity which stated that there is no abrupt transition from one order of reality to another. This in turn was identical to the law of Mean Terms, formulated by the Neoplatonist philosopher, Iamblichus, which held that 'two dissimilar terms must be linked by an intermediary having something in common with each of them'.[12] He cites as examples the role of daimons in mediating between gods and men; and the role of soul as mediating between eternity and time, and between the sensible and intelligible worlds.[13] Hidden in the theory of evolution, therefore, is a doctrine of daimons which owes more to tradition than to empiricism.

But apart from this sort of philosophical precedent for 'missing links', it seems simply to be the case that the need for continuity exerts as archetypal a fascination over the imagination as the idea of shape-shifting. We always construct a series of links between ourselves and the gods (or whatever we conceive to be the ground of our being), such as the Neoplatonic emanations, the medieval Chain of Being or the Roman Catholic saints, angels and Blessed Virgin Mary.

When Protestantism and, later, eighteenth-century Deism, did away with the links between us and God, it was easier to cease believing in Him; but it also left a vacuum which cried out to be filled with some new chain of being – and the theory of evolution exactly fitted the bill. The model for the evolutionary chain was not philosophical or theological, however. It was the mirror image of that devolutionary chain which in traditional societies is supplied by genealogy. When we trace our origins back to the gods or ancestors, we correctly derive history from myth, which is traditionally always prior. Evolutionism incorrectly tries to literalize myth back into history.

In Darwin's time, genealogy was, as it were, the current orthodox view of evolution: we were all descended from Adam and Eve. Instead of deliteralizing this fundamentalist devolutionary version of events back into myth, evolutionism swung to the opposite and equally literal pole, insisting on a fundamentalist evolutionary version. The impasse continues to this day, with the Darwinists at loggerheads with the Creationists, who are by no means beaten. In October 1999, the School Board in Kansas voted to remove the teaching of the theory of evolution from the school curriculum.

THE SCIENTIFIC PRIESTHOOD

But what, if not Adam and Eve, does the evolutionary chain link us to? The Darwinist answer, of course, is: to an ape-like ancestor in the first instance, and ultimately to protein molecules in the primeval ocean. The psychological answer is that it links us to a symmetrical but inverted version of the transcendent God it has done away with – it links us, that is, to an immanent goddess. Darwinists are not aware of her, but she is present in Darwin's vision of Nature as a cruel power, which his successors inherited. They still see Nature today in an unwittingly Romantic light as the irrepressible source of all forms of life ('through her prodigious fertility, her powers of spontaneous variation, and her powers of selection',[14] she can do anything that God did). When Jacques Monod wrote of the 'inexhaustible resources of the well of chance',[15] he was using a metaphor which traditionally belongs to the creatrix in her manifestation as the Soul of the World.

The goddess is particularly present in any ideology which emphasizes growth and development. As James Hillman has noticed, 'the evolutional terms of Darwinian biology . . . resonate with the person of the mother archetype'.[16] It is her perspective that 'appears in hypotheses about the origins of human life, the nature of matter and the generation of the world'.[17] If she was the archetype behind Darwin's model of evolution as bush-like, 'a rich radiation of varying forms',[18] it was another archetype – the Apollonic – which changed this model into something Darwin never intended. Evolution became identified not just with growth but with upward growth – an 'escalator' towards ever greater improvement. It seemed to offer biological proof of the Enlightenment belief that the human race follows the same pattern of growing up as the individual. Thus Darwin's disciples clearly saw a progression from childish native cultures to more mature Western cultures, to the most mature Western culture – the British – to the most grown-up individuals within that culture, namely the British scientists, who, by a happy coincidence, happened to be themselves.

Scientists, then, became a new sort of priesthood from whom all authority flowed. They themselves were quite explicit about this, promoting without irony the theory of evolution as a new 'gospel'.[19] Darwin's followers, such as Hooker, Tyndall, Spencer and Huxley, formed themselves into a secret enclave – the X club – with the express intention of taking over the Royal Society and pledging to 'place an intellectual priesthood at the head of English culture.'[20] Religions do not need scientific proof, and nor did theirs: the truth of evolution was really a revelation from the goddess by whom they had been unconsciously seized.

And it *is* true, if only because all stories, even tall ones, embody an imaginative truth. 'Everything possible to be believ'd,' asserted Blake, 'is an image of truth.'[21] Evolutionists are guilty of idolatry, not because they worship false images, but because they worship a single image falsely, fixing the wealth of Nature's metaphors in a single rigid mode and so obstructing the fluid, oceanic play of imagination, so appalling to Darwin, yet so essential for the soul's health.

GENES AS DAIMONS

According to Plato, we are randomly allotted at birth a daimon who determines our destiny.[22] It represents, in other words, that combination of Chance and Necessity which Jacques Monod in an influential book of that name, attributes to the key mechanisms of evolution (random genetic mutation = chance; natural selection = necessity). Monod seems to think that they are neutral, value-free scientific principles; but of course they are not – they are the usual 'goddess' in two of her most ancient guises. Chance is the blind goddess Fortuna whom scientists unconsciously acknowledge when, as they often do, they call chance 'blind' – something no abstract principle could be. Besides, chance is precisely what a scientific hypothesis is supposed to save us from.[23] It should at the very least be itself treated as a hypothesis to be established. Instead chance is unscientifically taken for granted as the background against which all inquiry is conducted. In short, it is a belief.[24]

Necessity is sometimes the all-powerful goddess Ananke, sometimes the three Fates who spin, allot and cut the threads of our lives. It is they who give us our daimons in their aspect of chance and necessity. But daimons also embody opposite aspects: *telos*, or purpose, as opposed to chance; and freedom as opposed to necessity.

The daimon is our imaginative blueprint. It lays down the personal myth we enact in the course of our lives; it is the voice that calls us to our vocation. All daimonic men and women are aware of personal daimons and their paradoxes. Both Yeats and Jung spoke of having daimons who drove them ruthlessly – often, it seemed, against their will – towards self-fulfilment; who gave freedom in return for hard service.[25] The same language of ruthless driving and brute necessity, but without the concomitant meaning and freedom, is used by biologists to describe genes.

Genes are literalized daimons. I am not of course claiming that they do not exist; but I am far from being alone in saying that their function and meaning is by no means as well understood as sociobiologists claim. They are shadowy, borderline, elusive, ambiguous entities – to judge by the amount of disagreement about them – and, as such, they satisfy the daimonic criteria.

They greatly exercise Richard Dawkins, a leading proponent of evolutionism. In language remarkable for its primitive anthropomorphism, he avers that genes 'create form', 'mould matter', 'choose' and even engage in 'evolutionary arms races'.[26] Like demons, the 'selfish' genes 'possess us'.[27] They are 'the immortals'.[28] We are 'lumbering robots' whose genes 'created us body and mind'.[29] This, surely, reminds us more of the sermon than of science. It certainly demonstrates the ubiquity of daimons, even (especially) when literalization prevents them from being recognized as such. Traditionally, our bodies have been seen as the vehicles of our personal daimon, our soul or 'higher self'. Now, by an amusing inversion, we are asked to believe that our most treasured attributes are simply pressed into the service of the genes: 'it is really our genes that are propagating themselves through us. We are only their instruments, their temporary vehicles . . .'[30] Given such an extreme ideology, it is no wonder that sociobiologists want to believe that genetic engineering will solve everything from cancer to drug-addiction to unemployment. But, as the Harvard geneticist R.C. Lewontin points out, not only is their ideology unrealistic, but all their 'explanations of the evolution of human behaviour are like Rudyard Kipling's *Just So* stories about how the camel got its hump'.[31]

14

The Composition of the Magi

HERMES TRISMEGISTUS

The idea of Beginnings is one of our most popular myths. Christian
culture is keen on beginnings – 'In the Beginning was the Word' – and
time began, or began to go forward, as it were, at the date of Christ's
birth. But myths begin 'Once upon a time', to indicate that there are no
literal beginnings, only myths about Beginnings. According to one such
myth, the Renaissance began in 1453 when Constantinople fell to the
Turks, and its scholars fled to the West, bringing with them the classical
texts which would revive humanistic learning.

In Florence, Cosimo di Medici employed agents to collect the newly
available Greek writings; and, in about 1460, a monk arrived from
Macedonia with a manuscript which was so exciting that Cosimo commanded his chief translator, Marsilio Ficino, to put aside the works of
Plato he had already assembled and begin at once on this new collection
of treatises.

It was called *Corpus Hermeticum*. Its author was Hermes Trismegistus,
'thrice-great' Hermes. Ficino had already heard of him from Cicero and
Church Fathers such as St Augustine; already knew that he was an
Egyptian sage, almost a god, of staggering antiquity. Indeed, he had
already placed Trismegistus at the very beginning of his 'genealogy of
wisdom', so that Orpheus, Pythagoras and the 'divine' Plato derived
their authority from him – and now here was a collection of his writings!

Since 'the great forward movements of the Renaissance all derive their
vigour, their emotional impulse, from looking backwards',[1] the discovery
of texts which may have been composed in a Golden Age of wisdom

from which mankind had fallen away – but which might now be recovered – caused a tremendous stir across Europe. Over the next two hundred years, many thinkers discerned in the Hermetic works the promise of a *prisca theologia*, an original and pristine theology which, earlier and therefore more sacred even than Christianity, offered a way out of the quarrels and schisms that beset Christendom after the Reformation.

It was especially well equipped to do this because in many ways Hermeticism seemed to anticipate Christianity; and, at the same time, it incorporated elements which resembled Platonism, Neoplatonism and Stoicism, and synthesized them into a religion which was all the more attractive for being free of temples or liturgy.

What Hermetic religion offered was a gnosis, a direct revelation of the divine. The treatises took the form of dialogues, much like Plato's, between a master and pupil in which the latter is led towards divine illumination. The thought was tortuous and difficult; but the mixture of poetry and intellectual rigour, magic and mysticism which passionately engaged the whole person held a powerful appeal for people who felt that religion, rather like modern philosophy, had become lost in cerebration and remote from an actual experience of God.

Hunchbacked, lisping, prone to melancholy, Ficino was also brilliant and charismatic. He inaugurated at his villa a philosophical centre which consciously imitated Plato's Academy in Athens. It was for a while the beating heart of Florence, as Florence was the heart of the Renaissance. Ficino was the first great Renaissance magus, a word that is meant to imply philosopher and wise man as well as magician. He translated, studied and taught the works of Plato, Plotinus, Proclus, Hesiod and, of course, the *Hermetica*; but he also practised astral – 'star' – magic.

FICINO'S STAR MAGIC

It is difficult for us to imagine how a magus viewed the stars, although not perhaps so difficult as it is often assumed – who has not been filled with some mystical intuition while letting their mind roam across a starry sky? At any rate, the stars that most interested the magus were those we call planets; and while he saw them as we do, as physical bodies, he also saw them as living beings moving gracefully against the backdrop of 'fixed stars' like animals (as the magus Giordano Bruno says) or like ensouled bodies. Sometimes he saw them as other worlds, each governed by a 'star-demon' or an angelic power.

Stars, in other words, were daimons, even gods, who were intimately connected to us by an invisible influence (*influenza*) as tangible and as potentially pestilential as 'flu. They moved our bodily humours like tides; their music set up deep resonances in the psyche. Venus was constellated in matters of the heart, Saturn in moods of melancholy, Mars in the impetus to battle.

For the young English magus, John Dee, 'effluvia' from the stars were celestial powers he could invoke after the manner of Ficino, directing their flow into the 'imaginative spirit' where they 'coalesce more intensely as in a mirror, show us wonders and work wonders within us'[2] – a marvellous picture of the lens of imagination concentrating and fusing the rays which emanate from the ruling daimons, whether they are depicted as planets, gods or archetypes. Indeed, perhaps the only way we can grasp the constant astrological awareness of the magus is to read it in psychological terms – to transpose the heavens and the unconscious and to imagine the night sky as within us and the unconscious without. No longer 'as Above, so Below', but 'as without, so within'. Giordano Bruno even anticipated this change of spatial metaphor when he compared the stars to soul-sparks floating in the infinitude of psyche – a Gnostic image Jung adopted as he became increasingly unhappy at having confined the psyche 'within' us. The stars move through the night as the archetypal images of the gods move through the collective unconscious, sky and psyche reflecting each other.

Ficino's astral magic was designed to draw down and direct the influences of the stars for one's own ends. It was continuous with older, medieval magic which, however, was aimed at invoking angels or demons and compelling them to do one's bidding. This gave rise to an overtly 'demonic' magic which seems to have appealed particularly to the northern European magi such as the Abbot Trithemius and his pupil Johannes Reuchlin, to Paracelsus and, notoriously, to Cornelius Agrippa. While Ficino recognized this kind of magic, which was at once more powerful and more dangerous than his own, he favoured a *magia naturalis* – a 'natural magic' which harked back to Neoplatonic theurgy and whose planetary influences were more abstract and spiritual.

They worked in two ways: either directly on the imagination of the magus or indirectly through one of the imaginative forces, such as the force of images (talismans), the force of music (number, proportion, harmony) and the force of words (incantations). But the essential *vis imaginativa* – force of imagination itself – was always present, the subordinate forces being used only as aids to heightening and communicating it.[3]

We can only guess at the actual forms of magic which Ficino almost certainly practised at his villa; but they would have involved elaborate and pious rituals, comparable to the Mass in their use of words, music, smells and sacred objects; and tailored to the planetary influence they were meant to invoke.[4] While playing the lyre, Ficino sang ancient Orphic hymns – in a solar ritual to the sun god Apollo for instance. In an atmosphere filled with incense, and surrounded by solar objects of contemplation such as gold and sunflowers, he and his colleagues called down the sun's power with poetic incantations and with talismans inscribed with the sacred characters of Sol (a man on a throne with ravens).[5] If the music was specially composed, the proportions of its consonant intervals corresponded mathematically – hence sympathetically – with the movements, distances or positions of the relevant heavenly bodies.

In a sense, the whole aim was to create an environment so sympathetic to the planetary influence that its attraction was automatic. The magus played a semi-divine role, manipulating his network of 'celestial images' at the level of *Anima Mundi* in order to infuse the divine powers of the intelligible world above into our sensory world below.[6] Either he was transformed by the experience or he brought about some transformation in the world. He might invoke the benign influence of Venus, say, on behalf of someone deficient in venereal qualities. His direction of that person's emotions, and the concrete alteration of their imagination, invites a comparison between natural magic and what we now call psychotherapy.[7]

The magus was an artist. He was fascinated by accounts in the Hermetic books of statue-magic – also practised by Neoplatonic theurgists – whereby daimons or deities were attracted into statues of themselves. Doubtless the Ficinians tried this, exerting all their artistic talents in those sights, sounds and sensory experiences associated with the god of their choice; but if the magi were artists who infused divine life into statues, the real magicians, I suspect, were Donatello and Michaelangelo.

WHAT PETRARCH SAW ON MOUNT VENTOUX

It is easy to see the affinity between natural magic and the arts. Both were different applications of imagination which was considered the chief faculty of the soul. The world Ficino inhabited and consciously created around him was a world of soul, a psychic reality. It was neither Hermetic, magical, artistic, Neoplatonic, polytheistic, psychological; but it was a unity of all these things which added up to more than the sum of them, a kind of religion which, when it historically failed, collapsed back into its constituents and enriched the now-separate disciplines of philosophy, art, psychology and (surprisingly) science.

None of this implies for one instant that Ficino was ever anything but Christian. No matter how much his Christianity was influenced by Greek and Latin writers, no matter how much of paganism he embraced, he remained a pious Christian – and this is true of nearly all the Renaissance magi, even though some of them did sail very close to the wind of heresy. It was just that his theology came from Plato: 'in this circle of chosen spirits, the doctrine is upheld that the visible world was created by God in love, that it is the copy of a pattern pre-existing in Him, and that He will ever remain its eternal mover and restorer. The soul of man can by recognizing God draw Him into its narrow boundaries, but also by love of Him itself expand into the Infinite – and this is blessedness on earth.'[8]

Although the idea of psyche, soul, is crucial to Neoplatonism, Ficino 'consciously modified it in this decisive point, the central position of the human soul'.[9] Soul was for Ficino 'the centre of nature, the middle term of all things . . . the bond and juncture of the universe'.[10] Its imagination took precedence over perception, just as the Romantics would later assert. For everything, said Ficino, is 'known *via* the soul, i.e. transmitted through psychic images, which is our first reality'.[11]

We are often told that the distinguishing feature of the Renaissance is its shift from a God-centred world to a man-centred world; and that it was the beginning of modernity in that sense of an exaltation of human ingenuity and will instead of submission to the will of God. This is not quite true. The fallacy probably began with the translators of Petrarch whose ascent of Mount Ventoux in April 1336 is another popular date for the beginning of the Renaissance.

At the top of the mountain, with a tremendous view before him of French Provence, the Alps, the Mediterranean – he opened a copy of St Augustine's *Confessions* at random and read: 'And men go abroad to admire the heights of the mountains, the mighty billows of the sea, the broad tide of rivers, the compass of the ocean, and the circuits of the stars, and pass themselves by . . .'[12]

Petrarch was stunned by the coincidence between these words and his own position. They were both a personal vocation and an expression of the new attitude of the Renaissance. From now on he would turn inward, not 'pass himself by' but concern himself wholly with the self – that is, with the *soul*. 'Too often translators have rendered "soul" and "self" in Petrarch's writings as "man", giving rise to the humanistic fallacy of the Renaissance – that it is a turning away from God or Nature to man.'[13]

When Petrarch came down the mountain he was also eschewing the spiritual path, the ascent of a St Augustine, and choosing a descent into the valley of soul or 'vale of soul-making', as Keats has it.[14] His otherworld journey would be an imaginative journey into the enchanted realm of classical antiquity, and especially the pagan myths, 'which were the core of his, and all the Italian humanists', apparent passion for classical poetry, history, biography, Platonic philosophy'.[15]

It was in Petrarch's sense – of man as soul – that Ficino's pupil Pico della Mirandola described man in his *Oration on the Dignity of Man*. When God had created the world, wrote Pico, he found he had no archetypes left with which to make man; and so he addressed his last creation thus: 'I have set you at the centre of the world, so that from there you may more easily survey whatever is in the world. We have made you neither heavenly nor earthly, neither mortal nor immortal, so that, more freely and more honourably the moulder and maker of yourself, you may fashion yourself in whatever form you shall prefer.'[16]

Here is a manifesto of the daimonic nature of Man. Our reality is primarily psychic, avers Pico; we are souls who have been given freedom, mutability and the power of self-transformation – not, we notice, by virtue of a post-Reformation will, but by imagination which 'now rose to the highest position on the epistemological spectrum, unrivalled in its capacity to render metaphysical truth'.[17]

THE ART OF THE CABALA

'The profound significance of Pico della Mirandola in the history of humanity can hardly be overestimated', enthuses Frances A. Yates. 'He it was who first boldly formulated a new postion for European man, man as Magus using both Magia and Cabala to act upon the world, to control his destiny by science . . .'[18]

Pico was a younger contemporary and pupil of Ficino. In 1486, at the age of only twenty-four, he composed nine hundred *conclusiones* – a catalogue of the Renaissance magus's basic beliefs – and challenged all comers to debate them with him. There were no takers. But the scheme his theses represented – a synthesis of all religious philosophies – influenced all the magi. In particular Pico added a new element to the union of Hermeticism, Neoplatonism and magic: the Jewish esoteric and mystical tradition known as Cabala. (It is usual now, after the scholarship of Gershom Scholem, to spell it Kabbalah – it simply means 'tradition' – but I will retain the Latin spelling as long as I am discussing it in a Renaissance context.)

Pico had learnt Cabala from the Spanish Jews, many of whom spread the Cabala in their own right throughout Italy after they were expelled from Spain in 1492 – a date which in Frances Yates's view is as important as 1453. It was Cabala, too, which gave a fresh impetus to the German Renaissance when Johann Reuchlin, having travelled to Italy to follow Pico, brought it back to Germany and, in 1517 – the same year that Martin Luther inaugurated the Reformation – published his *De Arte Cabalistica* which became 'the bible of the Christian Cabalists'.[19] For, like Pico, Reuchlin believed that Cabala, as an ancient wisdom descending from Moses, could confirm the truth of Christianity.

Kabbalah crystallized out of Jewish mysticism in medieval times,[20] reaching its height in thirteenth-century Spain among such luminaries as Abraham Abulaifa, Joseph Gikatila and Moses de Leon – who, thanks to Scholem, has been identified as the author of that most influential of texts, *The Zohar*.

However, it was the *Sefer Yetsirah*, or Book of Creation, written by a Jewish neo-Pythagorean between the third and sixth centuries AD, which laid the basis of the Kabbalah: the doctrine of the twenty-two divine letters of the Hebrew alphabet and the ten Sephiroth. These are the ten emanations or angelic powers in which God's creative power unfolds; or, they can be seen as the ten most common names of God, together forming His one great Name. They can be arranged in an interconnecting pattern to form a schematic 'Tree of Life', a ten-stage ladder of ascent from the lowest sphere of being to the Divine Source, encompassing in between all the possibilities of existence (the whole system is in any case bound together by a plethora of mediating angels, arranged in hierarchies, and each having a demonic counterpart).[21]

So the 'Tree' becomes 'a model for the nested hierarchies of the universe, a contrivance for imagining the ordered universe – in other words, a means of organizing the psyche by internalizing the knowable universe as a stairway to God'.[22] Climbing in meditation up the Sephirotic rungs, the Kabbalist steadily approaches union with God.

The second fundamental element of Kabbalism was the Hebrew alphabet, especially as it applied to the Torah (the first five books of the Old Testament). Every letter – every jot and tittle – of the Torah was sacred; it contained the names of God.[23] Gikatila thought that the whole thing was an explanation of, and commentary on, the Tetragrammaton, JHWH (= Jahweh, or Jehovah). He thought the letters were the mystical body of God who is the Torah's soul. In fact the Torah not only embodies the transcendent being of God, it is even the instrument of Creation – 'God looked into the Torah and created the world', says an early Midrash.

Moses de Leon discerned four levels of meaning to the Torah: the literal, the allegorical, the Talmudic and Aggadic, and, finally, the mystical. It is like a divine code which can be contemplatively deconstructed back through its surface layers to the hidden names of God and, at last, to the one Great Name, the original and unutterable ululation by which the world was made.

The Renaissance Cabalists were more intrigued by a procedure which seems to have been imported from German Hasidism and to have played only a minor role in classical Kabbalah. It was called *gematria*; and, like Ficino's astral magic, it could be used both contemplatively, as a means of self-transformation, and practically, for magical purposes such as the invocation of angels. In *gematria*, every letter of the Hebrew alphabet was assigned a numerical value so that words and phrases could be translated into numbers, which were then manipulated and permutated in a mystical or magical way that is no longer clear to us. It seems to have afforded a deep spiritual satisfaction to find, for instance, a numerical match between the words of a prayer, a phrase from the Bible and 'certain designations of God and the angels'.[24] At a time when mathematics as we know it was still bound up with sacred numerology and a belief in the objective and mystical power of numbers, it was not difficult to believe that an angel could be summoned and bound by words whose numerical value was equal to that of the angel.

Language for the Kabbalists is always mystical. It 'reflects the fundamental spiritual nature of the world'.[25] Speech reaches God because it comes from God. This belief is echoed, incidentally, but in a secular way, by the post-structuralist thought of people such as Jacques Derrida whose proclamation of a 'new thinking'[26] holds that all knowledge and meaning depend on conceptual relations, notably language. There is nothing but the great net of language, no meaning outside the relations between words, no 'I' capable of being in truthful relationship with the world. We do not speak or use language; we are spoken or used by it.[27] This is supposed to be a neutral quasi-scientific theory, a myth-free truth.[28] But far from being myth-free, its claims for a superhuman language are an unconscious recapitulation of the Kabbalists' primordial language. Yet, without the Kabbalists' mystical and transcendent understanding, this kind of deconstructionism denies any depths to art or heights to divinity. It is a debased image of Kabbalistic language, an arid form of determinism which may well turn out in the end to be trivial.

'Christian Cabalist' became synonymous with 'magus'. But Cabala was never without the other strand of Hermetic-Neoplatonic-magical philosophy in the constitution of the magus. There was a third strand, too, which I shall go on to describe: alchemy. Together, these strands were woven into a complex new religious philosophy which has been called occult Neoplatonism.[29] It promised a return to some pristine universal religion from which all religions had sprung – but centred on Christ. Its chief currents converged and, in a sense, came to a climax after the Reformation, after the Italian High Renaissance, in England during the last two decades of the sixteenth century, when the two Renaissance magi *par excellence*, Giordano Bruno and John Dee, were at the height of their powers.

15

Conjuring Angels

JOHN DEE'S JOURNEYS

Early in the year 1582, a man named Edward Kelley knocked on the door of a house in Mortlake on the outskirts of London. History has painted him as a shady character, a rogue whose ears had been clipped for the crime of forgery and a charlatan who claimed psychic powers and a knowledge of magic. Some of this may have been true. At any rate, the owner of the house in Mortlake, John Dee, was sufficiently impressed by Kelley to work with him for the next seven years.

Their task was to conjure angels. Using his profound knowledge of Cabala, and especially the magic of Cornelius Agrippa, Dee conversed with angels via the mediumship of Kelley. He kept diaries recording the conversations; and it was the publication in 1659 of excerpts from these, made by Meric Casaubon, which gave rise to the image of Dee in the popular mind as, at best, a deluded fool and at worst a diabolist.

Dee was in his fifties when Kelley arrived. He had already mastered all the elements of knowledge that constituted a magus, from Hermeticism to alchemy. At the age of only twenty-three he had lectured to packed houses in Paris[1] on Agrippa's three-world cosmos – the Intellectual or Supercelestial world influenced the celestial world via angels, and the celestial world in turn influenced the Elemental world (of animals, plants, metals) via the stars. Whereas Ficinian natural magic was linked with the Elemental world, Agrippan ceremonial magic was appropriate to the Intellectual world.

Dee had also lectured on Euclidean geometry and mathematics. He was no occult, marginal figure but the most celebrated philosopher of his day, not merely in England but in Europe, too – in his twenties and thirties he travelled widely through France, Switzerland, Italy, the Low Countries, and Hungary. He was astrologer and mathematician to Queen Elizabeth;[2] and, as a close friend of Gerard Mercator, he was influential in cartography and geography, and a pioneer in the science of navigation. His library at Mortlake was one of the largest in Europe. He was tutor to Robert Dudley, the future Earl of Leicester, and mentor to his nephew, Philip Sidney, from whose circle 'the Elizabethan poetic renaissance sprang'.[3]

The circle included the poet and diplomat, Sir Edward Dyer; Sir Francis Walsingham, whose daughter Frances married Sidney; and Sir Walter Ralegh whose half-brother Adrian Gilbert was the 'laborator' or resident alchemist to Sidney's sister Mary, Countess of Pembroke, at Wilton House – Mary was herself 'a great chymist', according to Aubrey's Lives;[4] and Gilbert was one of the few people privileged to witness Dee's experiments with practical Cabala.

In 1583 Dee and Kelley set off for Prague where Rudolf II presided over a kind of magi's utopia, especially encouraging alchemists – the street they frequented can still be seen – to gather from across Europe. The Sidney circle, meanwhile, acquired a new mentor: Giordano Bruno, originally from Nola in Italy. Ordained a Dominican monk, Bruno had soon got into trouble over his heretical views and, around 1576, had fled the country to roam through Europe as a missionary for the 'Egyptian' religion. This was nothing other than our occult Neoplatonism, derived from Ficino and Pico, but now with a strong admixture of Agrippa whose De Occulta Philosophia (1533) was virtually Bruno's bible.[5]

BRUNO'S FUROR

Bruno caused an uproar when he debated his doctrines with the doctors of Oxford University. He seems to have been a passionate, even a violent, man, and he advocated a correspondingly powerful, world-transforming magic. Just as the Cabalistic ladder of Creation lowered itself, like the Neoplatonic emanations, from the One, through the gods, to the stars, demons, elements and senses, so it could also be climbed by magical operations. The crucial link between this world and the celestial was the demons – which, however, were emphatically not devils, but neither were they angels[6] (except in Dee's sense). They were, of course, daimons – whom Bruno, like Dee, sought to draw down by incantation and by seals, or sigils.

Unlike Dee, Bruno's preferred procedure was to condition the imagination to receive the daimonic influences through magical images stamped on the memory; and this 'magically animated imagination'[7] was the key to his teachings. 'Bruno's language is excited and obscure as he expounds this, to him, central mystery, the conditioning of the imagination in such a way as to draw into the personality spiritual or demonic forces which will unlock its inner powers'[8] and so transform him into a god-like being. The ascent of the daimonic ladder required a *furor* of love – a mixture of fierce meditation, exacting ritual magic, and passionate, intense imagination in order to storm 'the black diamond doors'[9] of the deep psyche, releasing visions, revelations and even supernatural powers.

Although Bruno was in some ways an exceptional magus – he had given up his Christianity for example – the atmosphere surrounding him is not untypical: a pious Christian's regard for fasting, prayer and cleansing before ritual; a mystic's longing for direct knowledge of God; an intellectual's excitement, wrought up to the highest pitch by the monumental discovery of a religion older and more authoritative even than Christianity; a social reformer's joy at the possibility of a return to an 'Egyptian' utopia where everything was disposed harmoniously and wisely through a natural, scientific magic; an adept's awe at the promise of a higher magic which could initiate him into the divine Ideas of God Himself. Small wonder, then, that after the comparatively sterile intellection of medieval theology, occult Neoplatonism enchanted the finest minds of the Renaissance with a promise of transcendently resolving religious schism and restoring the Golden Age.

The Renaissance magi consciously placed themselves in a tradition which harked back, as they thought, to the Chaldeans, Egyptians, Orphics and Pythagoreans – essentially the same tradition as the Golden Chain of alchemy which anticipated the Romantics from Goethe, Schelling and Coleridge, for example, to W. B. Yeats, T. S. Eliot and C. G. Jung. Whatever the differences in their expressions of the tradition – this 'perennial philosophy' – certain tenets (if I may recapitulate for a

moment) remain constant: that the cosmos comprises a system of correspondences, notably between microcosm and macrocosm; that the cosmos is animated by a world-soul which links all phenomena together;
that the human soul is but an individual manifestation of the world-soul;
the chief faculty of the soul is imagination; and that, finally, the experience
of personal transmutation, of gnosis, is of the essence.[10]

SCIENCE AND MAGIC

If the Renaissance magi seemed to the later Enlightenment to be superstitious old sorcerers, at the time they seemed quite the opposite: daring,
fresh and hard-nosed, much as scientists appeared to young people early
in the twentieth century when education mostly consisted of studying
Latin and Greek. The idea of a dispassionate and practical magic
promised a release from the stifling and arid controversies of the old
theology, and a 'scientific' method for transcending this dull, sublunary
world to the clear air of visionary heights.

Science did not so much depose magic as emerge from it. The
sixteenth-century Swiss alchemist and magus Paracelsus, for example,
laid the foundations of modern chemistry and medicine. He operated by
natural magic on the imaginations of his patients – a kind of psychotherapy – in order to effect a cure. But he also treated their bodies in a
practical way. His world-view was alchemical and his approach, empirical.[11] Bruno was well ahead of his time in championing a Copernican,
heliocentric cosmos which, moreover, he suggested was not self-
contained but infinite, and inhabited by innumerable moving worlds.[12]

Conversely, the scientists of the seventeenth century were still imbued
with occult Neoplatonism. 'William Gilbert's theory of the Earth's
magnetism rested on his proof that the world soul was embodied in that
magnet; William Harvey believed that his discovery of the circulation of
the blood revealed the human body to be a microcosmic reflection of
the Earth's circulatory systems and the cosmos's planetary motions.'[13]
Newton's law of gravitation owed as much to the Hermetic philosophy
of sympathies as it did to science.[14] The very beginnings of empiricism
with Francis Bacon 'were rooted in the magical tradition'.[15]

A little watershed in the change from one world-view to another can be discerned early on in the speculations of Cornelius Agrippa about the magus's ability to produce through mathematics wonderful operations 'without any natural virtue'. He means 'without any innate power'[16] – that is, with purely mechanical methods. He cites legendary artefacts such as the flying wooden pigeon made by Architas, the moving statues made by Daedalus and the speaking statues of Mercurius described in the Hermetic treatise, the *Asclepius*.

But he is less interested in these things as particular devices than as instances of applied science. He is, in other words, perhaps the first man to see the possibilities of, and to desire, technology, in the modern sense of the word. This may seem strange, coming from the doyen of magic, who was not too fussy about the uses to which magic was put; who would even invoke demons, providing it worked. Yet this, too, I suppose, is characteristic of the technocrat.

THE UNCANNINESS OF NUMBERS

The magus was as much a scientist as an artist; and nothing expresses this ambiguity so well as his attitude towards numbers. All science derives from Pythagoras' and Plato's conviction that our diverse and apparently ever changing world is really obedient to certain unifying laws, embodied in eternal mathematical forms. The unruly movement of the planets, for example, ought to be able to be explained by a single geometrical model. However, mathematics led Plato to mystical vision. His successors among the Greeks and Arabs followed suit. They had all the maths necessary to develop a technology but disdained to do so: number was a qualitative way of arriving at, and contemplating, eternal truths – it was not a tradesman's measuring tool. Modern scientists, on the other hand, saw any mathematical constancies in Nature as merely representing 'a certain mechanical tendency towards regular patterning, with no deeper meaning per se'.[17] In other words, Plato's philosophy provided a basis for a world-view which contradicted his own basic assumptions. Somehow, mechanism and materialism had been built on his mysticism.

The Renaissance magus lay halfway between these two worlds. John Dee's mathematics in the 'lower' sphere of navigation and mechanical engineering was continuous with the higher 'mathematics' which gave access to the supercelestial world. Maths and numerology were the same thing. Numbers were Pythagorean personalities – 'perfect' or 'friendly', for instance, or even Unutterable (*alogon*). They were daimons (or inseparable properties of the daimons they were used to invoke), which manifested a 'mervaylous neutralitie'[18] between the sensory and supercelestial worlds.

Another watershed in the change of world-views can be seen in Johannes Kepler's struggle to reconcile his planetary measurements with the perfectly circular orbits prescribed by Hermeticism and Platonism. His reluctant adoption of elliptical orbits represented a shift from the qualitative and mystical view of the heavens to a quantitative and scientific view. Kepler came down on the side of mathematics as opposed to numerology and, indeed, in a fierce controversy with the Rosicrucian and alchemical philosopher Robert Fludd, was the first man to draw a distinction between the two.[19]

Unhappily, numbers were one of the reasons that, towards the end of the sixteenth century, the Renaissance magi began to fall into disrepute. Their arabic numerals – our modern numbers – had only recently replaced Roman numerals which were still used throughout the Tudor period, for instance to keep Government accounts.[20] To the uninitiated the new squiggles looked uncanny,[21] even diabolical. Mathematicians like Dee were in danger of being branded as sorcerers. It was shocking, therefore, but not in retrospect completely unexpected, when in 1583 a mob sacked his house at Mortlake and did considerable damage to his incomparable library.

There were broader reasons for the decline of the magi. The great new syncretic religion had come under attack from the very factions it had hoped to transcend. These were not Protestants or Catholics (there were magi of both persuasions); nor even the Puritans (Sidney was himself a leader of the Puritan party). Rather, they were the radical puritans who infested both sides, the narrow counter-Reformationist Catholics as much as the fundamentalist Protestants. At war with each other, they were perhaps relieved to combine forces against the religious philosophy of Ficino, Pico, Bruno and Dee. They had some powerful ammunition: certain disciples of Agrippa – John Faustus was an example – had followed him into a darker magic, a conjuring aimed more at power than at gnosis. The puritans were quick to tar all the magi with the same brush. Rather like some modern Christian fundamentalists, they were eager to detect the Devil wherever they could. Magic began to be discredited. Not, as C. S. Lewis points out, by science, but by a general 'darkening of the European imagination'.[22] As the light of the Renaissance was overshadowed by the growing number of witch hunts and by allegations of heresy and devil-worship, the whole movement of occult Neoplatonism foundered amidst 'clouds of demonic rumour'. 'The Renaissance magus turned into Faust.'[23]

Sir Walter Ralegh who alone, after Sidney's untimely death in battle, could assume the mantle of England's 'Renaissance man', was banged up in the Tower of London and left to eke out his days in alchemical experiments with his old friend Henry Percy, the 'Wizard Earl' of Northumberland. John Dee was squeezed out of public life and exiled to Manchester where he died lonely and destitute. In 1600, Giordano Bruno was burned at the stake in Rome.

The final blow to occult Neoplatonism was provided by one Isaac Casaubon, who, in 1614, proved with rigorous dating techniques that the ancient and most wonderful Hermetic writings, so lovingly translated by Ficino 150 years before, were not as old as the magi had supposed. They had been composed by a variety of Greek authors, combining elements of Neoplatonism, Stoicism, Jewish mysticism and Gnosticism between about AD 100 and 300. The fifteen dialogues did of course embody a timeless philosophy, and many of their elements were probably of considerable antiquity; but to specify their provenance as being 'before the time of Moses' had been a mistake. Their re-dating became, in the minds of the puritans, a debunking.

THE VEGAN SPIDER

Modernity began (let's say) in 1623, with the publication in Paris of a book called *Quaestiones in Genesim.* It was written by a thirty-five-year-old member of the Minimes Order – an off-shoot of the Franciscans – called Marin Mersenne. A friend of Descartes, an admirer of Galileo, a correspondent of all the savants in Europe, he launched with his book a thirty-year crusade against absolutely anything that smacked of paganism, polytheism and magical thinking.

Unlike other puritan thinkers of the time who were vitriolic about beliefs in daimons or talismans or magic, almost as if they were afraid of them, Mersenne was simply baffled by them. 'Belief in the power of magic images of the stars seems to him quite mad.'[24] He is not on the watershed between the Renaissance world-view and the modern – he has already crossed over.[25]

He condemns Ficino and Pico; he condemns the doctrine of *Anima Mundi*; he condemns Hermeticism and Cabala. Under his onslaught 'the life-blood of the Renaissance Magus drains away'.[26] Robert Fludd fought a spirited rearguard action in a long debate followed with intense interest by the intelligentsia of Europe – but he could not win. Every daimonic reality cannot but seem shadowy and insubstantial under the harsh glare of rationalism.

Dressed in black from neck to ankles, gnawing on his spare diet – he ate no meat nor dairy products – in the depths of his ascetic Parisian cell, Mersenne 'became the arachnoid center of the European learned world, always attacking the "magical" early Renaissance – especially alchemy – in order to further the "mechanical" later Renaissance'.[27] In religion he insisted on dogma; in science, on measurement – in both he called ceaselessly, like a fist coming down on the table, for *facts*. 'His is the position that allows no third place between theology and science, no place for psyche.'[28] After Mersenne, imagination was outlawed until the Romantics; psyche, until the depth psychologists. He inaugurated above all the characteristic feature of the modern world-view: literalism.

16

The Boar from the Underworld

VENUS AND ADONIS

The English Renaissance took place after the Reformation, largely during the reign of Elizabeth I. Just before her accession to the throne, her sister Mary had tried to reinstate Catholicism with a fanatical persecution of the Protestants – who arguably did not finally triumph until Oliver Cromwell replaced King Charles I. For a hundred years, England was convulsed by the savage competition for its soul between the old Catholic spirit and the new Protestant spirit, each intent on usurping the other.

However, the depth and passion of the conflict – not just socially but, above all, psychically – was held in suspense by Elizabeth. The two spirits 'were deadlocked, and in a sense spellbound, by her deliberate policy throughout her very long reign'.[1] She could not return to a Catholicism whose head, the papacy, had branded her the 'bastard of a heretic'; nor did she wish to. But neither could she endorse a Protestant revolutionary movement which had so terrified her sister Mary and whose logical conclusion was the abolition of the monarchy and civil war.[2] She managed instead to hold the two forces in tension; and it was this tension in part which fostered, and imbued with such urgency, the 'third way' – the occult Neoplatonism of John Dee and the Sidney circle.

A young poet of the time correctly divined this tension, as poets will, and set it down in a poem which, in turn, was taken from one of the oldest myths in Western culture. But he did what no individual can successfully do, unless he or she is the mouthpiece of the collective imagination: he changed the myth.

The myth in question was the story of Aphrodite, or Venus, and

Adonis. She is the goddess of love and reproduction behind whom stand all the great Middle Eastern Goddesses, through Astarte, Ishtar, Inanna, back to Tiamat in the Babylonian creation myth. In Elizabethan England the great Goddess was officially defunct; but she lived on, of course, in her Christian guise, as the Virgin Mary and even as her earthly embodiment, the Virgin Queen. There was a crucial sense, too, in which she was revered as the sacred social order, headed by and grounded in the Monarch, whether king or queen (hence the profound trauma suffered by England at the beheading of Charles I).[3]

Behind Adonis stands all the sons or consorts of the Goddess, especially Thammuz (Dumuzi) who spends half the year with Inanna, and half with her underworld aspect, Ereshkigal. Analogously, Adonis is supposed to spend half the year with Aphrodite and half with her underworld 'double', Persephone. However, when Aphrodite falls in love with Adonis, she refuses to return him to the Underworld. The enraged Persephone surges up from below in the shape of a wild boar and reclaims Adonis by killing him. The myth is about more than fertility. It is about the primordial relationship between Mother and Hero, unconscious and consciousness, the death of the heroic ego and its rebirth in union with the soul.

William Shakespeare alters this story at its core: instead of describing how Adonis reciprocates the passion of Venus, as in the original myth, he makes Adonis reject her. He becomes the chaste, moralistic, puritan ego which severs itself from the Love Goddess and ground of its being – and pays the price. This is Shakespeare's myth. It is about loss of soul, and it is the characteristic myth of modernity.

SHAKESPEARE THE SHAMAN

Ted Hughes, whose interpretation I am drawing on in this reading of Shakespeare's *Venus and Adonis*, reminds us that the poem would be instantly recognizable to a tribal culture as a shaman's 'call'.[4] It is exactly like a typical initiation dream in which the shaman (Adonis) is approached by a beautiful woman (Venus) who promises to teach him how to shamanize. If he refuses she is liable to kill or dismember him in the shape of an old woman or an animal such as a wolf (e.g. among the Goldi of Siberia). Shakespeare's shamanic animal is the boar, 'and his butchered self is reborn symbolically as a purple flower "chequer'd with white" '. (This is how the dead Adonis reappears in the poem.) 'In other words, his first long poem enshrines his shamanic rebirth into the service of the Goddess, the dream form of the cataclysmic psychological event which was the source of his poetic inspiration.'[5]

The dream of death and rebirth which marks a person out as having the shaman's vocation is paradigmatic of the situation within every individual when the ego rebuffs the love of the personal daimon, the self or (as I have been calling it) soul.

Soul always seeks union through love. If that love is rejected it goes on seeking union in whatever way it can, becoming increasingly distorted by repeated rejections, until it has no choice but to savage the ego with madness and death. But, again, these are precisely the initiatory experiences of suffering by which the ego is reunited with soul.

Shakespeare's shamanic call re-enacts this archetypal drama both for himself and for the tribe of the English. For, throughout history, the great shaman appears whenever the tribe, people or culture are threatened with extinction. He 'gathers up the whole tradition of the group, especially its earliest mythic and religious traditions, with all the circumstances of their present sufferings, into a messianic, healing, redemptive vision on the spiritual plane'.[6] Such is the vision of the collected plays of Shakespeare which, like ritual dramas (Hughes argues), attempt to heal at an imaginative level the rift in the English psyche.

Venus and Adonis was followed immediately by another poem, *The Rape of Lucrece*. The setting is ancient Rome, where the pure and almost saintly Lucrece entertains a friend of her husband's, Prince Tarquin. Possessed by uncontrollable lust, he rapes her and flees. She reports the crime to the authorities – then kills herself. Tarquin is banished, and the Roman monarchy brought to an end.

This simple tale is shaped by Shakespeare for his own ends. For example, he stresses Tarquin's horror at what he cannot stop himself from doing. He does not linger on the act of rape but rather on the way we are intended to understand it – as a sin deeper than 'bottomless conceit/can comprehend in still imagination'.[7] It is not only Lucrece who is defiled but also – and it is the same thing – 'his soul's fair temple', which is 'defaced'.[8]

The Rape of Lucrece is a symmetrical and inverted version of *Venus and Adonis*. In the latter, a voluptuous goddess loves a man who rejects her; in the former, a man loves a chaste human 'goddess' who rejects him. In *Adonis*, the hero is killed by a boar = Persephone = the 'other half' of the goddess he has spurned. In *Lucrece*, the hero, like a wild boar, kills (rapes and causes the death of) the goddess = his soul = his own spurned 'other half'. Both poems are 'images of the same act – the destruction of the soul: the tragic "crime" of the Puritan hero'.[9]

In *Measure for Measure*, Shakespeare makes explicit the notion that Adonis and Tarquin are like two rival brothers or two sides of the same person. The chaste and puritanical Angelo is suddenly seized by lust for the pure Isabella, and attempts to violate her. Thereafter, all the plays are like variants of the original double-myth. Their heroes (Hamlet, Lear, Othello, Coriolanus, Leontes, Timon and so on) reject their girl-friends, wives or mothers (Ophelia, Cordelia, Desdemona, Volumnia, Hermione and so on) and either go mad or act like madmen. Each hero is a different study of the moment when Adonis turns into Tarquin.

As Hughes sees it, *Venus and Adonis* is the source-myth of the old Catholicism; *The Rape of Lucrece* is the source-myth of Puritanism. Shakespeare has somehow 'identified and appropriated the opposed archetypal forms of the Reformation, the two terrible brothers that Elizabeth had pushed down into her crucible, under the navel of England, to fight there like the original two dragons of the island'.[10] But then he has done something even more unlikely: he has interpreted the Catholic myth from the Puritan point of view, and the Puritan from the Catholic point of view.

In *Adonis*, the Love Goddess is seen through the Puritan spectacles of a young Protestant who naturally reviles what he sees as a dangerous and whoreish demoness; in *Lucrece*, the young warrior god is seen through the eyes of the goddess as a lust-crazed maniac who will destroy her. Adonis fears for his soul just as Lucrece fears for hers.

CROMWELL'S DREAM, ENGLAND'S NIGHTMARE

Psychologically speaking, the puritan hero is in its radical form the modern literalizing ego, which strives to separate itself from the smothering mother, from the voluptuous feminine, from the soul's entanglements, from Nature herself – and to rise through clear imageless air to the rarefied spiritual heights. But the paradox is: the more it apparently succeeds in its ascent, the more it is cut off from its own vital roots in soul. And the more it is cut off, the more vulnerable it is to the backlash of the soul it has denied – a soul which, poisoned by the ego's rejection, returns as the boar of madness and destruction. If the ego is not killed – that is, forcibly initiated – by the boar (as Adonis is), it is possessed by the boar, as Tarquin is. He is the ego who – again, paradoxically – appropriates the very rage of soul that would destroy him, and turns the rage back against the soul, destroying himself in a deeper sense. The sin of the ego is to wish to sever itself from its own source; its tragedy is that it sometimes succeeds.

This is a clumsy way of describing the vexed relationship between a particular kind of ego and soul. Its most elegant expressions are found in myth, notably the Greek myth of Heracles and the Norse myth of Sigurd; but its most dramatic expression is found in Shakespeare's plays, and, incidentally, in the plays of Aeschylus and Sophocles who experienced a tension similar to Shakespeare's when in old Athens the 'goddess', polytheism, myth itself, came under attack from the new rational philosophers.

The literalizing ego is that perspective within myth which also drives beyond myth, tries to literalize itself and so deny myth. The puritan hero is in fact the historical embodiment of this drive. We can see Adonis moving from myth into history in the emergence of the natural scientists, who coldly detach themselves from the goddess as Nature; but who, like Tarquin, are secretly possessed by an uncontrollable fear and hatred of her – as the constant metaphors of rape and violence in their supposedly dispassionate discourses betray. Is it too much to see something of Adonis in the young Darwin, the Nature-lover who suddenly takes fright at the voluptuous advances of the goddess of the rain forest – and rejects her?

Isn't there a touch of the Tarquin in his attempts to tame her with bonds of classification and to ravish her with facts; the more so as he feels increasingly beleaguered by her bloody, threatening presence behind the smiling hedgerows?

At any rate, Shakespeare seems to have been aware of the ego's literalizing drive. For, while his two poems are reversed variants of each other, they are also sequential: *Lucrece* is what happens on the human and historical plane as a result of what has happened (or is always happening) on the divine mythic plane of *Adonis*. Shakespeare intimates that whatever takes place in imagination may well, if it is not imagined onward, if it is not allowed free play to permutate, be acted out in fact.

The struggle between Catholic and Protestant puritan, goddess and hero, was concentrated on the figure of Elizabeth. She was Virgin Mary to the monarchist Catholics but, to the republican radical Puritans, she was no better than the accursed Pope. One half of England worshipped her; the other half, consciously or not, wanted her dead. Shakespeare's regicides – Richard III, Macbeth, Brutus, Edmund – are like the nation's nightmare, like imaginative rehearsals to fend off the real thing. *The Tempest* is a final magnificent attempt to hold the national psychic schism in suspense and even to resolve it through the magic of its hero, the Renaissance magus Prospero who, Frances Yates tells us, is modelled on John Dee.[11]

At about the same time as *Macbeth*'s first performance, a schoolboy told his master of a strange dream. He had dreamed that he would one day be King of England. He was of course soundly flogged for such a blasphemous notion. But in a way his dream – and England's nightmare – came true. The boy's name was Oliver Cromwell; and, forty-odd years later, he presided over the killing of Charles I – 'his horror at what Divine Possession compelled him to do is amply recorded'[12] – and became Protector of England.

17

Mercurius

RED MERCURY

Red mercury appeared on the European black market in 1977. It was being smuggled out of the Soviet Union to Germany and Italy, and from there to such volatile countries as Lebanon, Iraq, Libya, Israel and South Africa. Rumour had it that red mercury was a high-energy catalyst which accelerated the chain reaction in thermonuclear devices. In effect, it made atomic bombs easier to build and – a terrorist's dream – small enough to fit into a suitcase.[1]

Western governments deny its existence. So does the Russian academy. But there is talk of a KGB report which concludes that red mercury does exist; and a letter certainly exists, signed by Boris Yeltsin, that gives a certain company the right to export red mercury. The Russian security minister spokesman, Andrei Chernenko, said in August 1992 that it 'does not exist at all'; two months later, he said that 'no major leaks' of it had occurred.[2]

Occasionally, however, samples are intercepted or 'recovered'. They seem to be pure mercury, or mercury tinged with brick dust, or various compounds of mercury. They seem, that is, not to be 'the real thing'. Yet these samples are also as much rumour as red mercury itself. If the whole matter is an elaborate hoax, it is one that has gone on for twenty-five years. It sometimes looks like an 'urban legend' – at any rate it is an authentic myth.

An English reporter pursued it for eighteen months. We saw him on television.[3] He found a Russian scientist willing to discuss red mercury. A new type of tiny neutron bomb, said the Russian, was within sight.

But the scientist did not turn up for a second meeting where more technical questions were to be asked; he claimed security had tightened up. Another Russsian scientist was found, but he would not go into detail over red mercury. A third promised to answer questions in two weeks' time, but two months passed before he made contact – and then he only indicated that red mercury made nuclear weapons more efficient. The scientists themselves seem to be in the grip of the legends and folklore surrounding red mercury. The reporter was still waiting for definite news at the end of the programme. Six years on, I am still hearing rumours – but still nothing unequivocal.

Red mercury is a modern version of that Red Tincture, or Powder, which is best known as *lapis philosophorum*, the Stone of the Philosophers. Almost as soon as the art of alchemy passed to Europe from the Arabs in the twelfth century, it began to be rumoured that a miraculous substance, possibly a 'stone', had been manufactured with the power of turning base metal to gold.

This was not such an outlandish idea as it seems to us. The medieval world-view held that everything possessed an innate disposition to per-fect itself. Thus all the lesser metals, such as copper, tin and lead, were striving – we might say 'evolving naturally' – towards the incorruptible condition of gold. Like red mercury, then, the Philosophers' Stone was only accelerating what was already a natural process in the base metal. By the same token, it was believed that the Stone was also the Elixir of Life, the universal panacea which accelerated our own innate growth towards perfection and bestowed immortality. Chinese alchemy was almost wholly preoccupied with the Elixir rather than gold-making.

Modern science has assumed that alchemy was a primitive form of chemistry, doomed to failure because of its 'impossible' aim of making gold. But true alchemists always insisted that their aim was precisely not 'common gold' but 'philosophical gold'. It was C. G. Jung who noticed that the *Magnum Opus* – the Great Work – of alchemy was as much a psychological operation as a chemical, concerned with self-transformation as much as with the transmutation of metals.

When Jung first came across alchemical material he found it 'rather silly'.[4] But, in 1928, his friend Richard Wilhelm sent him a book of Chinese alchemy, *The Secret of the Golden Flower*, which sufficiently intrigued him to begin collecting alchemical manuscripts. Gradually it dawned on him: 'the experiences of the alchemists were, in a sense, my experiences', he wrote, 'and their world was my world. This was, of course, a momentous discovery: I had stumbled upon the historical counterpart of my psychology of the unconscious.'[5]

Through alchemy, Jung realized that 'the unconscious is a *process*'.[6] The psyche is transformed or developed by the relationship of the ego to the contents of the unconscious. He could read this transformation from individual dreams and fantasies but, although he could sense some deep underlying pattern to the development of all personalities, individual case histories only provided tantalizing pieces of the jigsaw, and not the whole puzzle.

The Great Work, on the other hand, was a collective operation, a mythology built up over many centuries, and displaying a complexity and consistency of symbolism that no individual case could hope to match. The Opus, in other words, provided an archetypal model for what Jung called the central concept of his psychology: the process of individuation.[7]

The goal of individuation (over the course of a lifetime) was a union of consciousness with the unconscious – a union in fact of all the psychic opposites in the *self*. As I have mentioned, Jung doubted that it was possible to accomplish the self. It was a hypothetical goal, a kind of psychic wholeness for which the Philosophers' Stone (typically called 'the Stone that is no Stone') seemed an apt symbol.

THE TRANSMUTING POWDER

And yet, stories of some actual 'stone' were always present wherever alchemy was practised. In the fourteenth century, Nicholas Flamel, a Parisian notary, claimed to have come across a legendary alchemical text by Abraham the Jew which he spent over twenty years deciphering. It was, he says, the 'first preparation' which held him up; but once he had accomplished it, the rest was plain sailing. He records the exact time of his first 'projection', the application of the Stone to another metal: noon on Monday, 17 January 1382, in the presence of his wife Perrenelle. On this occasion he seems to have made only the 'white' Stone, because he transmutes half a pound of mercury into silver.

However, 'afterwards, following always my book, from word to word, I made projection of the red stone upon the like quantity of mercury, in the presence likewise of Perrenelle only, in the same house the five and twentieth day of April following, the same year, about five o'clock in the evening which I transmuted truly into almost as much pure gold, better assuredly than common gold, more soft and pliable . . .'[8]

Over the next thirty years or so, the poor notary and his wife founded and endowed with revenues fourteen hospitals; built three chapels; and enriched with great gifts seven churches – all in Paris, and as much again in Boulogne.

Two hundred years later, John Dee recorded in his diary entry for 19 December 1586 that his companion and 'scryer' (medium) Edward Kelley projected 'one minim' of his 'powder' upon an ounce and a quarter of crude mercury and produced nearly an ounce of best gold. Kelley never claimed to have made the Philosophers' Stone, or wonderful red transmuting powder. He said he had been led by a revelation to Glastonbury where he found it hidden in a wall. At any rate, he had a lot of success with it.

Edward Dyer attended a transmutation in Prague in 1588 which he later described to John Whitgift, the Archbishop of Canterbury. 'I am an eye witness thereof', he wrote, 'and if I had not seen it, I should not have believed it. I saw Master Kelley put of the base metal into the crucible, and after it was set a little upon the fire, and a very small quantity of the medicine put in, and stirred with a stick of wood, it came forth in great proportion perfect gold, to the touch, to the hammer, to the test.'[9]

Elias Ashmole quotes testimony that Kelley once took a piece of metal he had cut from a warming pan and, without touching it or even melting the metal – only warming it in the fire – he turned it to pure silver with a drop of 'Elixir'.[10] In fact, Kelley was so successful that Queen Elizabeth's chief counsellor, Lord Burghley, wrote to him in Prague, begging him to return to England; or, failing that, to send a portion of the transmuting tincture to Her Majesty – to help with the expense of building up the Navy against the might of Spain.[11]

THE GREAT WORK

In order to begin the Great Work of alchemy, you need a reliable guide, a recipe you can follow. But if you turn to the texts of the European masters who practised 'our philosophy' and wrote about it between about 1200 and 1660, you find that while they are all recognizable as descriptions of the same Work, no two are the same. All agree, for example, that the one thing required to begin the Work is the *Prima Materia*; but no one can agree on what this Prime Matter is, except that it shares many features with the Stone it is destined to become.

According to the *Gloria Mundi* (1526), each is 'found in the country, in the village, in the town, in all things created by God; yet it is despised by all. Rich and poor handle it every day. It is cast into the street by servant maids. Children play with it. Yet no one prizes it, though, next to the human soul, it is . . . the most precious thing upon earth and has the power to pull down kings and princes.'[12]

Clearly, then, the starting point of the alchemical process is not some literal substance; and this is borne out by the 'thousand names' of the Prime Matter, which include mercury, sulphur, gold, iron, lead, salt, earth, fire, water, air, dew, sky, cloud, sea, mother, moon, virgin, dragon, serpent, chaos . . .[13] Whatever substance was used – antimony trisulphide (stibnite) was popular – it was subordinate to some symbolic rather than actual 'essence'.

Just as mysterious was the 'secret fire' without which the Work was futile. It was *the* secret of alchemy. But, once again, it was as elusive as the Prime Matter, if not actually identical to it. It was a fire, yes, but a 'fire which does not burn'. It was also a 'water' – but one which 'does not wet the hands'.[14] It was the 'treasure hard to attain' which had to be extracted from the Prime Matter; and yet it was the agent which performed the extraction. Often it was called 'our Mercury' or Mercurius, a personification that indicated both the quicksilver which ran like a volatile spirit through the earth, and also the god-like earth spirit itself.

Mercurius was the essence of alchemy, invisible, unchanging, yet never the same. He was also identified with Hermes Trismegistus, the legendary founder of Hermetic philosophy and author of the Emerald

Tablet. This short gnomic tract was like the alchemists' creed, containing such key pronouncements as 'What is below is like what is above, and what is above is like that which is below, for the performing of the marvels of the one thing'; and '. . . separate the earth from the fire, the subtle from the gross, smoothly and with great cleverness'.[15] Alchemy was 'the Hermetic science *par excellence*'.[16]

THE RAVEN'S HEAD

At the very beginning of the Opus it is evident from descriptions of the necessary apparatus that something more than a chemical experiment is intended. The alchemist's array of alembics, retorts, cucurbits and the like were thought of philosophically as one vessel, the round or oval 'Hermetic egg' which was an emblem of the psyche itself. 'One the vessel, one the stone, one the medicine, and therein lies the whole magistery.'[17]

Although the Work was in one way a single operation, it was also divided into stages, variously called calcination, solution, separation, conjunction, mortification, putrefaction, sublimation, cibation, exaltation and so on. No one agreed on exactly how many stages there were (seven, eight, ten and twelve were popular numbers), but everyone agreed that there were three overriding movements: Nigredo, Albedo and Rubedo. Blackness, Whiteness and Redness. But even here there are variations, Viriditas (Greenness) before Blackness or Citrinitas (Yellowness) before Redness. 'Our matter', says Paracelsus, must turn 'blacker than the crow . . . whiter than the swan; and at last . . . more red than any blood.'[18] 'See to it that you prepare the couch of Venus carefully', writes Philalethes, 'then lay her on the marriage bed, and in the fire you will see an emblem of the great work; black, the peacock's tail, white, yellow and red.'[19]

Alchemical recipes read like plays or psychodramas. *Theatrum Chemicum*, or the Chemical Theatre, is the title of Ashmole's collection of treatises. The ingredients – earth, water, mercury, sulphur, salt etc. – cannot be taken literally. They are dramatis personae, more often called Sol and Luna (Sun and Moon), Rex and Regina (King and Queen). The Work is a waking dream, often a nightmare, in which the Prime Matter appears as a dragon, Sol is devoured by a green lion, the king is dismembered by wild animals or disembowelled by eagles.

Typically the Opus begins with an Ourobouros – a serpent biting its own tail – whose 'poison' separates the Prime Matter into two primordial principles, 'our sulphur' and 'our mercury', male and female, King and Queen, which are rejoined and again separated in the course of many distillatory 'circulations'. The Raven's Head appears, signalling the conjunction that is death and putrefaction, a sinking down into the 'black blacker than black' of the Nigredo. As the watery 'body' of the unified King-Queen is further heated, its airy 'soul' is seen to ascend to the top of the vessel, or 'heaven', whence it condenses and returns as a 'dew' to consummate the marriage of the Above and the Below. Months, even years, of circulations might be needed to cleanse and purify 'our body' before the sudden iridescence of the Peacock's Tail heralds the soul's readiness to raise it up in Whiteness, Luna rising in cold glory out of Sol's grave.

Whereas the Albedo represents the marriage of certain opposing principles, such as King and Queen, soul and body, above and below, mercury and sulphur, the ultimate conjunction of opposites is reserved for the Rubedo whose product is the Philosophers' Stone. This stage is inexpressible. It is analogous to the paradox of Christ's Incarnation, the impossible conjunction of two things utterly unlike (God and man). Or, we might say that while the Albedo is analogous to the Christian mystic's experience of rebirth, the Rubedo is a resurrection – for which Christ is the obvious symbol, and which Jung called the self. Alchemy had its own images: a miraculous stone, a monstrous winged hermaphrodite.

In his early encounters with alchemy it was obvious to Jung that the Philosophers were, as he would say, projecting the contents of their own unconscious psyches into the Hermetic egg. The persons and animals and processes they saw were like hallucinations thrown forward from the unconscious on to the blank screen of whatever 'matter' was simmering in the vessel.[20] Later, he was jolted into a new view by an 'astounding definition' of imagination he came across in Martin Ruland's *Lexicon of Alchemy* (1622): 'Imagination is the star (*astrum*) in man, the celestial or supercelestial body.'[21] In other words, he suddenly saw the Opus, not as a series of 'immaterial phantoms' but as something actual and corporeal, a 'subtle body'.[22] Imagination, he says, is 'perhaps the most important key to the understanding of the Opus'.[23] It is 'a physical activity that can be fitted into the cycle of material changes, that brings these about and is brought about by them in its turn. In this way the alchemist related himself both to the unconscious and the substance he hoped to transform through the power of imagination' which is therefore a 'quintessence', 'a concentrated extract of the life forces, both physical and psychic . . . [the artist] works with and through his own quintessence and is himself the indispensable condition of his own experiment'.[24]

Despite the almost alchemical obscurity of this definition, we can perhaps see what he is getting at: the Work takes place in a realm intermediate between mind and matter. It is a daimonic process, a 'chemical theatre' in which material processes and psychic transformations interpenetrate.

VOLATILE AND FIXED

Throughout the alchemical texts the cry resounds: '*Solve et coagula!*' Solution and congelation, says the *Mirror of Alquimy*, a collection of early tracts attributed to Roger Bacon, 'shall be in one operation, and shall make but one worke . . . For the spirits are not congealed except the bodies be dissolved . . .'[25] An analogous and equally central process was summarized in the oft-repeated slogan: 'Make the fixed volatile, and the volatile fixed.' As Bacon remarks: 'the spirit will not dwell with the body, nor be in it . . . Untill the body be made subtil and thin as the spirit is . . . then shall he be mingled with the subtill spirits, and imbibed in them, so that both shall become one and the same . . .' By constant repetition of this process, 'the whole body is made a spirituall fixt thing'.[26] But a 'fixed spirit' is as paradoxical an entity as the 'volatile body' which is its corollary – one of the many paradoxes, in fact, of which alchemy is composed and which converge on the Stone.

Chemically speaking, a liquid is heated and evaporates to a gas which rises, cools and condenses into a liquid which is then fed back into the original liquid – a circular operation known as reflux distillation. Alchemically speaking, 'our matter' was made volatile; its soul rose out of its body as if at death – only to return to the body, becoming 'fixed' and, at the same time, resurrecting the transformed matter. Psychologically speaking, reflux distillation is a wonderful model – perhaps the only one – for the dynamics of the psyche. As Jung might say, consciousness differentiates itself from, and ascends 'above', the unconscious 'below'. It then condenses around an ego which reflects – turns its light back on to the dark unconscious in order to differentiate further and to raise the unconscious contents into consciousness.

More simply, we can see in the alchemical operations (of which reflux distillation was only one) the whole self-reflecting and self-transforming nature of imagination. We can see the movements of soul, elusive and shape-shifting in itself, becoming visible as it is 'fixed' in matter, and then becoming invisible again as it is volatilized into spirit.

But we ought not to take this essential freeing of spirit from the grossness of matter too literally. For it is, historically, the misfortune of matter to be the principal vehicle of the literal perspective. However, while matter is concrete, it is never literal – a distinction as essential to alchemy as it is to ritual.[27] Thus the hidden agenda of the Opus was to free matter through 'distillation' and 'volatilization' from the opacity of literalism, and make it transparent to soul in a new 'subtle body', such as Jung discovered imagination to be.

Alchemy was as much the cultivation of 'double vision' as the fusion of substances; as much the interpenetration of literal and metaphorical as of mercury and sulphur. The double nature of imagining was expressed in that paradoxical principle the Philosophers called *Mercurius Duplex*, in whom duplicity was no less evident than doubleness.

THE MIRROR OF ALCHEMY

'He is all things, who was but one', writes Michael Sendivogius about Mercurius. 'He is nothing, and his number is entire; in him are the four elements, and yet himself is no element; he is a spirit, and he hath a body; he is a Man, and yet acts the part of a woman . . . he is life, yet kills all things . . . he flyeth from the Fire, yet Fire is made of him; he is water, yet wets not . . .'[28]

In Mercurius we see the characteristic which so excited Jung: he (or she, or it) is *coincidentia oppositorum*, a coincidence of opposites, the point at which all the contradictions which rend existence are resolved. He is the beginning, middle and end of the Great Work – prime matter, secret fire and Stone. He is the arch-daimon who rules the lesser daimons of alchemy (who are nothing else than images of him). 'Being invisible and incredible,' says Confucius of the mysterious Kwei-shins, 'they may be said to be abstruse; and yet entering into all things without exception, they may be said to be manifest . . . if you say they do not exist, they do; if you say they do exist, they do not . . .'[29] And exactly these paradoxes apply also to Mercurius, who is one's own soul and also the Soul of the World; as personal as a lover, as impersonal as a god. Like the Tao, he is everything and nothing, everywhere and nowhere. Like a Trickster deity he is both sublime and ridiculous, never allowing his spiritual side to become divorced from matter, never allowing the high mystical goal of the Great Work to become altogether divorced from its dark physical side.

Mercurius is an invisible spirit, says Basil Valentine in the *Twelve Keys*, 'like the reflection in a mirror, intangible, yet it is at the same time the root of all the substances necessary to the alchemical process'.[30] In effect, Mercurius is imagination – which also works, according to Plotinus, 'like a mirror so that by means of it the reflection of consciousness takes place'.[31]

The mirror is the most common image for the Soul of the World, too, because the mirror is, as it were, nothing in itself but only the sum of the images it reflects. Soul always manifests itself indirectly, as something other than itself, as nothing other than the images by which it is represented. ('Image *is* psyche,' said Jung.) Heraclitus explained that God is day/night, winter/summer – all the opposites: 'He undergoes alteration in the way that fire, when it is mixed with spices, is named according to the scent of each of them'.[32] Yet the idea is that these images are the reality while the objects we attach reality to, are in fact pale imitations of them. The symbol of the mirror runs through the Neoplatonic tradition from Plotinus to the alchemists, from Jacob Boehme's 'vegetable glass of Nature' to Blake's 'looking-glass of Enitharmon', to Yeats who combines Plato with Boehme when he asserts that the Holy Spirit 'wakes into being the numberless thought-forms in the great mirror'.[33]

The notion that the ground beneath our feet is, so to speak, fluid and shifting sends us flying to the philosophies and theologies of fixity and literalism to prevent ourselves from falling. But as soon as we make a definite assertion about the nature of reality, reality itself – soul, imagination, the unconscious and (the best model of all) Mercurius – immediately constellates its opposite. Whenever we think we have captured reality, and pinned the daimon down, he has in fact already slipped away; and we are left with an empty mask.

18

The Philosophers' Retorts

MERCURY AND SULPHUR

The sum total of individual alchemical texts forms a mythology in which each text, or myth, appears to be a symmetrical and inverted variant of its neighbour, as if they were all versions of some great original myth – which, however, remains hypothetical. Indeed, like the process of reflux distillation itself, the texts 'circulate' in the sense that they represent permutations of each other, just like the turning of a kaleidoscope which generates a huge range of patterns out of a limited number of elements.

This mythological permutating is a large-scale mirroring of the permutating – transmuting – 'circulations' at the core of each individual text, whose elements conform to the usual system of dual binary classification. Some of alchemy's basic pairs are shared with other mythologies –

Above	Below
Light	Dark
Male	Female
Spirit	Matter
Fire	Water –

while others, as we have seen, are unique:

Sol	Luna
Sulphur	Mercury
Rex	Regina
Fixed	Volatile

and so on.

Structuralists would call these elements 'signs', and would claim that nothing lies behind them, that they signify nothing beyond themselves. Alchemists would profoundly disagree. Mercurius underpins the alchemical enterprise as surely as Imagination underlies all mythologies. The Great Work, therefore, is a work of soul. It is religious. Its elements are the images, the daimons, of which reality is composed.

Students of alchemy are often bewildered by the mass of contradictions in the recipes. We read that our sulphur is a fixed body and, in the next breath, a volatile spirit; or that our mercury is at one moment water, at the next, fire. Such frustrating paradoxes can be resolved by remembering the principle of analogy. Sulphur: mercury:: fixed: volatile:: fire: water. But, at every 'circulation', the pairs of elements rearrange themselves such that the analogy which applies to the stage of Calcination, say, is reversed at Separation. Sulphur: mercury:: volatile: fixed:: water: fire.

A mythology, we recall, goes on permutating its elements and generating variants of its constituent myths until it is imaginatively exhausted – whereupon it springs up again in a different guise. The alchemical myth seems largely to have exhausted itself in Europe by the end of the seventeenth century; it was already dying out as a practical activity in the late sixteenth century. But it reappears in different guises, such as drama and science, as I will shortly suggest. Above all, it reappeared – as Jung realized – as the psychology of the unconscious.

If there is some overall aim of mythology, we remember, it is the attempt, never quite realized, to reunite Heaven and Earth. Alchemy has the same aim. Its symbol of reunion is the Stone in which all the pairs of elements are ravelled up in a grand marriage. No matter how unattainable the goal, the Work absolutely has a purpose in the way that all deep imaginative activity has one – not so much a fixed goal as a volatile Way. Alchemy is always going on whether we know it or not. It is the movement of the mythopoeic imagination itself. The alchemist merely collaborates with, and accelerates, the movement, just as an artist does. In his struggle to transform the world he is also transforming himself, making his own soul. Authentic art, then, always entails initiation, both for the artist and his client. It can only be made by the self's imagining and never by what sometimes looks like this – the self-serving fantasies of the ego.

COOKING METALS

Just as tribal myths are linked to initiation – they are often like prescriptions for it – so alchemy can be read as an initiatory process. More particularly, it is a kind of cooking of raw materials into a new kind of material, the 'Stone'. As we have seen, tribal initiation rites (at birth or puberty for instance) often consist of a symbolic cooking of the initiates, which works by analogy with the literal cooking of food. The 'natural', biological person is transformed into a 'cultural' individual. Alchemy is both like this and unlike this – it is an inversion of this process, as we saw in the case of shamanic initiation.

The alchemist is already a 'cultured' individual who neither cooks food nor is 'cooked' by others. He cooks 'metals' and thereby 'cooks' himself. We are in the most direct relation to food because we incorporate it; inorganic 'metals' are what we are in least relation to – not only can we not eat them, they are furthest from anything living, except a stone (which they are to become). The Work does not transform Nature into Culture, but Culture back into a super-Nature.

To perform this task, the Philosopher cannot use the ordinary fire which transforms raw Nature into cooked Culture; he needs a 'secret fire', an unnatural fire which will transmute inedible metals into an edible meta-Nature, the Elixir that will make him as immortal as the Stone and able to withstand any fire because he is himself composed of fire.

The initiation of the Philosopher is like that of a tribal shaman, who is likewise an acculturated individual returned to a super-Nature. The body of 'our matter', personified as Rex (King) or Sol (Sun) undergoes the equivalent of the shaman's dismemberment. He is violently divided, maimed, mutilated, torn apart – before being conjoined with Regina (Queen) or Luna (Moon). The re-forging of the shaman's body with 'iron bones' is analogous to the immortal 'diamond body' of Chinese alchemy.

However, many of the alchemical texts describe in different stages the *birth* of Sol; his mutilation in a way that is analogous to *puberty* rites; his *marriage* to Luna; his *death*, followed by roasting (cremation) or putrefaction (burial); and his subsequent resurrection. In other words, the stages of the Great Work are like the major rites of passage. A lifetime's initiations are compressed into the Work, which is therefore a greatly accelerated completion of the individual's *telos*, goal or self (except that the Work may itself last a lifetime . . .).

THE GROANING OF CREATION

Although the alchemists were, it seems, Christians – and their texts were full of Christian imagery (as well as, for example, Greek mythology and Hermetic philosophy) – they were more or less conscious of working in a kind of Christian underworld. While the Church emphasized spiritual ascent and separation from Nature, alchemy at once followed this pre- scription and at the same time kept it closely bound to its mirror-image: the descent of the soul and the need to remain connected to Nature, 'our matter'.

The traditional progress of Christian mysticism found a place in alchemy – but only as one of its variants. As each text seems to invert the operations of the next, alchemy emerges as a mythic recapitulation of the whole gnostic-Hermetic-Christian complex of myths which com- peted for orthodoxy in the first centuries of the Christian era. At the same time, alchemy's unique contribution might perhaps be described as completing the work of Christ who had redeemed humankind but who had neglected to redeem the fabric of Creation itself – which, as St Paul says, 'groaneth and travaileth' like the Soul of the World in the coils of matter's serpent.

It is difficult, in an age of specialization, to picture an activity like alchemy in which chemistry and metallurgy, mythology and theology, experiment and ritual, were all tightly compacted in the Hermetic egg. The Philosophers themselves could not decide whether to call the Work 'our art', 'our science' or 'our philosophy'. In a sense, we can only reconstruct it by recombining the elements into which alchemy was dissolved at around the turn of the seventeenth century. The retorts of the Philosophers metaphorically burst asunder at that time, releasing their myth-laden gases into the already charged atmosphere of Europe. The new empiricism was one strand fostered by alchemy, even while it was inimical to it. As Jung remarked, Paracelsus and Boehme divided alchemy between them into natural science and Protestant mysticism respectively. At the same time, alchemical imagery spilled over into poetry and drama, from Jonson and Shakespeare, Donne and Marvell, through Goethe, to Blake and Yeats. There has always been an air of mystery surrounding the emergence of English Elizabethan and Jacobean drama. Shakespeare and his contemporaries seemed to come from nowhere, suddenly throwing up a glittering fountain of plays full of incomparable imagery. Might they not have been simmering in secret, deep in the collective imagination, incubated under pressure in private retorts – before flying out, fully fledged, on to the public stage?

Artists, I suppose, understand alchemy best – the long struggle with intransigent materials, the fusing of subject and object in the fire of imagination, the synchronous mirroring of inner and outer worlds. But we are all prey to leaden despair, to mercurial mood swings, to sulphurous rage, to blocked fixities and manic volatilizations, to the blackness of depression, and to dreams of lacerating beasts, revelatory white ladies and a wise golden child – the *filius philosophorum*, son of the Philosophers, who is another synonym for the Stone.

But if depth psychology is one place where alchemy went – even the language of amplification, mortification, sublimation, projection, etc. is the same – another place is mainstream science, beginning with chemistry, of course, and ending with modern physics.

THE FOUR-FOLD UNITY

For example, the Philosophers' Stone is often described as, quite simply, the union of the four elements, *Mercurius quadruplex*. The Philosophers' Stone of physics is the grand unified field theory. It seeks to unify the four fundamental forces of Nature: electromagnetism, the 'strong' nuclear forces, the 'weak' nuclear forces and gravity. Electromagnetism was itself a preliminary conjunction made possible by the concept of energy. What looked like different things – electrical and magnetic forces, such as light and heat – were seen as manifestations of the same thing. Like Mercurius, energy came to be seen as something which could manifest in many different forms organized by fields.[1] Indeed, once Einstein had established the equivalence of energy and mass ($E = mc^2$), which means that they can be converted into one another, all Nature could be imagined as consisting of fields and energy.[2]

The unified field theory is as much an alchemical and metaphorical enterprise as it is a literal scientific project. Jung noticed how preoccupied we are with four-fold unities: the mandala – a circle divided into four quarters – seems to be an archetypal image of the self which appears spontaneously in dreams and fantasies. But since such a unity is an ideal construction, hard to actualize, it is tempting to predict that the unified field theory will not be attained. It is looking quite promising, as I write – the first three forces are all but unified. But the fourth, gravity, is proving recalcitrant. I suspect that, as the physicists move closer and closer towards incorporating it, so there will be ever tinier anomalies to prevent the final perfection.

The world of the subatomic physicist is full of alchemy, almost as if the Newtonian world-view, so opposed to the alchemical, had reversed itself back into alchemical mode but raised, as it were, to the second power. The modern Hermetic vessel seems to be the particle accelerator which 'circulates' its 'elements' – the particles – and accelerates natural processes. The alchemical interchangeability of spirit and matter becomes the interconvertibility of energy and mass. Separation and conjunction become nuclear fission and fusion, although the particle accelerator only 'separates'; conjunction, or fusion, is attempted in another Hermetic vessel: the doughnut-shaped torus.

Above all, the realm uncovered by the miles-long accelerator and its linked computers – how cumbersome and Victorian they will soon seem to us – is the *metaxy*, the in-between world: between wave and particle, observer and observed, mind and matter. At the furthest limits of matter no less than of mind the intermediate realm of 'subtle bodies' takes on new life. 'The physical and the psychic are once more blended in an indissoluble unity', wrote Jung in 1944. 'We have come very near to this turning-point today.'[3]

NEWTON'S GOLDEN TREES

Although Isaac Newton has traditionally been credited with piecing together the scientific world-view that spelled the end of alchemy, he also studied alchemy for more than a quarter of a century and conducted thousands of experiments – his alchemical manuscripts total some 650,000 words. His relative and laboratory assistant, Humphrey Newton, describes Isaac as rarely going to bed before two or three o'clock, while, during spring and autumn (astrologically significant times, perhaps) 'he used to employ about six weeks in his laboratory, the fire scarce going out either night or day, sitting up one night and I another, 'till he had finished his chemical experiments, in the performance of which he was most accurate, strict and exact. What his aim might be I was not able to penetrate into, but his pains, his diligence at these set times made me think he aimed at something beyond the reach of human art and industry . . .'[4]

Isaac seems not to have been entirely without success. In *Clavis* (*The Key*), he describes the process for making philosophical mercury, and his results:

I know whereof I write, for I have in the fire manifold glasses with gold and this mercury. They grow in these glasses in the form of a tree, and by a continual circulation the trees are dissolved again with the work into a new mercury. I have such a vessel in the fire with gold thus dissolved, where the gold was visibly not dissolved by a corrosive into atoms, but extrinsically and intrinsically into a new mercury as living and mobile as any mercury found in the world. For it makes gold begin to swell, to be swollen, and to putrefy, and to spring forth into sprouts and branches, changing colours daily, the appearances of which fascinate me every day.[5]

One of the greatest alchemists – certainly my favourite – was also one of the last. He wrote under the name Eirenaeus Philalethes, but his identity is unknown. In his treatise *An Open Entrance to the Shut Palace of the King* (1669 edition), he claims to have attained the Philosophers' Stone in 1645 at the age of twenty-three. He promises us the plainest description yet of alchemy's secret, which he calls the 'Sophick mercury', or 'our water' (compounded, typically, of 'fire'). *An Open Entrance* was Newton's bedside reading for twenty years. His copy, annotated on every page, can be seen in the British Library.

Newton's *Clavis* shares many concepts with the works of Philalethes. It could pass for a work *by* Philalethes. Indeed, at one point in Newton's manuscript a phrase is repeated as if Newton had made a mistake common to someone who is copying out rather than composing. Moreover, in William Cooper's 1678 edition of *Ripley Reviv'd* – five tracts by Philalethes – a treatise called *Clavis*, now lost, is listed among Philalethes's work. B. J. T. Dobbs, whose excellent research I am drawing on here, thinks that, on balance, *Clavis was* written by Newton. But in this slight confusion, in the interesting overlap, we might care to see another little watershed in the history of thought where, for a brief moment, the last great alchemist and the first great modern scientist are indistinguishable.

THE SECRET

The Great Work cannot begin without the secret – and yet it can, and did, begin without the secret because many Philosophers laboured for years in order to find the secret, experimenting with every conceivable substance and making valuable scientific discoveries along the way. The idea that there was some literal secret was as persistent as the idea of a literal Stone, tincture or powder; and, regardless of whether there was something literal or not, this idea was crucial to the sense of fascination and mystery without which the Work, like any long-term scientific project, could not be sustained. No one could volunteer for the years of effort and hardship the Work requires without the promise of uncovering a wonderful secret and, in its wake, a priceless treasure. This is one of the necessary deceptions of Mercurius who lures us with treasure of one kind, in pursuit of which – if we do not go mad or die (*'nonnulli perierunt!'* say so many texts – 'Not a few have perished!') – we acquire a greater one; or perhaps we find that the Work is itself the treasure, its own reward, like the ecstatic experience of the self-delighting circlings of the soul. At any rate, the Work bestows secrets that one could not have imagined before the Work began because one is changed in the course of the Work to someone one could not have imagined being before.

We know now, of course, that it is impossible to change one element into another, or base metal into gold (except by high-energy processes unavailable – in technological form, at least – to the alchemists). On the other hand, if it is possible to transform in the course of the Work the very structure of one's own psyche, who knows but that the very structure of matter might be reciprocally – sympathetically – altered, more especially if the Neoplatonists are right in saying that both matter and psyche are only different aspects of that world-soul the Philosophers understood as Mercurius. But in any case no self-respecting Philosopher would have allowed himself to be deterred by a little thing like impossibility. As a Christian, he was commanded to take up his cross and follow Christ: that is, to become like Christ – a task which, strictly speaking, is impossible. But only the impossible requires the superhuman effort. Only the impossible is, finally, serious.

'Transform yourselves . . . into living philosophical stones!' cried Gerard Dorn,[6] the speculative alchemist who so impressed Jung with his psychological awareness of the Great Work's purpose. But no matter how much we might wish to confine alchemy to the 'only psychological', the 'merely metaphorical', we will always be plagued by tales of some literal product such as red mercury or a grand unified field theory. We will always stumble over the Stone that is no Stone.

In his book *The Golden Calf,*[7] the seventeenth-century scientist Helvetius, physician to the Prince of Orange, relates that on 27 December 1666 he was visited at home in The Hague by a stranger in his mid-forties, average height, clean shaven, slightly pockmarked and dark-haired. He had come, he said, to take issue with Helvetius's published scepticism of alchemy and asked him if he would know the Philosophers' Stone if he saw it. Helvetius said he would not. The stranger produced a small ivory box and from it took 'three ponderous pieces or small lumps of the Stone, each about the bigness of a small walnut, transparent, of a pale Brimstone colour'[8] which Helvetius was allowed to examine. Eventually the stranger was persuaded to give the scientist a tiny piece, promising to return in the morning to show Helvetius how to project. But he did not return; and was not seen again.

'Nevertheless', wrote Helvetius, 'late that night my wife . . . came soliciting and vexing me to make experiment of that little spark of his bounty in that art . . . saying to me, unless this be done, I shall have no rest nor sleep all this night . . . I commanded a fire to be made (thinking alas) now is this man (though so divine in discourse) found guilty of falsehood . . . Nevertheless my wife wrapped the said matter in wax, and I cut half an ounce or six drams of old lead, and put it into a crucible in the fire, which being melted, my wife put in the said Medicine made up into a small pill or button, which presently made such a hissing and bubbling in its perfect operation, that within a quarter of an hour all the mass of lead was totally transmuted into the best and finest gold, which made us all amazed as planet-struck . . .'[9] He ran with his 'aurified lead' while it was still hot to a goldsmith who judged it the finest gold in the world, worth fifty florins an ounce. The gold became a *cause célèbre* – even Spinoza, the rationalist philosopher, visited the goldsmith who had assayed the gold, and inspected both the gold and the crucible in which the transmutation took place.

19

The Cosmos and the Universe

The revolutionary moment at which the modern world began – according to one popular scientific myth – was the publication in 1543 of *De Revolutionibus orbium caelestium*. Its author, Nicolas Copernicus, proposed that the Earth was neither static nor the centre of the cosmos. It moved around the sun.

The Greek word *kosmos*, probably coined by Pythagoras, is untranslatable. It has a double meaning suggesting the equal presence of beauty and order.[1] The medieval cosmos included everything from God and the angels to planets, humans and animals, like Plato's 'single living creature which encompasses all the living creatures within it'.[2] It was self-contained, vast, but finite. The Copernican revolution opened out this cosmos into a universe. The brilliantly lit, sacred hierarchy was blown away by the cold winds of dark secular space.

At least, this is roughly how we think of the revolution in hindsight, because our world-view is so scientific that we suppose the Copernican revolution to have been earth-shattering. At the time, however, it was not. Copernican heliocentricity was either ignored or taken on board in a speculative sort of way. The Elizabethan world-view remained medieval. If you thought the earth moved round the sun you were less likely to be a respectable scientist than a fringe philosopher of the Hermetic sort, like Giordano Bruno. Copernicus himself, in a passage immediately after his heliocentric diagram, invokes the authority of Hermes Trismegistus.[3] Nor did he think his announcement was of great importance – after all, the heliocentric scheme had been known since at least the third century BC, when Aristarchus of Samos put it forward.

SAVING THE APPEARANCES

It was not, then, Copernicus's hypothesis which caused a revolution in thought. It was actually the revolutionary claims of his successors, such as Galileo, that the heliocentric model was literally true – a move which was 'almost enough in itself to constitute the "scientific revolution"'.[4] It was for this, rather than the theory itself, that Galileo was famously persecuted by the Church.

For the ancient Greeks, hypotheses were devices for 'saving the appearances'. For example, the planets were believed to move at constant speeds in perfect circles. When observation contradicted this belief, hypotheses were devised to account for the deviations. Different hypotheses were advanced, for instance, depending on whether the planets were thought to move round the Earth or round the sun. The Greeks would have regarded as slightly cracked the decision by Galileo, Johannes Kepler (1571–1630) and the like to promote their hypotheses as 'facts'. Even more eccentric was their propensity, copied by us moderns, to make models (of the solar system, for instance) and then to interpret the model literally. The Arabs used the Ptolemaic hypothesis to make models of our planetary system. But they used the models purely for calculation. They would not have dreamed of confusing the model with the reality, whatever that might be. They would not, as critics of modern science sometimes say, have mistaken the map for the territory.

Beginning with Galileo, it took quite a long time for heliocentricity to become orthodoxy – about as long as it took for the new scientific method to triumph. Indeed, heliocentricity is even today the central symbol of modernity's triumph over antiquity: we claim to know more and to be nearer the truth than people in the olden days because we can prove that the Earth goes round the sun.

But in another way we have reneged on the truth by excluding aspects other than the literal. Our solar system will always be as much an imaginative as a literal space; the planets, archetypal images as well as balls of dust or gas. Most of us, consciously or not, still recognize this. Our moon is still mostly like the virgin goddess Diana, presiding over the velvety heaven of Night, and more responsive to flights of the imagination than to the launch of phallic rockets.

Besides, the great heliocentric proof of our progress has never really taken off, never really changed our perspective. We still live in a geocentric universe in which the sun rises, climbs, sets – in other words, moves round us. Perhaps we are merely as sensible as the Greeks and Arabs, able to entertain contradictory world-views simultaneously. Perhaps it is only the queer desire of the scientistic – that none of us shall escape disenchantment – which would make us think otherwise.

THE LIGHTED CATHEDRAL

The medieval cosmos was a series of spheres containing, in ascending order, Earth, Moon, Mercury, Venus, Sun, Mars, Jupiter and Saturn. Beyond Saturn was the sphere of the fixed stars, and then the *primum mobile* which dictated the motion of the other spheres. This was the model devised by the ancient Greeks, for whom there was nothing beyond the *primum mobile* – 'neither place nor void nor time', as Aristotle says.[5] Christianity adopted the scheme and added on God who was imagined as seated in the Empyrean, a sphere of fire above the *primum mobile*. While the Greeks held that each sphere possessed an Intelligence, analogous to the archons of Gnosticism or the star-demons of Hermeticism, Christianity allotted each sphere to the regulation of one of the angelic orders. Seraphs were in charge of the *primum mobile*, Cherubs in charge of the fixed stars and so on (the other orders were Thrones, Dominations, Virtues, Powers, Principalities, Archangels and Angels). Since Earth did not move, it did not need an Intelligence. It seems to have been Dante's brilliant suggestion that it has one in Fortune.[6]

In *The Discarded Image*, C. S. Lewis describes how medieval people regarded their cosmos. Whereas we are aware of the distance between Earth and the stars, they were aware of height. Whereas our universe is mathematical, abstract and unimaginable – a thousand light years and a million light years are equally ungraspable – their cosmos was vast, yes, but concrete, finite, imaginable – and beautiful, like a colossal cathedral.

Moreover, it was not dark, as ours is, but full of light. The translunary world – everything above the moon – was not a black and silent vacuity but dazzling, and resounding to the harmonious music of the spheres. Because the sun illuminated the whole cosmos, and even the stars have only reflected light, like the moon, the medieval world-view was in a way more heliocentric than ours. It is true that, from the point of view of the whole system, the Earth was at the centre; but, from the point of view of medieval men and women, they were not at the centre of things but on the rim. So, while we feel we are looking out when we look at the night sky, they felt they were looking in. And were it not for the blinding sun, they would have seen more of the awesome shining cosmic architecture which could only be glimpsed at night by starlight.

Some such view of the universe persisted for most people until well into the seventeenth century and, for some, into the eighteenth. Its last great embodiment appears as the background to John Milton's *Paradise Lost*, written in the 1660s. If Bruno was the first to postulate an infinite space, Milton was perhaps the first to conjure up the modern picture of outer space: Satan's journey from Pandaemonium to Earth meant crossing the dark immeasurable distance of Chaos. (He travelled by means of a 'mole immense' which turns out, disappointingly, to be a large bridge.) Suddenly the infinity of space was not just an idea but an existential challenge. The mathematician Blaise Pascal was the first scientist, but not the last, to feel the bleakness of 'the infinite immensity of spaces of which I am ignorant and which know me not . . . The eternal silence of those infinite spaces frightens me.'[7]

PARALLEL WORLDS

The infinity of space is the logical extension of Cartesian dualism: once subject is separated from object, there is no reason why the world 'out there' should not be removed indefinitely. Traditional Otherworlds are always finite because imagination is always self-limiting – it represents itself in terms of a particular spatial metaphor. The idea of 'outer space' has no such limits because it is an Otherworld which has been literalized to be continuous with this world. It is space which is not allowed to be metaphorical and is therefore undefined, unlimited, empty.

At the same time, since imagination can only be denied, not done away with, metaphor creeps back in. Albert Einstein suggested for example that space is finally – like imagination – self-limiting, 'curving' around to form a self-contained universe. Modern theorists, no matter how they disagree in detail, agree that our universe is not, as it were, infinite enough. They need more and bigger universes to fill the void. 'Wheeler suggests that an infinite number of universes follow one another in time; Zel'dovich speculates that a truly infinite array of empty spacetime may be pockmarked with temporary bubbles, quantum fluctuations, in one of which we live.'[8]

Best of all, Hugh Everett came up in 1957 with that boon to science fiction and ufology – the parallel universe theory. Of course, the idea of anti-matter (the usual reversed Otherworld) was a forerunner of his notion, which proposed that all possible quantum worlds are equally real and exist in parallel to ours.[9] This is the inevitable literalization of that spatial metaphor which locates the Otherworld next to ours, rather than above or below. But it is also a literal representation of the way a dominant myth is shadowed by all its possible variants, just as any conscious stance we adopt is permutated in the dreams and fantasies of the unconscious.

Even if we confine ourselves to our own universe, we can see how its literal reality is continually being re-mythologized. Weird neutron stars (pulsars), red giants, white dwarves, black holes – these are the daimons of a fairy-tale outer space which is filling up again with more and more brilliant galaxies, shadowed by more and more 'dark matter'. At the very edge of the visible universe, as if at the limits of imagination, unidentified flying objects have been observed. Called quasi-stellar objects, or quasars, they are the last word in astronomical daimons.

Quasars seem to radiate as much energy as a galaxy – billions of stars – and yet their fluctuating brightness over short periods suggests that they may be only as large as our solar system. Their light and radio emissions display very high red shifts – a kind of Doppler effect in light rather than sound waves – which imply fantastic recession-speed, close to that of light. Such fast, distant, powerful yet compact energy-sources can scarcely be imagined, let alone explained. Thus some cosmologists have been tempted to place quasars much closer to home, where they could have much more orthodox size-to-power ratios – in which case the equation of red shift with recession-speed (on which our cosmology depends) is blown out of the water.[10] The uncertainty surrounding the ambiguous, elusive, and even shape-shifting quasars points to the daimonic nature of our universe.

THE BIG PICTURE

It is no coincidence that the first great cosmological literalist, Galileo, was also the first to make extensive use of the telescope. Enhanced eyesight began to replace imaginative vision. Indeed, no one could have thought that a telescope was needed to see the stars until the idea of imaginative vision as the way the world is grasped was already waning. The bigger, more detailed, picture the telescope presents flattens the depth and qualitative meaning of the Otherworld into distance and quantity. Built for literalism, in other words, telescopes have literalism built into them. Their single vision breaks down the gorgeous carousel of astrological constellations into stars and galaxies known only by their numbers. The sacred heavens become secular space, for the divinity of the heavenly bodies cannot be seen more clearly by amplifying them, but only by imaginative insight. The telescope is the Cartesian instrument *par excellence*: it stretches the distance we can see, increases the detachment between observer and observed, and, in the process, creates the very universe it claims to be objectively observing.

Magnification, in the sense both of size and of quantity, has become the currency of modern cosmology and astrophysics. Their gods are big numbers, whether they refer to the remoteness of a quasar or the smallness of a quark. The 'horizon' of the visible universe is 15 billion light years away (a light year is calculated by multiplying the number of seconds in a year by 186,000 or 300,000, the number of miles or kilometres that light travels in a second). The size of a quark is some 10^{-15} smaller than the nucleus of an atom (which is already too small to go into here).[11] In the 'inflationary scenario' of creation, the universe expanded from 10^{-25} centimetres across after 10^{-35} seconds (time itself is said to have begun when the universe was 10^{-43} seconds old) to a light year across (186,000 miles/300,000 kilometres) after one second.[12]

Such fantastic sizes are not part of a recognizable world. We are all fascinated by bigness and smallness as long as they remain, like giants and dwarves, on a human scale. But the scientific numbers do not fill us with wonder like the architectonic beauty of the medieval cosmos; they only stun the mind and numb it and make it unable to think. It is as if they are the latest metaphors, posing as literal entities, for the non-spatial and timeless nature of the Otherworld. Instead of the concrete daimonic images we need to connect us to the Otherworld, we get the abstract idols of Big Numbers in the face of which we can do nothing except bow our aching heads.

The sums of the cosmologists remind me of nothing so much as the art of gematria, which in turn reminds us that the obsession with large numbers *per se* was a sign that true gematria had been debased to arid calculation, like that of the Schoolmen who famously pettifogged over how many angels can dance on the head of a pin. One Kabbalist, a worthy forebear of our cosmologists, deduced that the universe was constituted of 301,655,172 . . . heavenly hosts.[13]

The scientific preoccupation with size and number is concomitant with the 'inflation' of the heroic rational ego. This takes place when the ego denies soul and is thus ambushed from behind, so to speak, by the negative image of soul which captures the ego unawares, puffing it up with delusions of its own god-like self-sufficiency. Whenever size and quantity get out of control, we find egoism swelling to megalomania – the Bigger and the More of the tyrant's palaces and parades and pairs of shoes. I am not suggesting that the humble astrophysicist is like this; but I cannot help wondering whether psychological inflation is not, like literalism, built in to the very nature of the modern ego whose symbol, at its inception, was the magnifying telescope.

1.6×10^{-33} cm or 0.00000000000000000000000000000016th of a centimetre is, we are told, the smallest distance that makes any mathematical sense. It is called the Planck length. At this distance spacetime itself behaves like the 'virtual particles' which (we are told) appear out of nowhere in a vacuum. In this way might the universe have begun: 'a tiny bubble of spacetime pops spontaneously and ghostlike into existence . . . whereupon inflation seizes it and it swells to macroscopic dimensions'.[14]

Cosmologically, then, 'inflation' is 'a mechanism for converting a virtual quantum Universe into a full-blown cosmos and enables us to contemplate the creation *ex nihilo* ("out of nothing") of theology'.[15]

Psychologically, perhaps, inflation is a mechanism for converting the virtual notions of tiny unstable egos (about as thick as two short Planck lengths) into full-blown delusions of omniscience.

DARK MATTER

The rational ego cannot finally cut itself off from soul; but its denial of soul's myriad images leaves an empty void which, in turn, is mirrored – as soul is always mirrored – in the universe at large. The dark abyss of space punctuated by the tiny lights, like the gnostic soul-sparks, of dying suns is the image of the modern soul. Or, rather, soullessness – in the face of which the ego suffers that sense of alienation, rootlessness and lack of meaning which is the inevitable corollary of its inflationary belief in its own self-sufficient power.

To fill the void with ever-increasing numbers is a vain attempt to recapture a soul which, however, is impervious to quantity and can only be replenished by quality. No matter, for instance, how cosmologists multiply the stars and galaxies, they still find themselves short – in fact, about ninety per cent short – of the matter they need to account for the equilibrium of the universe. They have been compelled to postulate the existence of a vast amount of invisible 'dark matter'. Some of this could be the remnants of stars (such as black holes) and of planets, like Earth, which are hard to detect; but most of it has to consist of 'exotic kinds of particles, unlike any actually detected by nuclear physicists'.[16] These 'virtual particles' are extremely transitory and elusive yet all around us without our knowing it . . . We can see them for what they are by now, I hope.

The theory of dark matter tells us as much about the modern unconscious as about the cosmos. Jung noticed that whatever we suppress gathers in the unconscious and throws a 'shadow' over the world. Dark matter is precisely the shadow of the imaginative fullness we have denied to our cosmos. The daimons we cannot bring ourselves to admit return as dark 'virtual particles'. Like the psychological shadow, dark matter's massive invisible presence exerts an unconscious influence on the conscious universe.[17] It even threatens to slow down the expansion of the universe, to stop it and then to contract it in an apocalyptic counterpart to the big bang – the Big Crunch. Here is a myth which rehearses the inflated ego's primordial fear of the unconscious that will drag it back down and, like the dark destructive Mother, devour it.

20

The Weight of the World

In the mid-1970s Jacques Monod became the spokesman for a large number (probably the majority) of scientists with his book *Chance and Necessity*. He issues a clarion call to man, who 'must wake out of his millenary [*sic*] dream and discover his total solitude, his fundamental isolation. He must realize that, like a gypsy, he lives on the boundary of an alien world, a world that is deaf to his music, and as indifferent to his hopes as it is to his sufferings or his crimes.'[1]

Like his eighteenth-century predecessors, Monod claims to subscribe to a neutral, objective picture of the universe, only to demonize it – not, this time, as an unruly woman, but as a deaf indifferent alien. His view is Romantic (we are like 'gypsies') and tinged with self-congratulation, as if to say (as so many scientists do say): 'You might like to believe that the universe is a benign place but, I'm sorry, it is not. We scientists understand your need for false comforts and illusions; but we face facts, no matter how unpalatable – and the facts are that we are all alone in a hostile universe.' 'Hostile' is often used to describe the universe, contradicting the official scientific view that the universe cannot be hostile because it is made of simple inert matter. (Thus do the daimons always strive to re-animate the universe, by creeping in at ideology's back door.)

At around the same time as Monod's book, Steven Weinberg's *The First Three Minutes* described how the universe will end, all life becoming extinct. This sad fact means, for Weinberg, that our little lives are paltry and our values meaningless, except in one respect: we have the consolation of . . . science. 'Men and women are not content to comfort themselves with tales of gods and giants' – a sneer aimed, rather wildly, at religion and myth – 'or to confine their thoughts to the daily affairs of life; they also' – tumescent violins – 'build telescopes and satellites and accelerators, and sit at their desks for endless hours working out the meaning of the data they gather.'[2]

Weinberg apparently does not see the bathos: are lab technicians really the solitary and heroic bearers of all that is best in our culture? Neither, like Monod, does he see the humour in this, nor the hubris.

The picture of the lonely scientist braving an alien universe is a heroic myth. Other myths, even heroic ones – consider the myth of Odysseus – show us that we are very far from being alone. We are embraced by a network of relations, not just with living family and friends but also with helpful daimons and protective gods. Nature is not indifferent and dead but animate, personified and kindly. Even the universe can be as it was for the medieval age, full of gods and blazing with light, rather than Pascal's 'silent spaces'. In short, it is the heroic modern ego which feels itself to be alone; and the empty, hostile universe is a reflection of it.

THE EGO AND THE HERO

What psychology calls 'ego' is archetypally based. It is, we might say, the archetype of 'the drive to activity, outward exploration, response to challenge, seizing and grasping and extending'.[3] Its style of consciousness lies in 'feelings of independence, strength and achievement, in ideas of decisive action, coping, planning, virtue, conquest (over animality), and in psychopathologies of battle, overpowering masculinity, and single-mindedness'.[4]

The best portraits of ego are found in myths: the heroes. Achilles, Samson, Heracles, Oedipus, Sigurd, Odysseus, Perseus, Parsifal – these are the Graeco-Romano-Judaic-Nordic heroes who pattern the ego-consciousness of Western culture. And so it is important to ask: what hero or heroes underlie the distinctive modern 'scientific' ego; the ego I have been calling the 'rational ego', but which has been variously called the 'Heraclean ego', the 'northern Protestant puritan ego' (Hillman) and the 'heroic Enlightenment ego' (Midgley)? Archetypally, its background can be located in several myths, and the first of these is gnostic, a general term applied to many sects which flourished in the early centuries after Christ. They were loosely connected by their belief in the central importance of gnosis, knowledge, in the sense of a direct, existential experience of the Godhead.

Although Gnosticism was branded a heresy by Christianity, it was also a variant of Christianity. The Christian doctrine that God descended into manhood in order to save corrupt men is an inverted version of the gnostic doctrine that corrupt men have to ascend to the Godhead to save themselves. Gnosticism, in other words, is a necessary part of the total mythology surrounding Christianity; and, if it is suppressed, it will only return in another guise. It is not difficult to see that at least part of that guise is science.

For example, the gnostic myth of Sophia, which exists in many variants, can be outlined in a typical way as follows:[5] in the Beginning, thirty Aions emanate out of the primordial pair, Depth and Silence. Each Aion is a divine male–female couple; and the youngest, Sophia, separates from her male half and begins to search for gnosis – divine union – through a 'distorted intelligence': a conceited belief in the infallibility of her own intellect. This hubris causes her to fall from the divine world into the world of suffering and darkness, where she divides into two. Her 'higher self' returns to her other half while her lower self begins to generate demonic monsters out of successive states of mind – grief, fear, ignorance, bewilderment, and her longing to achieve divine union materialize as the elements of the created world (Sophia, 'Wisdom', is often the personification of *Anima Mundi*).

In one way, of course, this scenario is very different from our modern cosmos. But, in another way, it is curiously similar. The primordial elements are abstractions: Depth and Silence characterize the deep space of our own universe, or the conditions before the big bang. The pairs of Aions might be the blueprint for our own particle pairs of leptons and baryons, out of which Creation is formed. But more importantly, the myth of Sophia is behind our scientism, whose distorted intelligence seeks for truth and yet, in its hubris, is itself the cause of its separation from truth. Its literalism 'creates' the literal world it then proceeds literally to investigate. This pattern, prophetically laid down in Sophia's myth, is made more explicit as the myth continues: Sophia has no sooner created the world out of her own anguish than a demiurge – a creator Aion – called Jaldabaoth materializes and takes tyrannical possession of the agonized world. Sophia is now a prisoner in her own Creation.

Jaldabaoth is in a sense the son of Sophia. He is the paradigm of the rational ego which, grounded in soul, yet seeks to cut himself off from soul. He takes possession of soul's images (Sophia's Creation) and makes them literal – Sophia's imprisonment in her own Creation signifies the fixity of soul in its own images when they are literalized. The task of rescuing Sophia from the prison of literalism was assigned to an Aion antithetical to Jaldabaoth, a sort of good twin called Jesus – who raises Sophia up from the 'world of terror', becomes her 'sacred bridegroom' and whisks her off to Heaven. Here, then, is hope that the rational ego has another, redemptive side which can reconnect with soul.

GRAVITY

So much in the modern picture of the universe depends on gravity, which is credited with imposing order on the universe after the big bang. (In the mythic language of modern cosmology it was gravity which married spacetime to matter.) In medieval times, however, the effects of gravity were attributed to souls. Every thing from pebbles to planets had a soul, and every soul had a *telos* – an innate goal or aim. The oak was the *telos* of the acorn, which was attracted to the mature form of the oak. The *telos* of all the imperfect metals was gold. Objects fell to Earth because they were attracted to their natural element. They were 'returning home'. Thus things were held together by their souls; or, in later Renaissance thought, things were interconnected by an underlying soul, the Soul of the World.

Souls were expelled in the seventeenth century. Mechanistic science declared that the natural world was soulless, mere passive matter in motion. ' 'Tis inconceivable', wrote Newton, 'that inanimate matter should . . . operate upon and affect other matter without mutual contact . . .'[6] So, what then held everything in equilibrium and enabled one body to attract another? Newton drew on Johannes Kepler's theory of attraction to form a theory of gravitational forces which he could only conclude were an expression of God's will, 'an infinite and omniscient spirit in which matter moved according to mathematical laws'.[7]

It would not be surprising, given his alchemical proclivities, if Newton had in mind a spirit more akin to Mercurius than to God. Indeed, like Kepler, Newton and his theory of gravitation were suspected of trying (despite his denial) to reintroduce 'occult forces' or 'souls',[8] accused of returning science to the Dark Ages, and condemned as irrational until well into the eighteenth century when, at last, they were generally accepted.[9]

The mysterious nature of gravitation was put aside. Despite Newton's objection, it was simply assumed that matter had a power of attraction – although not, of course, through any sort of 'soul' – and this is more or less the way most of us imagine gravity today.

Einstein changed the picture altogether. He thought of gravity as less like a force and more like a field. But it is not a field within spacetime; it is a field which contains the whole universe, including spacetime. It underlies all things and the space between them. So, for example, the Earth no longer orbits the sun because it is being pulled by the sun's gravity; instead, it appears to go round the sun because the very spacetime in which it moves is curved by the sun's mass.[10]

'The cosmos is like a net which takes all its life, as far as it ever stretches, from being wet in the water; it is at the mercy of the sea which spreads out, taking the net with it just so far as it will go, for no mesh of it can strain beyond its set place.'[11]

If we picture the sea as the gravitational field in which the universe is extended like a net, we have something very like Einstein's image. But the quotation is in fact from Plotinus (IV, 3, 9); and he is describing the way the universe is extended in, and embraced by, the Soul of the World – which is the model from which Einstein's metaphor is unwittingly drawn.

Gravity has always been understood – not in the scientific sense but in the metaphorical sense, as the 'weight of the world'. People of a certain temperament have always been acutely sensitive to gravity. The Gnostics felt in every fibre of their being the deathly entrapment of gross, heavy matter. It was gravity which drew their suffocating flesh ever tighter around the frail soul-spark which alone could escape gravity and fly back to its source in the divine lightness.

The whole Newtonian universe can be read as a literal recapitulation of the gnostic cosmos. For no one understood better then the Gnostics the hostility of matter and, above all – Newton's key principle – its *inertia*. No one felt more keenly the *entropy* by which chaos triumphs over order, as the universe runs inexorably down towards heat death.

The Gnostics refused to collaborate with matter and gravity. They were ascetics who turned away from Nature and lived in desert places where they might nurture the soul-sparks that were in danger of extinction by the mire of Creation. Their lives were a long prayer, a hurling forth of their souls across the dense universe, back to their source in the light of God. The mystical journey was an initiatory pilgrimage, fraught with obstacles, through many spheres – often identified with planets governed by hostile archons. The end of the journey was gnosis, a knowledge as mystical and intimate as a marriage.

By comparison, the scientific method as a way of knowing is scarcely knowledge at all. It is an undeniably powerful tool; but its objectivity is a deliberate inversion of that passionate participation by which we really come to knowledge. Its detachment disqualifies itself from the essential journey of self-transformation without which knowledge remains emptily cerebral. Cognition does for wisdom, as the voyeurism of the astronomer counterfeits the Gnostic's vision.

NEWTON AND EINSTEIN

Just as the theory of evolution is, as we saw earlier, not so much an advance on the traditional belief in devolution, but a symmetrical and inverted version of it, so the Einsteinian universe is less a development of the Newtonian than an imaginative inversion of it, as if they were variants of each other. In fact, if Newton's universe is a symmetrical and inverted version of the traditional Otherworld, then Einstein's is a return to it: a fairyland where time, space, matter and causality – the four pillars of the Newtonian universe – are turned upside down.

Space and time are no longer independent and absolute. They are combined into spacetime and are relative. Time flows at different rates for observers moving at different speeds; it slows down near heavy objects (it goes backwards in black holes). Space itself is curved, and curves more sharply in regions of strong gravity. Matter has simply disappeared: the solid Newtonian atoms are largely empty. Matter is interchangeable with energy. Substance dissolves into probabilities and 'tendencies to exist'. Causality at subatomic levels disappears. Effects occur that have no cause. Things happen spontaneously or simultaneously or non-locally.

Non-locality is a return to a traditional idea. In 1982 it was shown that 'particles' of light from a common source continue to act in concert with one another regardless of how far apart they are; and this phenomenon is called non-locality. It implies that 'the entire universe which is thought to have blazed forth from the first light of the big bang, is at its deepest level a seamless holistic system in which every "particle" is in "communication" with every other "particle", even though separated by millions of light years'.[12]

This underlying unity of the universe is essentially a mystical idea. The notion of a single network of interacting particles is more particularly, of course, an echo of Stoic and Neoplatonic doctrines concerning the interconnection of all things in the world-soul, and their ultimate origin in the One from which everything emanates.

The world-soul was in even greater evidence during the 1990s when it became fashionable to think of the universe in terms of 'information' – a vast informational process, in fact, of which the human mind is a by-product, a part with the potential to understand the whole.[13] 'Mind' or 'life' need not be limited to matter but might be based on 'plasmas, electromagnetic field energy, magnetic domains in neutron stars'[14] and such like. There might be a 'supermind' encompassing all the fields of Nature – a kind of 'field of fields' – which has existed since Creation and which converted the chaotic big bang into an orderly cosmos. It is not a supernatural God but, as Paul Davies puts it in *God and the New Physics*, 'a directing controlling universal mind pervading the cosmos and operating the laws of nature,' while our minds are 'localized "islands" of consciousness in a sea of mind . . .'[15]

Here is another reinvention of the world-soul in which individual souls participate while also having access to the whole. The difference, however, is that soul, with all its imaginative power, has become 'mind', defined vaguely as a 'supercomputer', a rational super-consciousness capable of processing a limitless amount of information. Some scientistic 'futurists' are prey to strange fantasies of omniscience whereby mankind will one day have access to the totality of 'information' by merging with the supermind.[16] This will not take place mystically, however, but mechanically: we will have found a way to transfer our minds into devices or substances more durable than the body and so become immortal. Such literalistic doctoring of traditional religious ideas, to gratify the craving of the scientistic ego to perpetuate itself, would scarcely be worth mentioning were it not such a widespread fantasy.

The more we literalize the Otherworld, the more weird and potent are the shapes in which the daimons are compelled to return. A good example would be those strange anti-stars called black holes. Like highly compressed models of Einstein's universe, they seem to prove many of his predictions; or, conversely, they are products of an Einsteinian imagination – they are certainly archetypal images, whether or not they literally exist (the nearest possible black hole is Cygnus X–1).

SINGULARITIES

A black hole is created by a star which has collapsed on itself and become so compressed by gravity that all the space in its atoms has disappeared. The result is a 'singularity', which may be only a kilometre across but which has all the mass and gravitational pull of many suns. No one knows, or can even imagine, what a singularity is like – all the laws of physics break down at this point. Nor can it ever be directly known because nothing can escape from it, not even light which is, as it were, bent back completely by the singularity's supergravity. Its existence is inferred from the erratic movements of stars in its vicinity and from random stuff, such as X-rays, which is thrown out by whatever matter is sucked down it, as if down a giant plug hole.

The hole is not the singularity. It begins at the 'event horizon', the area around the singularity beyond which nothing can escape. Anything which crosses this horizon is, within a fraction of a second, crushed into nothingness by the singularity. However, because of the relative nature of time, which slows to nothing at the speed of light, anything crossing the horizon will, from the viewpoint of an observer outside, take an infinite amount of time to reach the centre. If we could watch a spaceship enter the black hole, it would appear to be 'frozen' inside. Its occupants meanwhile would experience instant obliteration, unless . . . There has been speculation that, were a singularity to be spinning at the speed of light, it might be possible to pass through it, into . . . well, something else. Another universe, perhaps. At any rate, the idea of a singularity provided cosmologists in the 1960s, such as Stephen Hawking and Roger Penrose, with a model for the source of the big bang. It solved the problem of what was 'before' the big bang because, with spacetime infinitely curved at the point of the singularity, time did not yet exist and space was shrunk to a point.

It is easy to see that whatever else a black hole is, it is a complex nexus of mythic resonances. It is an Otherworld where everything is, as usual, reversed and where, as in fairyland, time is distorted (a second becomes a year, or vice versa). Yet it is also a daimonic zone – a portal to the Otherworld, to 'another universe' (in which the black hole is reversed into a 'white hole'). It is invisible, yet its influence, like an archetype – like a god – is all the more powerful for being unseen, unknown and unknowable. Like Hades, who pulls us down to a death which is also life in another world.

As a daimon in a soulless cosmos, a black hole can only manifest itself demonically, as a devouring goddess or a Charybdis-like monster that whirls everything in its vicinity to oblivion. It is incomparably smaller than a star – smaller even than a white dwarf – but its power is commensurately greater. It shape-shifts – Hawking and others have proposed black holes as small as an atomic nucleus. It is like the *sol niger*, the black sun of alchemy. It is a materialistic image of the God of the *via negativa*, the Unknown God who dwells in the unfathomable abyss. It is a negative image of the One beloved of the Neoplatonists.

21

Fafnir's Blood

Because the heroic ego is grounded in soul and cannot finally – try as it might – be separated from soul, it can itself be seen as a way of imagining, even if that way is, as it were, anti-imagining. It gives that sense of individuality which Westerners treasure. It gives us that literalness we seem to need in order to feel that the world really is real. Above all, perhaps, it is that part of the psyche which imagines deeply into separateness, uniqueness and aloneness.

The birth of the heroic ego is sometimes described in myths of a Fall, such as that of Adam and Eve. It is a sin to go against God and to seek self-determination; but it is necessary to commit this sin – O *felix culpa* – if we are to become free, and to render thereafter free service to God. It is the reduplication of the Fall which is pernicious – the hardening of the heroic ego into a single rigid style which excludes God altogether, along with any other reality which is not literal.

THE LIVER-EATING VULTURE

The earliest Greek tragedy we have – Aeschylus' *Prometheus Bound* – is the story of a Fall. Prometheus is a titan who steals fire from the gods and is punished by Zeus, who chains him to a rock in the Caucasus mountains where his liver is torn out by a vulture every day and renewed every night. The play defines the tragic hero for subsequent tragedians as one who defies the gods. We admire the hero because he wishes to be free to carve out his own destiny; we shudder because he is guilty of *hubris*, spiritual pride, which is to believe that one is self-derived, free of the gods, almost oneself a god. In the modern secular age we are most of us, however modestly, guilty of this.

The classical hero has one divine parent. He is half man, half deity. When the gods are done away with, the divine half of man is assumed wholly by the human half. Psychologically, we say that the ego suffers an influx of unconscious contents which it is unable to accommodate unless it drastically inflates itself, arrogating to itself archetypal powers that should be held at a distance because they are the property of the gods. This is the ego's hubris, its *folie de grandeur* and, ultimately, its megalomania. But no matter how much power it seizes, it is never satisfied, always driven further by the vulture-like gnawing of its own limitless hunger.

'The only myth the modern age has contributed to civilization'[1] is very like the cautionary tale of Prometheus. It grew up around a historical figure, a minor Renaissance magus, and became increasingly mythologized, and widespread, through pamphlets, travelling morality plays and puppet shows. The story was adopted by Christopher Marlowe for his play *Doctor Faustus* (1591), and by Goethe for his long alchemical tragedy *Faust* (?1774–1831).

The original John Faustus was supposed to have exchanged the traditional magus's pursuit of knowledge as gnosis for knowledge as power and gratification – the mythic root, perhaps, of scientism rather than science. For Faustus's soul is not inadvertently lost but wilfully sold to the Devil. He chooses to deny soul, which is therefore left with no choice but to return in the end as the demons who drag him off to Hell.

HERACLES IN THE UNDERWORLD

On the other hand, James Hillman has identified the archetypal background of our modern Western ego as Heracles (the Roman Hercules).[2] He cannot bear daimons or images. He cannot think about death. His twelve labours are largely taken up with slaughtering or enslaving the fabulous beasts that embody the otherworldly powers of imagination. Only Heracles would clean out the Augean stables, an image of the soul where images gestate in warmth and putrefaction.

His attitude to the Underworld, so crucial in understanding any relationship to soul, is what would now be called dysfunctional. Where other heroes go to be initiated or instructed, Heracles goes on the rampage. Club in hand, he forces Charon to carry him across the river Styx. On the other side, the shades of the Dead flee from him in terror, just as our dream images flee from us when we wake into our rational egos. Hermes, guide of souls, is conducting Heracles down, of course, presumably in some embarrassment. For when Heracles draws his sword at the appearance of the Gorgon Medusa, he has to gently point out to Heracles that she is a phantom, an image which cannot be literally killed. This does not stop Heracles from wrestling with Hades' herdsmen and killing their cattle in order to feed the shades with blood – an attempt to literalize them back to life. Finally, he drags the guardian of Hades, the three-headed dog Cerberus, up into the daylight world where it does not belong.

Heracles seems unable to imagine. 'Rather than die metaphorically, as initiation demands, he kills literally, even attacking death itself (he wounds Hades in the shoulder)',[3] writes Hillman. Indeed, the myth mentions that Heracles specifically asked to be initiated into the Eleusinian Mysteries before his last dangerous labour of capturing Cerberus. Only initiation, by assimilating us to death, enables us to pass freely through the Underworld. But he was refused permission or, as variants of the myth claim, permitted only to partake of the Lesser Mysteries (which were specially founded on his account).

The lack of initiation is disastrous. It means that Heracles remains a daimon-killer, constantly denying the imagination, the Underworld and death. And this is precisely the pattern of the rational ego. Daimons make it mad because its sanity requires something 'real' it can bludgeon with a club. 'So it attacks the image, driving death from his throne, as if recognition of the image implies death for ego . . . Heracles in Hades shows us that iconoclasm [image-breaking] is the first move of murder.'[4]

The Heraclean way is not the only way to behave. Other heroes represent other styles of ego, notably other ways of relating to the images of soul as expressed in their relations with women – Perseus and Andromeda, Orpheus and Eurydice, Cadmus and Harmony, Jason and Medea, and so on. Odysseus has a devoted wife, Penelope, who waits for him while he is lost and wandering; but he also has intense relationships with other, very different kinds of women: the innocent Nausicaa, the witch Circe, the sorceress and goddess Calypso and, above all, the goddess Athene herself, who guides him and protects him from the wrath of Poseidon whom he has offended. 'He recognized all these women', concludes Book 22 of *The Odyssey*.

Odysseus' epithet *polytropos*, meaning 'of many turns' or 'turned many ways', suggests his flexibility, his ability to adopt many stances and perspectives and to relate to soul, as to women, in multiple ways. He is not strong like Heracles, or even like Ajax and Diomedes. He has no army like Achilles and Agamemnon. He only contributes one ship to the Trojan war. He is not keen on fighting, and not above feigning madness to avoid going to war. He is always called wily, crafty, devious. He dresses as a beggar when he returns home in disguise, like a classic fairy tale where the beggar is really the king. He can be conventionally heroic, but he is also content not to be, to be only human (he refuses an offer of immortality from Calypso).

When Odysseus encounters the Underworld, he needs no violent initiation, no dismembering. It is as if he is already acclimatized. He goes there only to learn certain facts. Actually he does not go there – he summons the Underworld to him, filling a trench with the blood of cattle so that the Dead might drink it and thereby take on enough temporary substance to speak to him.

THE CHARRED ANKLE-BONE

Like Heracles, the Germanic hero Siegfried has been an unquestioned model of the heroic type for centuries. It has rarely occurred to us that we should not perhaps be like him. In the Norse version of his myth, where he is called Sigurd, he kills the dragon Fafnir, who guards the treasure, and bathes in the dragon's blood. The blood confers invulnerability; but it does not touch a tiny spot on Sigurd's back where a linden leaf has fallen. Like Heracles' strength, Sigurd's superhuman immunity to harm is a sign of the hero. It is an exact parallel to the immunity of Achilles in Greek myth.

Achilles' mother, the goddess Thetis, roasted him to burn away his mortal parts. He would have died like his six older brothers, had not his father Peleus snatched him from the fire and replaced his charred ankle-bone with one from a giant's skeleton.[5] Other versions say that Thetis dipped him in the Styx, which made him invulnerable except for the place on his heel where she had held him.

To be invulnerable is a mixed blessing. It means that you do not let anything in. It means that you are as immune to the metaphorical death of initiation as you are to literal death. You are imprisoned by your own heroic perspective, confined to a single perspective. This, almost by definition, implies the rigid rational ego, carapaced against death – where 'death' means any other of soul's perspectives, such as the hero would acquire in the course of initiation. The rational ego always denies death, as the puritan fixes his eyes on life everlasting and the scientist dreams of perpetuating a deathless human consciousness in machines.

But to return to Sigurd . . . Like Heracles, he specifically misses out on initiation. As soon as he slays the dragon he receives the equivalent of the shaman's call: a summons from the Otherworld in the shape of Brynhild who is a beautiful valkyr, one of Odin's warrior maidens. She is waiting in a tower surrounded by a wall of flame, which Sigurd alone can breach, thanks to his magical horse – the ancestor of the shamans' 'spirit horses'. They fall in love, naturally. Sigurd then leaves Brynhild in order to perform the daring deeds that will make him worthy of her. Here the initiatory ordeals should begin, dismembering his rational ego and literal perspective in order to reunite him with his soul. But nothing of the kind happens. Sigurd forgets Brynhild, and marries a housewifely type called Gudrun.

I have described in more detail Sigurd's loss of soul and its dire consequences in *Daimonic Reality*. It is enough to say here that Brynhild is tricked into marrying Gudrun's brother, and Sigurd's blood-brother, Gunnar. On their wedding day, Sigurd suddenly remembers everything. Brynhild, his true love, begs him to flee with her, but he refuses because of his duty to Gudrun and Gunnar. Such an action adumbrates the priority that the northern Protestant ego gives to ethics over the erotic. Having once forgotten Brynhild, Sigurd now wilfully denies her. To deny one's soul is to be severed from the very source of life. Yet it is impossible finally to be separated from soul. And so Brynhild has no option but to reunite with Sigurd in the Otherworld – that is, she engineers his death. She tells Gunnar that Sigurd is after his blood. Thus Gunnar persuades his youngest brother to murder Sigurd with a sword thrust through the single vulnerable spot on his back.

BALDUR'S DREAM

It is a striking fact that the literalistic perspective which denies myth is itself represented in myth – we might say, contained imaginatively in myth where it cannot literalize itself and so cause Heraclean havoc in the realm of images. Nevertheless, that the literalizing drive of the rational ego will in the end carry it out of myth into actuality the modern world amply attests. Sometimes, what is enacted in the heroic sphere recapitulates, in variant form, what happens in the divine sphere. We saw something of this sort in Shakespeare's *The Rape of Lucrece* which replayed on the human plane what had already occurred on the mythic plane of *Venus and Adonis*. Analogously, the myth of Sigurd echoes another myth set among the gods rather than the heroes, whose symmetry with Sigurd's myth, together with the usual inversions, suggests that they are variants of each other.

I am thinking of the myth of Baldur who, as Sigurd is a 'solar hero', is as near a sun god as Norse myth has, always described as fair of face, bright, radiant.[6] His twin brother Hod was his opposite: blind, slow, a god of darkness. Baldur's death is the greatest tragedy to befall Asgard because it sets in motion the chain of events that leads to Ragnarok, the world-ending conflict.

In the *Edda* poem, *Baldrs Draumar* (Baldur's Dream), we learn that Baldur had ominous dreams which alarmed the gods (presumably they were premonitions of his death). As a result, his mother Frigg extracted a promise from everything in the world not to harm Baldur. Only the mistletoe was overlooked. But it was so small and insignificant – how could it hurt anyone? One day, however, as the gods were playing at throwing things at Baldur for the pleasure of seeing them fall harmlessly to the ground, Loki approached Hod and offered to help him participate in the game. Perhaps Loki was irritated by the gods' flaunting of Baldur's invincibility; perhaps he was just about his usual, gratuitously malevolent business – at any rate, he pressed a dart made of mistletoe into Hod's hand and guided his aim. Hod hurls the dart, and Baldur is killed.[7]

We can see parallels with Sigurd, who is invulnerable except in one place where the linden leaf lay. Baldur is invulnerable, not in himself, but because everything outside him agrees not to harm him, except for the mistletoe alone. He is a sort of inside-out version of Sigurd. Perhaps these perfect radiant sun-like figures are always doomed because they are inseparable from their own shadows, who must always, like the nightmares no one can avoid, try to undermine them and pull them down into darkness and death.

The tiny invulnerable spot on the skin, the little chink in the hero's armour, is where death can get in. Death is not, we recall, opposed to life but is the corollary of birth. Death is another kind of life, the life of the soul. The insignificant, weak spot – the wound, scar, Achilles' heel – is often, from the soul's point of view, the most significant. It is only the Heraclean hero in us who ignores or despises it; who overlooks the dream about the insect bite, the squashed beetle, the tiny stain on the carpet, the spot of blood on the snow, the irritating ulcer on the lip, the little leak in the pipe, the loss of strength from the haircut. But it is in such little details – little daimons – that soul is most present; or it is through those tiny cracks in the fabric of reality that we can travel, or suddenly drop, into the Underworld.

Encounters with the Sidhe often include a 'touch', or a 'stroke', which leaves us tender, scarred, even witless. Contact with UFOs or 'aliens' often includes a zap from a beam of light or a ray-gun, which leaves the contactee dizzy, sick, disoriented, 'touched', numb or irradiated. Shamans receive their vocations through just such sudden blows. They are all 'wounded healers'. Once we are struck by the gods, we are called to heal ourselves through an otherworld journey, a descent into the depths.

All daimonic events are like this. They stand at the boundary between worlds, where we can either fend them off by ignoring, ridiculing, 'explaining' them; or we can follow them down into the imaginative treasure-house of Hades. Whatever seems especially trivial or absurd can sometimes be the best way into deep insight.

22

The Myths of Machinery

While pondering the literalizing effect of the telescope on the universe, I began to wonder whether other technical inventions had a similar effect. Or, as with the telescope, I wondered if it was the other way round: perhaps technology was caused by, rather than causing, an increasing literalism. More likely, technical innovation and literalism are synchronous, each implying and reinforcing the other. At any rate, I wondered about the three most telling inventions of the Renaissance, a little before the telescope appeared.

THE CLOCK, THE MAGNETIC COMPASS AND THE PRINTING PRESS

The invention of the mechanical clock took Europe by storm. It had two outstanding characteristics. Firstly, it ran by itself. This so impressed the Western mind that it not only provided a new, clockwork model of the universe, it also invited us to believe that the model was a literal description – the clockwork model of the universe became the universe.

Much of the glamour of clockwork was owing to its imitation of animism: self-moving machines look as if they have souls. Thus mechanism generally replaced the old view of Nature as animate and became itself the model for the workings of Nature, whose soul is now superfluous, just as materialists consider souls to be surplus to the requirements of mechanical, wholly material bodies.

The clock's second key feature was its magical ability to grip the most fleeting of the gods: Time. Suddenly time was separated from the cyclical rhythms of Nature to become a detached, visible, linear thing. We too were separated from time. Instead of living with time – the past a matter of imagination and memory; the ancestors, even Eden, cosily near us – we found ourselves carried along by an objective time whose clocks coldly measured the generations and, like a telescope, pushed the past back into precise but remote distances. Time was always metaphorical – 'a moving image of eternity', as Plato says – till clocks made it literal.

The magnetic compass also seemed magically to move by itself. Like a little daimon, it guided us beyond the edge of maps and allowed us to sail into the Otherworld without losing ourselves. But the whole idea of the Otherworld is that we should lose ourselves in one sense in order to find our selves in another. The new compass made the Otherworld measurable, an actual place – made it into *this* world. Imaginative space was literalized into geography.

The clock gave us a sense of gaining some purchase on time, an Archimedean point from which we could lever ourselves out of slavery to natural rhythm. The compass did much the same for space, freeing us from the tyranny of the unknown, of not knowing where we were. Both inventions were central to the Renaissance feeling of expansion and human control. The third key innovation – the printing press – epitomized this sense of a world opening out. In particular, it increased literacy which reduced dependence on a literate elite and fostered individual freedom.

What the printing press diminished was the richness of oral culture. Grey print was inimical to colourful speech. It promoted the notion of objective, 'black and white' fact, in the face of which the traditional oral weaving of fact and fiction, literal and metaphorical, began to seem merely subjective, fanciful and insubstantial. (Traditional truth, we remember, was polarized by Western culture into literal fact and metaphorical fiction, the latter being discarded in favour of the former.) We even begin to doubt our memories when they are contradicted in print. Remembering became a dying art. The bards who could recite three-day-long poems were replaced by books. Our multifarious imaginings about the past were fixed in single definitive versions. Myth gave way to history; memory itself was made literal by machinery.

Machines are now more 'magical' than ever since so many became electronic. Computers have provided a new model for the brain. We happily talk about our mental activity in terms of 'neural programming' or 'hard wiring'. Such metaphors are useful for further imagining. For instance, we can begin to wonder whether we 'store' memory in 'databases' or whether the brain gives 'feedback'. The problem with such metaphors arises when they die. A dead metaphor is one that is taken literally. We are tempted to identify the brain with a computer, just as we once came to believe that the universe was the machine it had been compared to. This sort of abuse creeps in all over the place. Chemical interactions occur in our DNA, yet we ascribe consciousness and intention to them when we use words like 'communication' and 'information' – 'as if to say that "DNA contains the necessary information" is to say something as straightforward as that it contains the necessary carbon and hydrogen'.[1]

WHY TRIBES REJECT TECHNOLOGY

When soccer was introduced to the Gahuku-Kama of New Guinea, they played as many games as it took for the number of defeats and victories between the two teams to be equal.[2] Traditional cultures desire unity and equilibrium rather than change. This is one of the chief reasons why they resist development and its epitome, technology. Their 'rejection of history'[3] means that they can exist in the same way for thousands of years – we think of the Australian Aboriginals' 40,000-year-old culture – as opposed to the mere four hundred years of Western culture whose very principle has been change.

This conservatism makes traditional cultures vulnerable to that chauvinism which still exists in outlying (and not so outlying) parts of Western societies: any stranger is considered dirty, uncouth, barbaric, perhaps a witch, probably sub-human. 'Conversely, the internal social structure has a tighter weave, a richer décor, than complex civilisations', Lévi-Strauss remarks. 'Nothing is left to chance in them, and the double principle that there is a place for everything, that everything must be in its place, permeates moral and social life. It also explains how societies with a very low techno-economic level can experience a feeling of well-being and plenitude, and how each of them believes it offers its members the only life worth living.'[4]

Another reason why traditional societies resist development is their relationship with Nature. We have already seen that, like us, they distinguish between Nature and Culture, and set a high value on the arts of civilization brought to them by the mythic culture-hero. Unlike us, they do not subscribe to a belief in the unconditional priority of Culture over Nature which our idea of development implies. For them, Nature is not just pre-cultural and sub-human, but the supernatural habitat of the ancestors and gods. It is hardly surprising then if a technique or tool which interferes with, or alters, this relationship with Nature is rejected.

A tribe like the Menomini of the Great Lakes region were perfectly aware of agricultural techniques such as ploughing, which would have given them a greater abundance of their basic food, wild rice. They refused to employ such techniques because they were 'forbidden to wound their mother the earth'.[5] Other cultures might reject a technical improvement because of the disruption it would cause to their structures, intricately woven out of systems of metaphor and analogy. For example, the pottery of the Dowayos is notoriously poor and would greatly benefit from a semi-kiln firing technique. They doggedly refuse to introduce this method and continue to heap up their pots and fire them inefficiently because this process parallels the 'heaping up' of circumcision candidates.

To change one element in the analogical system is to disintegrate the whole. Once the Yir Yoront of Northern Australia adopted the undoubtedly more advanced iron axes, they lost all their economic, social and religious institutions which were linked to the possession, use and transmission of stone axes.[6] Analogously, there is no doubt that the technical inventions of the Renaissance – its clocks and telescopes and compasses – contributed greatly to the disintegration of the precise system of correspondences and hierarchies which made up the medieval cosmos.

Where tools have found a place in traditional societies, they are usually wielded by men. This is not, as we often suppose, because men are physically stronger than women; it is because the opposition Nature/ Culture is homologous with female/male – that is to say, Nature: Culture:: female: male. Accordingly, activities which require direct contact with Nature, such as gardening, or with natural products, such as pottery and weaving, are reserved for women. As soon as dealings with Nature need the intervention of Culture in the form of tools or machinery (above a certain level of complexity, at least) men take over. Women plant and weed; men work the lawn mower.

TEKHNE AS ART

The word 'technology' comes from the Greek word *tekhne*, which does not mean 'the application of science' but rather the opposite: it means 'art'. It was *tekhne* that Plato's Demiurge used when he made our cosmos in accordance with the ideal version of it which already existed in the intelligible world of Forms. But *tekhne* does not imply our modern notion of 'fine art'; it was skill or craft – a marriage of art and science, perhaps, such as all traditional societies practise.

There is no technical reason why traditional cultures should not develop an advanced technology – ours did, after all; and the Greeks certainly had the know-how. But they would have been baffled by our propensity to dominate Nature. Indeed, they would have thought it blasphemous. Their technology stopped at the level of artefacts and tools which remained personal, partaking of the souls of their owners with whom they were often buried at death. Our technology went on to become a kind of independent force, divorced from soul – a machinery which not only desacralized Nature but which could only arise amongst a people for whom Nature is no longer sacred. Machines turn daimonic power into literal force. They tempt us to believe that we can attain freedom from Nature altogether through a self-sufficient Culture. They tempt us, that is, with hubris. The danger is, that such pride will come before a fall – a fall into enslavement by the same machinery we created to free ourselves.

Our most popular technologies were often described as 'magic' when they first appeared. In fact, they are literalizations of magic. They seek to simulate mechanically (electronically etc.) the supernatural powers traditionally associated with daimons or their human counterparts, the shamans.

Guns and bullets supply the ability to do occult harm at a distance; telephony and radio supply the ability to communicate telepathically over long distances (the telescope is a kind of second sight, a way of seeing what is happening far away); X-rays and surgery literalize the shaman's ability to 'see inside' his patients, to diagnose their illness and to extract, manually or by sucking, the cause of the disease. Above all, the shaman's supreme powers are his ability to fly; his ability to travel at will into the Otherworld and to bring back a description of it; and his enlightenment. These three powers find their literalized counterparts in aircraft, television and electricity respectively.

Ever since the ancient discovery that amber (the Greek *elektron*) can carry the mysterious charge we now call static electricity, we have speculated about the possibility of a strange power inherent in the world. In the same way that natural magnets were seen as being inhabited by souls, this power was essentially a spiritual power which nevertheless had a material aspect that could cross over, so to speak, and affect us. In short, it was a daimonic power similar to, if not identical with, the Soul of the World – which, after all, has exactly this attribute of mediating between spiritual and sensory worlds.

In the early eighteenth century it was investigated as electricity. Although the scientists were confident that it was a natural force, the symbolism and much of the nomenclature used to describe it came from alchemy. Electricity was 'the ethereal fire', 'the quintessential fire', the *medicina catholica*, the universal medicine, and the 'cheap thing to be found anywhere'. That it was already seen in a double light, like the Philosophers' Stone, as both an elixir or panacea, and as a 'fire', is evidenced by 'the utterly promiscuous use of electrotherapies in the treatment of disease from the mid-eighteenth century until well into our own'.[7]

But it was as 'fire', as a source of light, that electricity particularly seized the imagination. This was because light was traditionally seen as being of two kinds: firstly, the natural light of the sun and of fire; secondly, a 'light of Nature', an inner or spiritual light which could shine suddenly in the darkest night, surrounding every visitation or vision (as it still does today in apparitions of ghosts, angels, Virgin Marys, UFOs, etc.). Metaphorically it is identified with moon- or starlight rather than with sunlight.

Electricity was at first identified with this light of Nature. But the closer science came to harnessing it, the more its elusive volatile nature became, as alchemy says, fixed. Its mystical properties were distilled away, leaving only the dross of ordinary light. Illumination, we might say, was literalized into mere light, whose profane brightness and crassness were inimical to the dim, secret and sacred light in which true enlightenment occurs.

THE GLAMOUR OF TELEVISION

Television's strange power to addict us stems from the fact that it is a literalization of imagination itself. It presents us with artificial visions and *ersatz* Otherworlds. We gaze enchanted at the 'little people' on the screen. But its images are not, as in authentic imaginative experiences, more real than everyday reality – they are less real. They correspond to that state of 'vague image-ridden illusion',[8] that *eikasia*, which Plato desribes as the perception of the prisoners who are forced to stare at the back wall of his Cave, on which mere shadows of reality flicker: 'the lowest and most irrational kind of awareness',[9] as Iris Murdoch calls it.

This is the most pernicious thing about television. It is not the content of its programmes, which mostly literalize the psychopathology of myth – endless soap operas about 'underworlds' of disease and crime, hospitals and cops, sex and death, that titillate and trivialize. Rather, it is the form of television, the medium itself, whose naturalism falsifies reality. I write feelingly because I am a chronic TV addict who finds it difficult to switch off the set even at two a.m., when I'm dead tired and there really is only rubbish on every channel I have access to. How can this be?

When we are fed images which are not, as Plato would say, representations of the eternal Forms, which are not, as we might say, Art, then we remain – our souls remain – unnourished. We crave more images, and more; we have to stay for the end of the story, no matter how banal or predictable – all in the hope of that satisfaction which contact with an authentic Otherworld, whether through our own or through others' imaginations, gives us. Television cannot supply this. The longer we watch, the sicker we feel at the surfeit of pre-cooked, re-heated and 'endless proliferation of senseless images'.[10]

I do not want my remarks on technology to sound like a Luddite rant. I am not against technology, and, like most people, have reason to be grateful for it in all sorts of ways. I only want to recognize that when it is divorced from *tekhne* – which is also a divorce from the imaginative roots of all technical endeavour – technology can lead to the kind of manic proliferation that is the counterpart of our collective ego inflation and loss of soul. We always want *more* to satisfy our craving – more machines, more images and, now, more 'information' – as if this quantitative 'more' could fill the aching void; as if 'information' were knowledge.

This is the drawback to a world-wide web of information. However useful a tool it is, it will never become the world-soul it is unconsciously imitating because it is a web spun out of our own entrails. Computer technology is so forceful that it is getting above itself, driving towards the literalizing of daimonic reality. Its 'chips' are little souls to animate everything from 'smart' toasters to bombs; its cyberspace is a fantasy Otherworld; 'virtual reality' is a literalistic and mechanical counterfeit of daimonic reality. We are fooled by the cleverness of computers into thinking that we can create the Otherworld and manipulate it. But the Otherworld is not our creation – if anything, it creates us. Nor can we manipulate it – we can only be transformed by it.

If I wanted to identify the archetypal, mythic background to technology, I would have to distinguish between the Industrial Revolution and the Electronic Revolution. In Norse mythology, the gods employ a giant to build their dwelling-place, Asgard. Giants are slow, dim-witted and prodigiously strong. This is how we might think of the great enginery of the industrial age. We might also think of Prometheus, the fire-stealing titan. For the fire he stole was not sacred fire but, as it were, functional fire. The sort of fire, perhaps, which made the steam which drove the titanic Victorian machines. Sacred fire was first kindled by Hermes, who invented fire-sticks. His first application of his new discovery was the burning of sacrifices to the gods. Hermes is the god of the Philosophers' secret fire, the light of Nature, illumination, while Prometheus presides over electric light.

Hermes is also, I suspect, behind the 'information revolution'. He is, we remember, the god of crossroads and boundaries; of mediation and of communication. If we revere him he gives us hermeneutics, insights and wisdom; if we do not, he deceives us (he is a great Trickster) through messages that seem true but are really false. Since he travels, uniquely among the gods, from Above to Below, from Olympus via our world to Hades, his dimension is depth. We relate to him through the depths of soul whose movement is slow, labyrinthine and downwards towards death. If we deny Hermes his vertical movement, he begins to spread horizontally, to speed up, until he is girdling the Earth like Puck (who did it in forty minutes). Hermetic revelations become literal signals, from satellites above to cables below, whose transmissions criss-cross the globe, growing faster and more garbled by the minute in a wild attempt to return us to that knowledge of eternal things which can never, alas, be cobbled together by no matter how many trillions of bits of information strung across the world.

THE FLIGHT OF THE SHAMAN

Mankind has always dreamed of flying. Indeed, mankind has always flown – in its dreams. All cultures believe, or have believed, that the soul can leave the body and fly. Out-of-the-body experiences are still commonplace. Many shamanistic societies say that their shamans leave their bodies to travel into the Otherworld. But, they say, this only goes to show how degraded the shamanistic art has become; for, in the olden days, the shamans were so powerful that they could fly in their bodies. When the Oonark Eskimos were told that men had landed on the moon, they were unimpressed: 'That's nothing,' they said. 'My uncle went to the moon lots of times.'[11] Once these real, imaginative flights had been ruled out by modernity as impossible, the myth had to be laboriously enacted through the building of aircraft, and even of space rockets.

Paradoxically, it was one man's quest for self-transformation which led to the invention of a new kind of flying machine. Arthur Young designed the Bell Model 47, which was awarded the world's first commercial helicopter licence. But he had come to see the helicopter 'chiefly as a metaphor for the evolving spirit – the winged self which he now began to call the "psychopter"'.[12]

'I experiment with the self instead of with the machine', wrote Young; and, aware of the essentially alchemical nature of his enterprise, 'Bell has become a laboratory in which I try to distill my self. The helicopter is only the vessel . . .',[13] only a clumsy approximation to something more profound, the 'winged self' which 'the helicopter usurped – and what the helicopter was finally revealed not to be'.

In myth, heroes often fly. Sometimes they shape-change into a bird – although gods such as Odin or Zeus are more likely to do this – but more often they acquire a flying horse, a magic carpet, winged sandals and so on. Such flights no doubt recall the aerial adventures of shamans who, in Siberia, 'ride' their drums as horses into the Otherworld; or, in North America, decked out in feathers, imitate the eagle's soar and stoop.

The first man to fly by his own skill was Daedalus, whom Greek myth credits with the invention of the saw, the potter's wheel and the compass for drawing circles (unless he stole them from his apprentice, Talos). At King Minos' request, he built the labyrinth on the island of Crete to contain the Minotaur. When Minos imprisoned him, Daedalus escaped, together with his son Icarus, on wings he had manufactured. He was not a hero or shaman capable of magical flight, but a craftsman who constructs the means to fly. He shows us that technology is not intrinsically antagonistic to myth, but is itself a part of myth. Daedalus provides, that is, the archetypal background to modern technology.

He is very like Volund who, in Norse mythology, was captured by a king who wanted exclusive use of his incomparable craftsmanship. Volund's leg sinews were cut so that he could barely walk, and he was confined to an island. But he secretly made himself a set of wings, and escaped.[14]

He had another reason to make wings: he had lived for seven years with a ravishing Valkyr, who had appeared in the shape of a swan. She had voluntarily put aside her swan's cloak in order to be a wife to Volund. However, as in the tale of the seal wife, she had grown nostalgic for her Otherworld, Valhalla, where the dead heroes dwell; and, putting on her swan's skin, she had flown away. Volund's wings enabled him to fly off in search of her.

Like a shaman, Volund has an otherworldly partner and can fly. But his flight is not supernatural as a shaman's is – it is artificial. Volund is not a shaman but another marginal, uncanny kind of person. He is a smith.

The archetypal smith is Hephaestus (Vulcan), armourer to the Greek gods. Like so many smiths, he is lame. He is also ugly and hot-tempered, yet he is married to beauty itself, Aphrodite (Venus), the goddess of Love. Yet she is unfaithful to him, especially with Ares (Mars), the god of War. Like Hephaestus, technology is only obsessive and dangerous perhaps when love is taken away from it by war.

Tekhne manufactures with love, according to blueprints laid down by imagination. Technology can be the wings which carry Volund into the Otherworld, there to be reunited with his daimonic wife. It can even mediate between us and the gods: Daedalus built an apparatus in the shape of a cow in which Minos' wife, Pasiphae, concealed herself in order to copulate with the god Poseidon who had assumed the shape of a bull. Daedalus understood the power of technology and the dangers of its immoderate use. He warns Icarus to fly neither too low, near the sea, nor too high, near the sun. The boy famously disobeys: he flies too high; the sun melts the wax in his wings; he plummets to his death. He is an allegory of the overweening ego which, detached from its paternal grounding, abuses technology, is tempted into hubris – high-flying pride – and is plunged into destruction.

23

The Invention of Walking

COLERIDGE LEAPS THE GATE

The English Romantic movement began (if you will allow this conceit) at the beginning of June 1797, when the twenty-four-year-old Samuel Taylor Coleridge set out from his cottage in Nether Stowey, Somerset, to walk to Dorset. The last forty miles took the future writer of 'Kubla Khan' and 'The Rime of the Ancient Mariner' about a day and a half. At a field gate that still exists, he paused to look down over the little valley of the river Synderford, across a field of corn, to his destination. Set in a grove of beech trees, it was a square, brick, Georgian house, called Racedown Lodge. He could see a woman's figure working in a vegetable garden. She looked up. Coleridge vaulted over the gate and hastened through the corn towards her.[1]

I have opened this chapter with a description of Coleridge because he epitomizes those aspects of Romanticism which most concern this book. Principally, he defined the Romantic imagination both for his own generation and for the next – for Shelley, Keats and Byron, that is, no less than for his friend Wordsworth. He arrived at his view of imagination mainly by observing himself; but also by reading German Romantics such as Fichte, Schiller and Schelling – whose work he sometimes paraphrased. As a result, he was dogged by accusations of plagiarism, against which he defended himself by saying that he had formed his ideas before reading his German contemporaries – largely by reading the same sources as they.

Firstly, he claimed to have been deeply influenced by the Neoplatonists and especially by Plotinus whom he loved to quote – a claim substantiated by Charles Lamb who reports that at school Coleridge would hold forth on the mysteries of Iamblichus or Plotinus while the other boys stood about in admiration.[2] He was also influenced by the latest philosophy: Immanuel Kant's *Critique of Pure Reason*, which had appeared in 1781. Surprisingly, Giordano Bruno had a profound effect on him and connected him, as well as the German Romantics, back to the occult Neoplatonism of the Renaissance.[3] Above all, he had long been planning an essay on the early sixteenth-century mystic, Jacob Boehme, who, more than anyone, was responsible for the Romantic rediscovery of imagination.[4]

That first sight of Coleridge was something that Dorothy Wordsworth, then twenty-five, never forgot. Nor did her brother William. 'We both have a distinct remembrance of his arrival,' he said forty years later; 'he did not keep to the high road, but leaped over a gate and bounded down a pathless field by which he cut off an angle.'[5]

For Coleridge it was the beginning of two of the greatest friendships of his life; for Dorothy and William he seemed 'a sort of incarnation of the Romantic poetic personality. His impact was physical as much as intellectual. It was not merely his writing: it was his talk, his face, his darting intelligence, his eyes, his warmth, his supreme attention and response to everything around him . . . "He is a wonderful man," wrote Dorothy. "His conversation teems with soul, mind and spirit." ' Wonderful. 'It is a word used repeatedly by both Dorothy and William of Coleridge and not used lightly by either of them.' The friendship forged over the next fortnight between the three of them 'became, in terms of literary influence, the most important of their lives; and as a combined force it would prove the most powerful in the history of English Romanticism'.[6]

Coleridge's eye, wrote Dorothy, 'has more of the "poet's eye in a fine frenzy rolling" than I ever witnessed'.[7] She is quoting from *A Midsummer Night's Dream* (V,i) in which Shakespeare set out what might be the definitive description of the Romantic poet. The passage was often quoted (according to Samuel Palmer) by William Blake:[8]

> The poet's eye, in a fine frenzy rolling,
> Doth glance from heaven to earth, from earth to heaven;

And as imagination bodies forth
The forms of things unknown, the poet's pen
Turns them to shapes, and gives to airy nothing
A local habitation and a name.
Such tricks hath strong imagination . . .

The poet can travel in imagination, it seems, from earth to heaven and back like a shaman on his spirit horse, ravelling up the Above and the Below, and giving shape to imagination's 'things unknown'. In common with all the Romantics, Blake would balk at the description of them as 'airy nothing' because the forms bodied forth by imagination are more real to him than tangible facts.[9]

A 'PASSION OF AWE'

Coleridge recognized two kinds of imagination which he called primary and secondary. He held the Primary Imagination 'to be the living power and prime agent of all human perception, and as a repetition in the finite mind of the eternal act of creation in the infinite I AM'.[10]

The secondary imagination was an echo of the primary, the same in kind but different in degree, which we employ consciously. Fancy, on the other hand, was almost the opposite of imagination, more mechanical than creative, being 'no other than a mode of memory emancipated from the order of time and space'; and, like memory, receiving 'all its materials ready made from the law of association'.[11]

The Primary Imagination, as W. H. Auden explained earlier, is only concerned with sacred beings and events.[12] Some of these seem to be universal – for example, the moon, fire, snakes, Darkness, he suggests. Others seem to belong to a particular culture – kingship and horses for the English, say, or the Pleiades and the jaguar for Brazilian tribes. But, for Westerners, most sacred beings or events are an individual matter and unintelligible to anyone else. 'A hand lighting a cigarette is the explanation of everything; a foot stepping from the train is the rock of all existence . . . but two quiet steps by an old man seem like the very speech of hell. Or the other way round.'[13]

Auden's sacred beings are archetypal images. They are daimons. They can be beautiful and wonderful, dreadful and horrifying, providing only that they fulfil one condition: they must arouse 'a passion of awe'. Encounters with daimons seize us, absorb us, possess us. We do not observe them objectively – there is no subject and object – because the ego is annihilated, and we are fused with the sacred being. It is in us and we are in it. We are not ourselves, but rather 'beside ourselves'. The word 'awe' is shorthand for this experience.

It is made possible because the imagination with which we respond to sacred beings is the same in kind as the imagination which produces them. Imagination underlies both us and the daimons. This is why our individual and personal encounters are also felt as universal and impersonal: from one viewpoint they come from an imagination that we contain; from another, they come from an Imagination that contains us. The Primary Imagination is, as Coleridge says, a repetition in us of the divine creative act.

Whereas the categories of the Primary Imagination are 'sacred' and 'profane', those of the secondary imagination are 'beautiful' and 'ugly'. In other words, the secondary imagination – which is not passive in the face of the sacred beings, but active – is able to evaluate them aesthetically, to reflect upon them and to express the original awe in the rites of homage we call Art.[14]

Between Shakespeare and Coleridge, however, imagination suffered a severe setback. It suffered in particular from the ascendancy of Reason – which was really rationalism – at the so-called Enlightenment that flourished in eighteenth-century France, and whose roots lay with Bacon, Galileo, Mersenne, Descartes, Hobbes, Locke and Newton. Thomas Hobbes, for example, 'at times came near to equating the imagination with madness'.[15] If he had attacked it openly he might have found an opponent with courage and skill to combat him. But his method was more insidious and more damaging: he simply assumed that imagination was pretty much the property of children, lunatics and the uneducated. No one, that is, of any importance.

Although Hobbes was an Elizabethan – he was born in 1588 – his mind, like that of Mersenne in France, was modern. 'He never missed an opportunity to cast doubt or contempt on any form of mental activity that was not strictly rational.'[16] Indeed, it was part of his propaganda always to take for granted that rational thinking was characteristic of the modern mind and to denigrate the 'superstition' and 'credulity' of the past. 'No one was ever busier, emptying "the haunted air and gnomed mine", giving rational explanations of phenomena that had once been attributed to gods or daemons.'[17] In the face of his monumental *Leviathan*, which appeared in 1651, it suddenly seemed impossible to go against Hobbes and to espouse imagination without allying oneself with unreason and the mental darkness of the olden days.

At about the same time, an unprecedented gulf opened up between educated and popular culture. (It remains to this day, along with the superior, Hobbesian tone that rationalists adopt when confronted with anything they regard as superstitious belief.) Thomas Browne's *Vulgar Errors* and John Aubrey's *Remaines of Gentilisme and Judaism* were not unsympathetic to the superstitious past or to the contemporary beliefs of simple people; they were simply conscious of inhabiting a different mental world, from whose outlook the imaginative life of the uneducated, its myths and music, its deities and daimons, were barely culture at all.[18]

THE COUNTRY LIFE OF JEAN-JACQUES ROUSSEAU

It is not insignificant that Coleridge arrived at the Wordsworths' on foot. He was a prodigious walker – they all were – who thought nothing of covering thirty miles a day. Wordsworth had already walked across the Alps into Italy.[19] But recreational walking was a relatively new thing. It was an expression of the enthusiasm for 'democratic' action which sprang up in the wake of the intense revolutionary excitement that had charged the whole of Europe since the fall of the Bastille in July 1789 – the subject of the sixteen-year-old Coleridge's first substantial poem. Thus, from about 1790 onwards, young toffs dressed as tramps wandered the countryside, staying at rustic inns and earnestly engaging 'the common people' in conversation.

Strictly speaking, however, walking in Nature had been 'invented' a little earlier, by the Swiss-born philosopher Jean-Jacques Rousseau who had died in 1778. He was a key Enlightenment figure and a friend of

Denis Diderot, who would become the director of the great *Encyclopédie*. And it was while he was walking to visit Diderot in prison that he had a sudden inspiration: the world was not – as the Enlightenment thinkers insisted – getting better. It was getting worse. Progress and science were leading mankind up the wrong path.

The only hope was to return to an unsophisticated condition of sincerity, equality and kindness – to leave civilization, in other words, and to go back to Nature. In the 1750s Rousseau practised what he preached by taking up a simple life in the country where the nobility and the intelligentsia visited him from time to time, amazed at the way he walked everywhere instead of riding. Rousseau charmed them with his 'natural' philosophy, making them feel, temporarily at least, that industrialization was ruinous to a Nature which was not wild and threatening but benign and garden-like, an open Book where everyone could read and feel the sublimity of the Creator.

After Rousseau, the tension between town and country, analogous to the tribal tension between village and jungle, habitat and wilderness, was polarized so that city values increasingly tamed and 'civilized' the country until the second half of the twentieth century – when the wilderness ambushed civilization from behind, returning as 'urban jungle' and no-go areas peopled, as of old, by alien tribes.

Rousseau is the kind of Enlightenment thinker we can sympathize with. A few of his colleagues – Voltaire, for instance – turned on him bitterly, calling him a Judas. But this was because Rousseau saw clearly how extreme Enlightenment rationalism was a quasi-religion, a scientistic parody of the stultifying Catholicism it despised. He called its proponents 'overbearing dogmatists, ardent purveyors of atheism'.[20] His was the true Enlightenment spirit, which rejoiced in the pure clean air of sweet reason and natural science, cleansed of institutionalized religion and murky superstition alike.

THE CALL OF THE WILDERNESS

To thinkers like Rousseau, Nature's 'garden' was a pure counterpart to a corrupt civilization. Analogously, they did not demonize imagination like the rationalists, but allowed it a place as long as it was not too 'enthusiastic', not too wild and bumpy. The Romantics, on the other hand, took a mountainous view of Imagination, commensurate with their ideal of Nature. For the Enlightenment had done its work, and the Romantics were so little oppressed by Nature after two centuries of rationalism that they longed for it again – and the wilder the better. Coleridge swapped comparatively tame walks through the Quantock hills for dangerous fell-walking among the peaks of the Lake District.

At the same time, everywhere in England was tame compared to the great wildernesses of North America, and so the idea of wildness took on a peculiar force there. (Coleridge himself planned a Utopian community on the banks of the 'Susquahannah' in Pennsylvania.)[21] 'In wilderness is the preservation of the world', wrote Thoreau, following the lead of his mentor, Ralph Waldo Emerson, who, in his essay on Nature (1837), advocated a new relationship with the land, one of living participation rather than one of domination: 'Standing on the bare ground', he wrote, 'the currents of the Universal Being circulate through me; I am part or parcel of God.'[22]

This mystical view of Nature increasingly caught the popular mood. It became commonplace to call the wildernesses 'the cathedrals of the modern world'. They were holy places; and secular pilgrimages – what we now call tourism – were made to the Lake District in Wordsworth's lifetime, just as they were to the Black Forest in Germany and, in America, to Yosemite Park whose chief protector, John Muir, was a disciple of Emerson's and an out-and-out Nature worshipper. But even as he was describing, in 1869, the western mountains as God's outdoor temples, the transcontinental railway was completed, bringing the wilderness under threat. Muir lobbied vigorously for National Parks, and the first – Yellowstone – was created in 1872.

It was in those days that the foundation of so many people's preference for a country walk over a church service on Sundays was laid. Nature had become once again, to the Romantic eye, a place that was both wild and sublime, a source of the divine; a place where educated young men could find adventure, freedom and otherworld encounters with rustic folk and customs which polite society had ignored; a place where daimons once more emerged from their woods and streams and mountain fastnesses.

But rationalism had so polarized the traditional ambiguity of Nature that the pendulum could always swing from the Romantic view back to the rationalistic. We saw such a swing take place in the young Darwin as he contemplated the wildness of South America. His response was poetic; his delighted exclamations at its beauty might have come from the notebooks of Coleridge. Then, suddenly, it seemed too much, too wild. Beauty dropped her mask to reveal chaos beneath.

Darwin panicked. There were 'unnamed animals staring him in the face'. He retreated behind the walls of rationalism and stayed there, feeling besieged by Nature, fearful, and sickened by the sight of a peacock's feather. But it was not of course Nature who was so hostile, as scientists so often believe; it was his own wild imagination – and all the wilder for having been held down by a rational classifying consciousness – which subverted him at every turn, taunting him perhaps with the dark suspicion he could never admit: that the nauseating feather could not have 'evolved', but was the handiwork of an invisible Artist.

24

The Romantic Philosophy

THE *TABULA RASA*

What, meanwhile, was the official philosophical view of imagination in the eighteenth century? As a result of Descartes's dualism, the most pressing philosophical problem had become the relationship between ideas in the mind and objects in the world. Although Descartes had divided the two, he still believed that we are born with certain ideas stamped on our minds. But, in 1689, *An Essay Concerning Human Understanding* appeared. It was by John Locke, who had been writing it for twenty years. He expressed his debt to Descartes, especially for his clear and rational style, but he did not agree with him about innate ideas.[1] Locke redefined the mind; or, rather, he revived Aristotle's idea that the mind was a *tabula rasa*, a blank slate like 'white paper, void of all characters, without any ideas'[2] on which experience writes. And this, I suppose, is still the common view of the mind.

What is the role of imagination in such a mind? David Hume, Locke's eighteenth-century successor, described it: imagination simply reproduces the sensory experiences impressed on the mind so that we can think about them when they are absent. Its creativity is limited to moving these impressions around and constructing new configurations. Above all, imagination allows us to believe in the continuity of the existence of objects in the world because, through imagination, they continue to exist even when we are not directly experiencing them.[3] But none of this implies that we can really know about the world. We can only know our impressions of it. And any order we impose on them – cause and effect, for instance – is purely arbitrary, an illusory order suggested by the association of ideas which is only a habit of imagination.

Immanuel Kant was badly shaken by this analysis. He had thought that Newton's description of the world, for instance, was pretty much certain knowledge. But, if Hume was right, there was no such thing as certain knowledge. He developed therefore a new model of mind, one that does not passively receive sense data, as Locke and Hume had said, but one that actively assimilates and structures them so that we know objective reality exactly to the extent that reality conforms to the fundamental structures of the mind. The world we attempt to grasp, that is, corresponds to principles in the mind because the only world we can grasp is already structured by those principles. 'All human cognition of the world is channelled through the human mind's categories.'[4]

Kant is here thinking in the tradition that comes from Plato and anticipates Jung. His categories are relations of Plato's Forms and Jung's archetypes, each of which should be seen, not in a static, monolithic way, but in a dynamic way as a pattern and perspective we see the world through – in effect, the world we see.

After Kant, it became clear that science can never establish absolute, objective truths because, on the one hand, it is itself a product of mental structures which are themselves relative; and, on the other hand, its method of observing produces that very 'objective reality' it is trying to explain.[5] (This is a truism for Postmodernism whose motto might be: 'All human understanding is interpretation, and no interpretation is final.')[6] There are no facts independent of the perspective from which the mind views them. It was Kant's insight that our compulsion towards mechanistic impersonal explanation is in us, not in things; and it was Max Weber's 'to see that it is historically a specific kind of mind, not human mind as such, that is subject to this compulsion'[7] – a specific kind of mind I have been calling the rational ego.

KANT'S IMAGINATION

Kant agreed with Hume's estimate of the imagination which worked more or less mechanically by associating ideas. But he called it the empirical or reproductive imagination and sharply distinguished it from the productive or transcendental imagination. An 'active and spontaneous power', this imagination was 'fundamental to our perceptual understanding of the world, which is universal and the same for everyone'.[8]

He thought imagination was a mystery. But he repeatedly tried to make the mystery clearer. In his *Critique of Judgement* he asks how we recognize man as a member of a particular animal species.[9] In a way that is incomprehensible to us, he says, the imagination is able to reproduce the image of an object out of countless similar ones. It seems to be able to unconsciously compare images, as if superimposing one on another to form a coincidence of those which are the same and so arrive at 'a mean contour which serves as the common standard for all'.[10]

If this were performed consciously it would mean measuring thousands of men and, by a kind of 'Identikit' procedure, arrive at a picture of the average man. But although a computer might work like this, the imagination does not. 'It is an intermediate', says Kant, 'between all singular intuitions of individuals, with their manifold variations, and the generic idea . . . a floating image for the whole genus, which nature has set as an archetype underlying those of her products that belong to the same species but which in no single case she seems completely to have attained.'[11]

In this way, imagination lies between the intellect and the senses, between abstract concepts and concrete percepts. Without a mediating imagination our sensory experience would be intellectually unorganized and therefore chaotic; while our intellectual life would suffer from sensory deprivation and therefore be empty.[12]

Kant's description of this transcendental imagination's mysterious workings goes back, of course, to the Neoplatonic Soul of the World which similarly bridges the gap between the ideal Forms in the intelligible world and the sensory objects of the physical world. It also foreshadows Jung's collective unconscious whose archetypes, unknowable in themselves, are paradoxically knowable through particular manifestations of themselves – that is, through archetypal images.

THE UNIVERSAL MIND

The modern Western mind is still largely dualistic, still built on Cartesian-Kantian lines, still very much the rational Enlightenment model. But at the same time as it was being finally formulated by Kant, a new outlook was emerging and developing with Goethe, Fichte, Schiller, Schelling, Tieck and others – the German Romantics who so influenced the likes of Coleridge in England and Emerson in America. In their own separate ways they all held in common 'a fundamental conviction that the relation of the human mind to the world was ultimately not dualistic but participatory'.[13]

This conception of the mind was implicit, as we have seen, in Kant's insight that knowledge of the world is determined by deep unconscious principles. But whereas he still confined these principles, as it were, to the human subject alone, the participatory conception suggested that 'these subjective principles are in fact an expression of the world's own being, and that the human mind is ultimately the organ of the world's own process of self-revelation'.[14] Reality is not separate, self-contained and thus able to be 'objectively' examined. Instead, it unfolds and becomes intelligible to itself with the active participation of the human mind.

Fichte, who has been called 'the father of Romanticism', believed in 'a transcendent, infinite world-spirit of which the human individual is a mere spatiotemporal, mortal expression, a finite centre which derives its reality from the spirit, to perfect union with which it seeks to attain'.[15] Schelling thought that Nature was an absolute being working towards self-consciousness[16] – a popular idea elaborated by Hegel and his followers who saw the whole universe as unfolding its meaning, coming to know itself through human minds and progressing to a higher state. Or, rather, the universe as Creation is itself an unfolding expression of a universal Mind or Spirit (*Geist*) which finally realizes itself in the human spirit, or comes to consciousness of itself in the human mind.[17]

Reality was variously thought of as world-soul or spirit, imagination and Nature. Goethe's *naturphilosophie*, for instance, maintained that Nature permeates everything, including the imagination. Such a notion helped the scientific Goethe to reconcile empirical observation with the artistic Goethe's spiritual intuition in a science of Nature which he thought superior to Newton's single, objective and literal view of the world. Nature and Imagination were as if the outside and the inside of the same thing. Analogously, Schelling declared that there are not two kinds of stuff in the world – mind-stuff and matter-stuff – but only one: the imagination which underlies both ideas and things, and also in a sense creates both Nature and Art.[18]

Imagination for Kant was an active function rather than the passive faculty it had been for Locke and Hume. It constituted the world as it appears to us. But for Romantics such as Schelling and Coleridge it was a creative function, constituting the world as it really is.[19]

Central to this function is the way imagination enables us to see the universal in the particular – to see things as symbols, which have the power both to embody an idea, feeling or intuition perfectly, and also to point to some meaning beyond itself. A symbol is an expression *par excellence* of Blake's double vision. Anything can become a symbol at the moment when it is so wrought up by imagination that it suddenly opens up like a window on to another, infinite world while yet remaining in this world. It is a 'still point' where the finite and infinite, conscious and unconscious, conjoin. The concrete particular is transparent to the universal archetype and the archetype is bodied forth in the particular.[20]

Kant and Schelling both held such ideas about symbols; but it took poets such as Coleridge and Wordsworth, rather than philosophers, to include as an essential part of imagination the passion of awe we feel in the presence of a symbol that ravels up such 'an aweful adorable omneity in unity'.[21] It is typical, too, of the extraordinary, exuberant yet melancholy Coleridge that he stresses something philosophers rarely mention, namely the joy imagination brings, even while he is lamenting its loss. 'Dejection: an Ode' is that paradoxical item – a creative poem about the failure of creative power. The soul sends out 'a sweet and potent voice' which is nothing other than the 'luminous cloud' of joy. It comes from within and is intimately connected with imagination. Without joy we merely see; and though we may see that a thing is beautiful, we do not *feel* it to be so. 'It is joy which converts a perception to a feeling, and it is this that is lost in the loss of the shaping power of the imagination.'[22]

25

Boehme and Blake

GOD'S MIRROR

Coleridge's distinction between fancy and imagination probably came from Jacob Boehme who scorns *phantasia* as the deceptive illusion of the ego, enticing the soul away from God and towards its own selfish desires. By contrast, *imaginatio* is the creative energy of God Himself by which He inspires the universe into being. God, says Boehme, is actually unimaginable in Himself, a 'groundless abyss',[1] which, however, desires to manifest itself – as if God wished to know Himself. In fact, He does come to know Himself – by begetting a 'mirror' in which He is reflected and by which He achieves self-consciousness. The mirror is *wisdom*, the beginning of all manifestation out of the ineffable and unmanifested Godhead, and also the essence of the Divine Imagination.[2]

Born in 1575, in Gorlitz, Upper Lusatia, Boehme belongs, strictly speaking, in the chapter on the Renaissance magi. He is placed here because he is the crucial link in the Golden Chain which connects the magi to the Romantics. It was the discovery of Boehme by the German Romantics and, independently, by Blake and Coleridge in England which initiated the resurgence of Imagination over Reason.

A shoemaker by trade, Boehme was happily married with several children – an unlikely background for the extraordinary series of books, from *Aurora* to *Mysterium Magnum*, which he produced between about 1614 and the year of his death, 1624. There is no doubt that he possessed enormous erudition in the usual areas – alchemy, Neoplatonism, Gnosticism and Cabala[3] – but the turning-point in his life seems to have been the three mystical 'illuminations' he experienced in 1600.

According to Boehme's friend, Abraham von Franckenberg, the first illumination was brought on by the sudden gleam on a tin or pewter vessel, which arrested the shoemaker and caused him to see 'into the secret heart of nature, into a concealed divine world'.[4] He had the sense of being embraced by divine love as if, he recalled, life had been resurrected from death.[5] Because he worked in the 'occult' tradition of the magi, which seemed to do most justice to his own gnosis, he fell constantly under suspicion of heresy. How painful this must have been to a man who was so devout a Christian that he strove always to harness his alchemical and Neoplatonic ideas to Christian theology. The results were necessarily idiosyncratic.

For example, the 'wisdom' which is the empty mirror of God's self-consciousness is assimilated to the Trinity. The 'abysmal' God begets the Son or Logos out of His emptiness in order to reflect Himself; but His very act of begetting a Son in whom He is reflected is a giving birth to Himself as Father. Both Father and Son are bound together by the Holy Spirit. So far so good: God knows Himself in Himself. But to know Himself outside Himself – as other than Himself – He requires a body. A 'fourth' must be added to the Trinity's three in order to reflect the Trinity as a whole and enable it to realize itself. This fourth is Wisdom as the divine Sophia. She is God's Imagination and the Magical Body with whom He clothes Himself and through whom He imagines the universe into existence.[6] She is the 'celestial' or 'subtle' body of God from which the physical body – our universe – emanates.

This is only a glimpse into Boehme's vast and profound metaphysical system. We can see the alchemical influence in the way that wisdom transforms itself like the mercurial prime matter: it is both mother of the Trinity and daughter, both beginning and end of the creative process, just as the self-circling energy of Imagination perpetually generates and dissolves images of itself. We can see, too, a Neoplatonic tendency in the way that Sophia is, like the world-soul, an intermediate plane between the One (now a three-personed God) and the world. Boehme explicitly described Sophia as the realm which, lying between Heaven and Earth, participates in both; a realm of transition and transformation, where spirits are transmuted into bodies, and bodies into spirits.[7]

Boehme believes as a matter of course that human beings are microcosms in which everything that occurs in the macrocosm, or universe, is reflected. But he goes further: man is the mirror-image of God Himself. He holds the power of the divine Imagination. Although man has always existed as a kind of Platonic idea in the mind of God, he was only made manifest – in the person of Adam – by the Son, or Logos, in conjunction with Sophia, or the Divine Mirror of Wisdom. Adam was originally a wedding of the masculine Logos and feminine Sophia, a man-woman or androgyne.[8] This tells us that our primordial psychological constitution is a conjunction of opposites, symbolized by masculine and feminine principles.

The human task – the Imitation of Christ – is an alchemical one: imagination transmutes us into an image of Christ; or, rather, the soul 'imagines into Christ' while God, in turn, 'imagines into the soul'. Finally, imagination has the paradoxical power to carry us beyond all its images, including God, to the ineffable *Ungrund*, the formless unity of the 'God beyond God'.[9]

'ENERGY IS ETERNAL DELIGHT'

In Boehme's system, imagination holds everything together. Adam's exile from Eden, his Fall, occurred because he abused his imaginative powers. He would be redeemed, as we are, by the 'second Adam' – Jesus Christ, who is Imagination made flesh.[10]

Exactly this 'theology' was taken up enthusiastically some two hundred years later by William Blake whose 'Jesus the Imagination' stood at the centre of his lyric poems and prophetic books. If he was called mad in his lifetime (even Wordsworth who should have known better called him that)[11] we can see now that it was Shakespeare's 'fine frenzy', the divine madness expounded by Socrates. The difficulty of his poems, with their obscure allegories and catalogue of invented personages, is owing to the fact that he did not have an existing, living system of symbols to work with. He admires, even envies, Milton for *Paradise Lost*; but he knows that the epic poem set in Biblical symbolism is no longer possible. 'He was a man crying out for a mythology', wrote Yeats with some justice, 'and trying to make one because he could not find one to his hand. Had he been a Catholic of Dante's time he would have been well content with Mary and the angels . . .'[12]

Nevertheless, when one reads Blake, Yeats continued, 'it is as though the spray of an inexhaustible fountain of beauty was blown into our faces'.[13] Kathleen Raine calls Blake the only poet to have created a Christian polytheism,[14] an architectonic mythology made from pieces of Swedenborg and Norse myth, alchemy and Hermeticism, Neoplatonism and Boehme – all fused in the white heat of his imagination.

Blake's enthusiasm for the Neoplatonists was tempered, as it was for Boehme, by an uneasiness concerning their emphasis on the transcendence of the spiritual over the material. Both Blake and Boehme wished to remain close to matter, even to redeem it. Both found a way of doing this through alchemical thinking where spirit and matter, soul and body, are never separated for long but continually interpenetrate.

Blake's *The Marriage of Heaven and Hell* – practically 'a manifesto of the philosophy of Paracelsus and Boehme'[15] – is an alchemical marriage. 'Without contraries is no progression', he wrote. Yet, what literary critics often regard as his most original contribution to thought is the very heart of alchemy, namely the 'conception of a single existing principle operating through contraries'.[16] This was – unsurprisingly, given their common alchemical background – an idea of Boehme's, too. He also imagined God, at times, as an eternal fire which included the abyss of hell and its devils. Blake adopted this notion in rather a Nietzschean way, which inverted the usual Christian order and made the angels insipid agents of conventional Christianity, while the devils became agents of imaginative fire, whose 'Energy is Eternal Delight'. 'He cried again and again that everything that lives is holy, and that nothing is unholy except things that do not live – lethargies, and cruelties, and timidities, and that denial of imagination which is the root they grew from in old times.'[17]

Blake believed in innate ideas. We do not, strictly speaking, learn anything new; rather, we bring everything we have into the world with us. While Plato believed that knowledge was really recollection, and that art was imitation, Blake went further: both knowledge and art are recreation.[18]

As if he had completely recollected the Divine Ideas at an early age, Blake's viewpoint never changed. The lyrics of his adolescence and 'the comments which blister the margins of books he read on a sickbed at seventy, are almost identical in outlook'.[19] From the beginning he held up John Locke, Francis Bacon and Isaac Newton as 'symbols of every kind of evil, superstition and tyranny'.[20] Against Bacon's empiricism and Locke's rationalism, he raised a perpetual outcry: 'Mental things are alone real.'[21] These things are also called forms or images – the products, in other words, of imagination.

LOCKE'S SPECTRES

Lockean philosophy distinguished sensation from reflection – which classifies the sensations and develops them into abstract ideas. These in turn afford generalizations by which we form patterns out of the mass of sensory data. Blake thought that 'to Generalize is to be an idiot. To particularize is the Alone Distinction of merit.'[22] Stick to the particular image, says Blake, because to reflect on sensation in the Lockean way is mere memory, producing a 'spectre' of the original image; a copy of a copy, as Plato would say. Distinct perception of actual things is infinitely superior to attempts to classify them into general principles.[23]

The Lockean idea of reality is simply a consensus based on the lowest common denominator, as if a farmer and a painter looking at a landscape were to arrive at a true picture by subtracting the agricultural qualities from the farmer's perception and the artistic ones from the painter's.[24] We see at once that this is not possible to do, nor worth doing if it were – we end up with a shadowy landscape so generalized as to be non-existent. We end up, in fact, with some sort of perfectly objective world composed of non-mental and unperceived units, such as atoms. But an atom, says Blake, is 'a Thing which does not exist'.[25]

In this snub to our modern atomists – the philosophical materialists – Blake means that it is nonsense to try and annihilate the perceived differences in forms by asserting that they are all built out of units of 'matter'. The reality of the world does not consist of a generalized grey fog of identical bits; it consists of vibrant, living, colourful forms. Nothing is real beyond the imaginative patterns we make of our reality. Hence there are as many different kinds of reality as there are people. 'Every thing possible to be believ'd is an image of truth.'[26] Even Locke shows us one facet of truth. For the belief in the mind's essential blankness is itself an enduring myth, an archetypal image which, however, cannot be taken literally.

DOUBLE VISION

When Blake saw the sun as a heavenly host rather than a golden guinea, it was more real because more imagination had been infused into it. The guinea sun is the generalized abstract sun in which we find our lowest common denominator; the heavenly-host sun is the visionary sun, as much created as perceived. The visionary has passed through sight into vision. Imagination sees through, not with, the eye. 'May God us keep/ From Single vision & Newton's sleep.'[27]

But it is worth repeating that Blake's double vision encompasses the guinea sun – to see only the heavenly host, to take the vision literally, would be as crazy as Blake thinks it is to see only the guinea sun (a madness we nevertheless call normality). Locke's blank-page mind is inert; Blake's mind sees through the eye and actively grasps the world with creative exuberance. That he really did this is evidenced, of course, by his art.

We might call the Blakean double vision a Hermetic consciousness, for which there are no dualistic problems of subject and object, consciousness versus the unconscious and so on. Hermes travels freely between upperworlds and underworlds. His stone herms are erected at crossroads, marking the fact that he is god of all borderlines.[28] Every daimon who appears at a boundary – whether between sleeping and waking, between day and night, at the turning of the year or at crossroads, on bridges or shorelines – is a face of Hermes. This is why to come to terms with daimons is also to develop a Hermetic way of thinking, a borderline perception which sees this world and the Otherworld simultaneously – which sees the one in the other, and vice versa, intertwined like the serpents on Hermes' thyrsus.

Indeed, the idea of 'double vision' should not, finally, imply seeing two things at once or translating one thing into another. It should be a single mode of seeing, as it were built into the eye, in which the doubleness of things – as in the best metaphors – is apparent at a glance because we are simultaneously seeing, and seeing through.

26

Remembrance of Things Past

PROUST'S MADELEINE

In Marcel Proust's novel, *À la Recherche du Temps Perdu*, the narrator famously dips a little bun – a madeleine – into his cup of tea and eats it. No sooner has he tasted the madeleine than a shudder runs through his body, followed by a sensation of exquisite pleasure as if, he says, love had filled him with its precious essence. He feels something inside him begin to heave up, 'something that has been embedded like an anchor at great depth'.[1] He does not know what it is, but he can feel it mounting slowly. And yet still it will not surface. Ten times he leans over the abyss and tries to summon it up, until suddenly the memory returns: 'the taste was that of the little crumb of madeleine which on Sunday mornings at Combray . . . my aunt Leonie used to give me, dipping it first in her own cup of . . . tea'.[2]

And so he learns that long after things seem dead and gone, 'the smell and taste . . . remain poised a long time, like souls, ready to remind us, waiting and hoping for their moment, amid the ruins of all the rest; and bear unfaltering, in the tiny and almost impalpable drop of their essence, the vast structure of recollection'.[3]

From the memory of Aunt Leonie, he proceeds to remember her room, her house, her garden; then the whole town, its streets and houses and gardens – his whole childhood 'taking their shapes and growing solid, sprang into being . . . from my cup of tea'.[4]

Proust's experience is familiar to all of us: a taste or smell transports us to another world. The journey into the past is an otherworld journey available to us all. Usually we make raids on the past to pull out a face or fact; sometimes we make more leisurely trips, dreamily remembering a childhood holiday or some other happy time. This kind of memory is analogous to Coleridge's fancy, a more or less mechanical association of images, and quite different from Proust's recollection – which is analogous to imagination. Unlike voluntary journeys down Memory Lane, Proust's narrator is seized by an involuntary encounter with the past, like one of Auden's sacred events. It is like an experience of the Primary Imagination, before which he is passive and awed, and on which he immediately sets to work in an active way, analogous to the secondary imagination, in his attempts to recall the initial recollection. In fact, the relationship between recollection and imagination is so richly interfused that it is as difficult to separate them as it would be to separate, in Proust's novel, autobiography and art.

THE MEMORY PALACE OF MATTEO RICCI

It was just such an interpenetration of memory and imagination which characterized the classical 'art of memory' by which Matteo Ricci, a Jesuit missionary to China in the 1590s, amazed his hosts, reciting back to them, after only one reading, four or five hundred Chinese characters.[5]

The technique was to picture the memory as a theatre or palace in which each thing to be remembered was assigned an image, the more grotesque, comical, hideous or ridiculous the better, because it is these attributes we seem to be able to recall most easily. These striking images were then arranged in clusters, *tableaux*, or 'rooms' so that, in order to remember everything – the points in a speech, for instance – one had only to 'walk' around the mental palace, visiting each room and collecting each memory from its image in turn.

However, Ricci's use of the art of memory was more or less mechanical, a simple data retrieval trick. The more profound art, used by the Renaissance magi, was to imprint planetary images and themes from classical myths on the mind, in the same way as mnemonic images, but now for the purpose 'of reflecting the universe in the mind' and 'to acquire universal knowledge, and also powers, obtaining through the magical organization of the imagination a magically powerful personality, tuned in . . . to the powers of the cosmos'.[6]

Psychologically speaking, the art of memory could be described as 'both a retrieval system and a structured model for laying out the groundwork and hierarchies of the imagination on archetypal principles. The ordering rubrics that provided the categories were mainly the planetary Gods and themes from classical myths.'[7] The art of memory reminds us that memory is a dynamic place, a theatre, where the images we store take on their own life, interacting like the gods and myths of which they are composed, creating new connections and new imaginative configurations that we do not merely remember but recollect.

FREUD'S FANTASIES

The experience of recollection is so powerful that we are convinced of its truth. But, whereas Proust would never claim literal truth for his recollection, never claim that it was factual – never claim, perhaps, that it was possible in the end to be factual about memories of childhood, people other than novelists (most people, probably) believe that memory is a reliable guide to literal truth, to the historical past.

Freud, for example, concluded on the basis of his female patients' clear recollections, as well as their dreams and their free associations, that they had been 'seduced' as small children by their fathers. But when patients whose early histories were well known to him reported similar memories (which could have no basis in fact), he began to smell a rat: paternal seduction – we now call it child abuse – could not possibly be as frequent as he had been led to believe. He surmised therefore that women were 'remembering' what they wished to have happened.

It sounds shocking to us now, the idea that a daughter could wish for 'abuse' from her father; but, according to Freud, they had during their 'Oedipal period' so passionately desired that their fathers be in love with them, that they vividly imagined it was so. 'Later, when they recalled the content of these fantasies, it was with such intensity of feeling that they were convinced that this could only be because of events which had actually taken place.'[8]

It sounds shocking to us because we have become aware of how common child abuse is. In the 1980s, when it was rediscovered, so to speak, it seemed to be everywhere. It was even compounded by accusations of 'satanic ritual abuse', reminiscent of medieval witch-hunts.[9] Moreover, adults began to come forward, claiming that they had been sexually abused as children. They had not realized it until they underwent psychotherapy, and then, in the course of their treatment, sometimes under 'regression hypnosis', all these memories of abuse had surfaced.

The retrogressive epidemic spread like wildfire across the USA and, to a lesser extent, across western Europe. Every third person, it seemed, was a 'survivor' of childhood sexual abuse. The newspapers were full of it; TV chat shows and documentaries rehashed all the details; a spate of movies dwelt on it; every other novelist leapt at the chance to spice up a jaded plot. At the same time, Freud was criticized for his representation of child abuse as fantasy, and accused of turning a blind eye to the horrendous scale of the phenomenon.

Then slowly, inevitably perhaps, doubts began to arise. By the early 1990s, many people were claiming that they had not in fact been abused after all. They had 'imagined' it; they had been pressurized into believing it by their psychotherapists, who had convinced them that they 'remembered' abuse. Some of these memories, especially under hypnosis, were startlingly clear – yet the 'victim' admitted that they could not have happened. Indeed, another set of victims appeared: those who had been falsely accused of abuse – victims of what was now called 'false memory syndrome', as if it were a disease.

But although the balance has tilted for the time being in favour of the falsehood of 'recovered' claims of childhood abuse, there are still plenty of people who maintain that they were abused and had simply, because of the extremely traumatic nature of their experience, forgotten it. That is to say, they had repressed or denied the memory of it. But other 'survivors' claim that no matter how traumatic the abuse has been it is impossible to forget it.

In England, the Brandon Report, which appeared on 1 April 1998, was sharply critical of recovered memory, especially by hypnosis or 'truth drugs', and claimed that genuine abuse is not forgotten or, if forgotten, remembered spontaneously without aids or prompting. But one can sense, too, another agenda behind this report. It was produced by psychiatrists who, notoriously, disapprove of psychotherapists. They tend to hold a materialistic view of the psyche, believing that it can be reduced to the brain so that psychic disorders are really organic disorders best treated with drugs. They simply do not recognize many psychotherapeutic assumptions, least of all the possibility of recovering repressed memories. They certainly did not know how to counter one victim called Caroline Malone, for example, who appeared on the BBC news on the same day as the release of the Brandon Report, to attest to her own memory of sexual abuse recovered by hypnosis – and then corroborated by the confession of her abuser.

The ambiguity of the situation is exactly analogous to that of the many people throughout the 1980s and 1990s who claimed to have experienced 'missing time' as a result of a close encounter with a UFO. Regression hypnosis was often used to try and fill in this gap in their memory; and, more often than not, they 'remembered' being abducted into the spacecraft of sinister little grey aliens who performed painful operations on them and stole ova or sperm.

The same debate surrounds the abductees as the adult survivors of childhood abuse. There is no doubt that some abductees only remember an abduction scenario after repeated hypnotic regressions and continual prompting, just as therapists have been accused of inducing 'memories' of abuse in the past. Others recall their abductions spontaneously, without the use of hypnotism.

No one who listens to the traumatized victims' accounts of their abductions can remain unmoved or unconvinced that something real did occur. But whereas scientism writes off the experiences as imaginary or organic (for instance, 'temporal lobe seizure'), and ufology writes it up as extraterrestrial invasion, there is a middle way by which we can think of them as *bona fide*, real, but not literal, journeys into the Otherworld such as traditional cultures have always taken for granted.

The weakness of memory, and its strength, is that it is not simply a record of events in the past. It takes events and mixes them up with fantasies and imagined events. It is tricky and deceptive. While we think of memory as passively storing events which can be pulled out at any time, like files, it is secretly at work, changing the shape of its contents.

It confabulates. It even makes things up altogether, like imagination. Greek mythology makes Memory – Mnemosyne – the mother of the muses who preside over the arts. It was understood, that is, that memory is pregnant with imaginative power. Never a mindless data retrieval system, she is always an adorner, a myth-maker, a falsifier of facts and a literalizer of fictions.

Memory is the form Imagination takes when it wishes to impress us with its reality. Imagined persons and events are indeed real, as I have perhaps been over-insisting. But imagination does not – quite rightly – trust us in our unimaginative and literalistic way to treat them as real. So it presents them as non-imaginative and literal – and we believe that they actually happened. But no matter how vividly we 'remember' them, they did not necessarily happen. Their reality is mythic, not historical. 'These things never happened; they are always', Sallust reminds us. This was Freud's insight into his patients' 'memories', and the beginning of depth psychology's recognition of a daimonic reality that is not literal.[10]

Such a reality is the norm in traditional cultures, of course, whose myths are presented as events which happened in the past, notably in the Beginning; and whose rituals, closely related to the myths, are concrete re-enactments – recollections – of seminal events in the past, notably the creation of the world. Yet no one takes these past events literally. It is as if they know that the idea of the past is a device to confer greater reality on myth and ritual.

THE HYPNOTIC MEMORY

The recent popularity of hypnosis as a key to unlocking the past is interesting. Hypnosis itself is far from being well understood. Debate about it is as polarized as the debate about the reality of the 'memories' it throws up. One faction says that hypnotic trances are real – although it is uncertain how exactly they are induced. The opposition asserts that they are not real, only very relaxed states in a susceptible subject. Whatever memories are retrieved from a hypnotic state, therefore, are either accurate accounts of events, says the first faction; or, says the second, they are more or less consciously fabricated by the subject. Once again, we do not have to side with either faction.

We have only to recognize that hypnosis, the child of nineteenth-century mesmerism, is one technique among many for inducing an altered psychic state – that is, for entering the Otherworld. Traditional methods include fasting, prayer, pain, drugs, disease, music, chant and meditation in order to induce trance, possession, ecstasy, vision. Those who have a talent, or even a vocation, for such states are called mystics, poets, mediums, witch-doctors and shamans. But I have argued else-where[11] that everyone needs some contact with the Otherworld, whether through dreams, imagination or vision, because such contact is essential to that initiation without which our lives are not in the fullest sense lived.

From the daimonic point of view, the desire for regression hypnosis comes from a desire to literalize the mythic past. We wish to literalize our epiphanic encounters with daimons and turn them into close encounters of the third (or is it fourth?) kind; we wish to literalize our childhood sufferings and turn them into traumas. We long to find that moment When Things Went Wrong. Sometimes hypnosis will take us back beyond childhood, before birth, to a 'past life' in which we find the cause of our present disorders.

All this is necessary, in a way, because one of the soul's most potent myths is the myth of Origins, the myth of How It All Began, whether the Creation of the world or the birth of a neurosis. But it *is* a myth, and should not be confused with history, as if things began at some moment in time. To adapt Sallust's remark: 'These things never *began*; they are always' – and they are always beginning. The idea of beginning is always present as a possibility in the psyche.

This is why the principle activity of gods and ancestors in tribal cultures is placed in the past. They are never active in the present. The present beliefs of traditional cultures are founded on stories of long-ago deeds of creation, or of war against evil spirits, or of the introduction of the civilizing arts. The retelling of the myths and re-enactment of rituals keeps this past constantly present – reflects the fact that it is always going on in the collective psyche.

Instead of literalizing the past, we might imagine it in terms of Plotinus's *epistrophé*, 'turning back' – 'the idea that all things desire to return to the archetypal originals of which they are copies and from which they proceed'.[12] Instead of tracing an image back to its 'origin', we imagine it back into its archetype. Psychologically speaking, we ask ourselves: what is the archetypal background to this dream image or that pattern of behaviour or those symptoms? What god is in them or behind them?

This method of reversion leads us out of purely personal constraints and back into a wider, collective, more mythic context where our private aggravations can expand and gravitate towards their grander mythical counterparts; where the bonds of the literal event can be severed, opening it into metaphor and multiple meanings; where history is dissolved back into myth; where our personal lives are connected back to the impersonal gods and we become at once less self-important and more important as selves.

FORGOTTEN MEMORY

Freud's brilliant insight was that, in order to untangle a fouled psyche, it was no good simply trying to remember the moment when things went wrong. There had to be an abreaction – an involuntary and concrete reliving of the primal trauma. Not a memory, in other words, but a total experience of recollection, as vivid as Proust's recollection after he tasted the madeleine.

This reminds us that, just as forgetting is the shadow of remembering, so the involuntary remembering of Freud's abreaction is the corollary of that involuntary forgetting he called repression. It is difficult to distinguish between what we have merely forgotten and what we have repressed – what we cannot remember voluntarily because we have involuntarily repressed it so that, in trying to recall what we are simultaneously determined to forget, memory is at war with itself and a battle rages between consciousness and the unconscious.

Freud investigated the forgotten (in hysteria); he documented the tiny forgettings we pay no attention to, the slips in everyday life, and showed how they were fissures in consciousness which led down to unsuspected depths of psychopathology. Jung went down even further, and discovered a collective unconscious as overlooked as its historical antecedents, whole forgotten areas of psychology, such as alchemy, which had slipped the mind of modern Western culture.

From the point of view of remembering, of consciousness, forgetting is at best a nuisance, at worst a festering repression. But forgetfulness has its own perspective which belongs with sleep, dreams and, ultimately, death. Underworld experiences, from dreams to alien abductions, resist being remembered because they do not want to be forced under the yoke of an imperious ego-consciousness. Remembering our dreams is often, as I have suggested, a process of dragging them into the daylight and trussing them up in explanations and interpretations. Forgetting may well be a necessary counter-movement – a move into darkness, loss of consciousness and the awakening into a different consciousness, a dream consciousness which can scarcely remember the everyday waking world.

Forgetting might be the way the unconscious remembers. When soul wishes to remind us of its presence, it opens a crevice in the base of consciousness through which the one thing we absolutely must remember slips – and we forget. Forgetting what we think is important might be a remembering of what is important.

27

The Still Sad Music of
Humanity

ANAMNESIS

The Greeks called truth *aletheia*, which means 'not forgetting'. According to Plato, truth was acquired by *anamnesis*, or recollection. Every soul before birth inhabits a divine realm to which it will return after death. Just as it is about to become incarnate in this world it drinks from Lethe, the river of Forgetfulness, so that it can remember nothing of its divine origins. This motif is not unique to the Greeks – a Jewish legend, for instance, says that we are struck on the mouth by an angel before birth so that we cannot speak of our pre-natal glory.

Whenever in the course of our lives we encounter something we know instinctively to be true, we are recollecting some part of the fullness of knowledge we possessed before birth in the intelligible world. Learning is remembering. Not cognition, but recognition. Far from coming into this world with minds like blank slates waiting to be written on by experience, we come with the backing of a whole pantheon; we come as microcosms of a whole macrocosm of knowledge. Our little memories, writes Yeats, 'are but a part of some great Memory that renews the world and men's thoughts age after age, and . . . our thoughts are not, as we suppose, the deep, but a little foam upon the deep'.[1]

For Yeats the great Memory is very like the Soul of the World. Conversely, Jung sometimes pictured the collective unconscious as a Great Memory in which the past of the entire race is stored. In both cases Memory is meant in the Platonic sense, as the source of *anamnesis* – the Primary Imagination, in fact, out of which we are born and to which we return. In the *Meno*, Plato celebrates the secondary imagination as *anamnesis*, 'a power of working at a barrier of darkness, recovering verities which we somehow know of, but have in our egoistic fantasy life "forgotten" '.[2]

There is, as we have seen, imagining in recollection, and recollecting in imagination, and we cannot with any certainty separate them. This goes without saying in artistic activity; and so I will by way of illustration make a small excursion to the west of England, to one of the seminal images of Romanticism: Tintern Abbey.

TINTERN ABBEY

I remember – with all that that implies – visiting the place as a schoolboy. Close to the river Wye, the Abbey is low-lying, gloomy, ruined; but also majestic and undeniably mysterious. I was studying William Wordsworth's poetry at the time (though with no very lively interest) and I knew vaguely that he had written a famous poem about Tintern Abbey, which was the centrepiece of the *Lyrical Ballads* – Coleridge's brainchild which, published in 1798, was the manifesto and first example of English Romantic poetry. I could picture the poet gazing on the holy site (was it ruined then? I assumed so) and seeing 'into the life of things'.[3]

I was quite wrong of course. The poem has a long title including 'Lines composed a few miles above Tintern Abbey' and the 'above' does not mean 'overlooking', it seems, but upriver, well out of sight of it – something I should have known if I had remembered the poem better. So I have to switch my image from the Abbey to the young William (he's twenty-eight) and his sister Dorothy (a year younger) who are sitting a few miles away on the banks of the Wye. While she packs up the picnic, he pulls out a notebook and begins to write, occasionally pausing to look up at the beautiful landscape.

He seems to be painting a word-picture of his surroundings; but, it turns out, he is doing nothing of the kind. He is writing about a previous visit, five years ago, to the very same spot. Is the poem about how much has changed and how ruinous time is and how the housing estate has destroyed the green fields? It is not. The opening twenty lines or so are a hymn to the way everything is still the same as when he first saw it. But of course it isn't: William is looking through his past, his memory, at the present scene and his poem is really about recollection and its relationship to imagination – a relationship central to the subject matter of the Romantics.

Furthermore, the poet's finest moments are not inspired by Nature, as we imagine a good Romantic should be, but by the memory of it. In between the two visits, he tells us in the poem, he has often thought about this spot; and so intense is the recollection, or his ability to invoke it, that he enters that 'blessed mood

> In which the affections gently lead us on,
> Until, the breath of this corporeal frame
> And even the motion of our human blood
> Almost suspended, we are laid asleep
> In body, and become a living soul:
> While with an eye made quiet by the power
> Of harmony, and the deep power of joy,
> We see into the life of things.'[4]

Wordsworth's poetic trance, occasioned by a memory, is heightened to a recollection – and then to re-creation. As much as he values the 'aching joys' and 'dizzy raptures' of his first, more youthful visit to the place, he values more the later remembering – the 'emotion recollected in tranquillity', as he says in the Preface to the *Lyrical Ballads*. Then he is able to concentrate on those images which are most meaningful; and the consequent feeling is more powerful in the absence of the thing that aroused it than in its presence. He has learned to look on Nature 'not as in the hour/of thoughtless youth; but hearing oftentimes/the still sad music of humanity'.[5]

There seems to be a further stage still to the poetic trance, a 'sense sublime' in which he ceases his active seeing into the life of things, and becomes passive again, less a subject than an object in the face of

> A motion and a spirit, that impels
> All thinking things, all objects of all thought,
> And rolls through all things.[6]

This vision of 'something far more deeply interfused/whose dwelling is the light of setting suns' is the authentic vision of the Soul of the World, the Imagination of Nature itself.

Wordsworth's recollection of this mystical vision, which is itself brought about by recollection, is the poem's climax. Even so, he is not finished. He also pays tribute to Dorothy and recollects forwards, as it were, by anticipating future rememberings of the present scene which will comfort her in times of pain or grief. He claims to be able to manage without Nature because he can hear the language of his former heart and read his former pleasures – that is, remember everything – by looking into her 'wild eyes', as if her eyes were windows of her soul in which all her memories, and therefore his, could be discerned.

Coleridge said of Wordsworth that part of the secret of his poetry was that he had always retained his vivid child-like vision of the world. He never quite lost the awful dizzy sensation he often had on the way to school when he grasped a wall or tree to prevent himself falling into the 'abyss' of a world which seemed to have no existence outside himself, so shadowy and insubstantial did it seem compared to the images in his own mind. But he only did what we all to some extent do: perceive the present through a past memory, which intensifies into a recollection – a reliving of the past – that in turn imaginatively transforms the present. Neither Wordsworth nor we can perceive Nature directly without, as he remarked, 'half-creating' it.

TIME REGAINED

It would be useful on the whole to distinguish between everyday remembering, when we dimly recall the past, and the Wordsworthian and Proustian remembering, when the past represents itself in all its fullness, sometimes joyfully, sometimes – abreaction – unbearably. As I remarked earlier, we might call the first kind of remembering memory, and the second, recollection. 'Memory is immediacy', wrote Søren Kierkegaard, '. . . whereas recollection comes only by reflection.' For example, homesickness is owing to memory; the art of recollection is 'to be able to feel homesickness notwithstanding one is at home'. Recollection is a kind of reduplicated memory, supercharged by imagination.

When we think again of Proust and his madeleine dipped in tea, we can see dimensions which were not apparent before. The incident is carefully placed at the end of the book's opening section and used as a device for examining the nature of memory and its ability to restore and redeem what Time has destroyed. But it is also a device for recalling the narrator's whole childhood, together with most of the characters who will appear in the course of the book, like an overture to the approaching symphony. His recollection is as much an act of creation, or recreation, as one of 'simple' remembrance.

Like Wordsworth, Proust is less interested in the contents of memory than in the act of remembering itself. They are both fascinated by the way the mind cuts into itself, transcends itself, to arrive at a visionary state outside itself. How paradoxical it is, thinks Proust, for the mind to seek its past within itself. For, in one sense, an image of the past precedes the act of remembering; and yet, in another, it does not – the past image is only an 'airy nothing' until it is anchored by the recollecting present:

'What an abyss of uncertainty whenever the mind feels that some part of it has strayed beyond its own boundaries: when it, the seeker, is at once the dark region through which it must go seeking . . . Seek? More than that: create. It is face to face with something which does not so far exist, to which it alone can give reality and substance, which it alone can bring into the light of day.'[7]

The past, it seems, can only take on reality in the present by a creative act of imagination.

28

The Desert and the Rose Garden

THE CLOUD OF UNKNOWING

The late Middle Ages saw a new breed of explorer set off for uncharted territory. The place they were interested in was a wilderness, a desert, 'so still, so mysterious, so desolate', said Johann Tauler. 'The great wastes to be found in it have neither image, form, nor condition.'[1] 'A still wilderness', reported Meister Eckhart, 'where no one is at home.'[2] Two centuries later, it was still unspoilt, according to a Carmelite friar named John: 'A wild and vast solitude where no human being can come', he calls it; 'an immense wilderness without limits. But this wilderness is the more delicious, sweet and lovely, the more it is wide, vast and lonely; for where the soul seems to be lost, there it is most raised up above all created things.'[3]

This desolate Otherworld is not, of course, a literal place. Tauler, Eckhart and St John of the Cross are all mystics. Their wilderness is a state of mind – or, better, of soul. The road there was named the *via negativa* by Dionysius the Areopagite who was originally believed to have been an Athenian disciple of St Paul's, but is now thought to be a Syrian monk of the late fifth century. He outlined two ways of approaching and knowing God: the Affirmative Way (or, as Charles Williams says, the Way of Affirmation of Images) and the Negative Way (the Way of Rejection of Images). Dionysius was as much a disciple of Neoplatonism as of Christianity, and so his two Ways reflect the tension between them, and were an attempt to reconcile them. This is why his writings, though they were enormously influential – especially on the medieval mystics – were also received with some uneasiness. They have 'always hovered over Christendom like the unfooted Bird of Paradise – admired, worshipped, and yet by some distrusted'.[4]

Broadly speaking, the Affirmative Way recognized that all images were good and from God, who could therefore be known through the order of the world; and that there were hierarchies of angelic beings – Christianized daimons – which linked us to the Supreme Being. The Negative Way asserted that all images of God were false images because nothing whatsoever could be predicated of God, who was unknown and unknowable, shrouded in impenetrable darkness – a 'cloud of unknowing' as one anonymous medieval mystic memorably expressed it. Thus, 'the one Way was to affirm all things orderly until the universe throbbed with vitality; the other to reject all things until there was nothing anywhere but He. The Way of Affirmation was to develop great art and romantic love and marriage and philosophy and social justice; the Way of Rejection was to break out continually in the profound mystical documents . . . of the great psychological masters of Christendom.'[5]

Yet both Ways co-exist – 'one might almost say co-inhere, since each was to be the key of the other'[6] – with no Affirmation so complete as not to need definition, discipline and refusal; and no Rejection so absolute as not to leave a few residual images, like the handful of beans and cupful of water the extreme ascetics needed to sustain their barest of lives.

SPIRIT AND SOUL

The two Ways represent a fundamental tension in the human condition, two predilections which have been traditionally expressed in a variety of ways: masculine and feminine, Classical and Romantic, Apollonian and Dionysian, Yang and Yin, right brain/left brain – almost any pair, that is, listed in a dual symbolic classification. The terms I have chosen are 'spirit' and 'soul' because they resist being taken literally, are central to Western culture, and are properly religious – in a pagan sense (the Greek *pneuma* and *psyche*) as much as in a Christian. They are not terms which can be precisely defined because they are neither substances nor concepts, but symbols; and the best we can do to distinguish between them is try to evoke their different characteristics.[7]

Spirit directs us to the Negative Way, driving us upward, beyond all images, towards the transcendental One, Truth, God. Its religions are the 'major' monotheisms. It disparages soul's religion as polytheism or animism – or does not recognize it as a religion at all. For soul's movement is downward to the Underworld, towards the immanent Many.

Whenever we sit down to serious intellectual work or to spiritual meditation, it is soul's daimons which distract us with anxiety and disturbing memories, and provoke us with daydreams and desires. From the 'pure intellect' and 'pure act' of Augustine and Aquinas, to the 'pure Reason' and 'pure Being' of Kant and Hegel, spirit always pursues purity. Pure science literalizes the pursuit: uncontaminated by the world, its super-hygienic laboratories secularize the mystic's cell; the fantasy of pure objectivity parodies the holy man's self-annihilation.

Not only purity but order, clarity, enlightenment are spirit's watchwords. Let's get things straight, let's be clear, let's be rational, wipe the slate clean, make a fresh start, says spirit. But soul is always at its side, obscuring, muddying and muddling. For soul favours the labyrinthine way of slow reflection, not rapid thought. Things cannot be made straight because they are intrinsically crooked and ambiguous; cannot be spotlit because they are intrinsically twilit; cannot be wiped away because they are harnessed to a long history whose traces cannot be kicked over. Soul holds spirit back, and down, making it mull things over and attend to the details here and now, rather than flying off into some grand future plan.

The universe is ultimately simple, elegant, unified, says the spirit of the scientist in his Apollonic way; no, says the soul of the artist in Dionysian ecstasy or Hermetic duplicity, it is complex, grotesque, multiple and full of anomalies. All images are false, says spirit; no images are false, says soul – only false perspectives on images. Where soul sees symbols, windows on to another world, spirit sees idols, like walls.

Spirit always leads us into literalism. Its mystics set out like the Desert Fathers for actual wildernesses, or make literal ascents of actual mountains. If soul ascends it does so metaphorically, like Dante in *The Divine Comedy*, and not before it has negotiated the dark forest and spiralled through the infernal regions. Blake was greatly influenced by a Swedish Inspector of Mines named Emanuel Swedenborg (1688–1772) who was privy to the activity of spirits. Whereas Blake had visions of daimons whom he understood metaphorically, as insights out of which to make art, Swedenborg saw spirits whom he understood literally, as revelations out of which he made a religion. This is the difference between the visionary soul and the mystical spirit.

THE ONE AND THE MANY

Nowhere does the tension between spirit and soul show itself more clearly than in the ancient philosophical debate about the One and the Many. The ancient Greeks argued that although the universe is made up of many distinct or discrete particulars, it is none the less a *uni*verse and not a *multi*verse. There must be, they felt, a single general principle that unites the particulars – otherwise the world would simply be a jumble of separate items without order, meaning or unity.

Thales thought it was 'water'; Anaximander called it 'the indefinite'; Xenophanes, 'One God'; Heraclitus, 'fire'; Pythagoras, 'number'. Each of these principles was 'a self-animated substance that continued to move and change itself into various forms. Because it was author of its own ordered motions and transmutations, and because it was everlasting, this primary substance was considered to be not only material but also alive and divine'[8] – in short, a daimonic principle which would become the Soul of the World.

The alternative was to start with a multiplicity of fundamental principles which, when combined, would form the objects of the world. Empedocles postulated four: earth, air, fire and water. Anaxagoras suggested an infinite number of minute, qualitatively different seeds. Leucippus and Democritus proposed the existence of an infinite number of changeless atoms moved mechanically by Ananke (Necessity).

In a sense the two opposites are reconciled in Thales' sublime (to modern ears, absurd) dictum, which not only expresses the co-existence of the One and the Many, but also insists on the commensurability of one impersonal principle and many personified principles, like a harmony of science and religion: 'the world is composed of water, and is full of gods'.

'It is characteristic of human reason to seek unity in multiplicity',[9] wrote Plato. His Forms were designed to solve the problem of the One and the Many – to explain how many things can share a common quality and how we, whose sensory experience is in flux, can have knowledge as opposed to mere opinion or belief (knowledge comes by *anamnesis*, returning to the Forms). But the problem remained knotty: 'the relation between the single Form and its many particulars or instances is explained variously, and never entirely satisfactorily, by metaphors of participation and imitation. On the whole, the early dialogues speak of a "shared nature" and the later ones of imperfect copies of perfect originals.'[10]

The conundrum of the One and the Many is central to theology: spirit longs for one God, soul insists on many. But the argument between monotheism and polytheism is unequal because it is started in the first instance by spirit and its monotheistic perspective. Polytheism has no word for itself; it does not understand monotheism's condemnation of it as an undesirable relativism; it shrugs and says that there are many perspectives belonging to many daimons or deities – and that's simply the case. Plato and his fellow philosophers will never quite solve the problem of unity's relation to multiplicity because the 'problem' is posed in the first place by spirit – which then tries to 'solve' it. From a daimonic point of view, there is no problem.

As we might expect, successful religions find ways of holding the One and the Many in tension. The ancient Greek, Hindu, Egyptian, Mesopotamian and Native American religions are all 'polytheistic'. But they have in practice been 'composed of men and women who worship one God or Goddess, or at least they worship one at a time – Athene, Vishnu, Ra, Baal, Wakan Tanka'.[11] Both psychically and spiritually, then, it seems sensible to adopt a polytheistic theology and a monotheistic practice – to accept many gods but to revere one at a time. This procedure may well mesh with the autonomous movement of the psyche itself, in which different gods or archetypes are constellated at different times of our lives. 'Myths may change in a life, and the soul serves in its time many gods.'[12]

A religion like Christianity is certainly monotheistic in relation to pagan polytheism; but in itself it is far from monotheistic. Under pressure from the fragmenting tendency of soul, its spiritual God was almost immediately impelled to become a Trinity. Behind a Christian mask, the Virgin Mary, saints and angels have always been venerated in a pagan way among Roman Catholics. It was part of the Protestant mission at the time of the Reformation to restore a proper monotheism, and puritans of all denominations went at it with a vengeance. Even so, as the deeply puritan Calvin despairingly put it, 'surely, just as waters boil up from a vast full spring, so does an immense crowd of gods flow forth from the human mind'.[13] It is precisely the puritan refusal to accommodate the daimonic Many which leads to rigid dogmatism, paranoid defensiveness and fanatical fundamentalism.

THE PERMUTATIONS OF PROTEUS

The Renaissance magi were preoccupied with the relationship of the One to the Many in various ways. First, they imagined their own version of the Neoplatonic doctrine of the emanation of the Many from the One. They viewed the process less mystically and more poetically – as a dismemberment of Osiris, Attis or Dionysus. The descent of the One into the Many 'was imagined as a sacrificial agony, as if the One were cut to pieces and scattered'.[14] Creation itself is a cosmogonic death and dispersal of a single deity, followed by a resurrection when the Many are 'recollected' in the One.

Secondly, they were fascinated by the figure of Proteus, even though he only appears briefly in Greek mythology, notably in *The Odyssey*. He is a kind of sea-god, a sort of seal-man whom the hero Menelaus is advised to capture and consult in order to break the spell that is withholding from him favourable winds. Disguised in sealskins, he and his three companions creep up on Proteus as he sleeps among his seals, and seize him. Immediately the god changes successively into the shape of a lion, serpent, panther, boar, running water and leafy tree. But Menelaus knows that the secret is to hold him fast until he is forced to appear in his own shape, and to give his counsel.

For the magi, Proteus was a symbol of the mercurial One who can become many by shape-changing; a reminder that one god can be immanent in the world and present in all its multifarious images so that

art, too, can celebrate the deity; and an allegory of the need to hold fast
to the one god, even if he appears in dangerous guises, in order to
uncover the truth. Proteus was an image of the resurgent Neoplatonic
notion that 'poetic pluralism is the necessary corollary to the radical
mysticism of the One'.[15]

Thirdly, Ficino, Pico and their successors were struck by Plotinus's
comparison between the unfolding of the One and the Many, and the
effect of multiple mirror-images[16] –

> . . . Empty eyeballs know
> That knowledge increases unreality
> Mirror on mirror mirrored is all the show[17] –

which suggested to them that the whole is repeated in every part, that
every god therefore is inherent in every other, and all of them rooted in
the One.[18] It was not only a mistake to worship a single god, it was not
possible because (as Plato had explained in *The Sophist*) the gods are
alternately divided and conjoined by a dialectical movement which puts
them through changing configurations.

The magi delighted in constructing new and surprising configurations
of gods. Ficino believed that each deity could be unfolded into a triad[19]
– Venus unfolds into the three Graces, for example (Botticelli's *Primavera*
depicts this) – and, at the same time, each triad of deities could be
combined to form nine 'new' gods and goddesses. Mercury, Venus and
Apollo combine to make Mercury-Venus, Mercury-Apollo, Apollo-
Venus, etc.

We can see in this polytheistic combining a kind of depth psychology,
a recognition that the components of the psyche – the gods – kaleido-
scopically change in relation to each other, always forming new patterns,
new mythical variants; and that to collaborate with this dynamic construction and deconstruction was to exercise that imagination in whose free
play the soul delights and seems to have no other end.

However, when the magi began to construct composite gods such as
Hermeros (Hermes/Eros), Hermathena (Hermes/Athena), Hermer-
cules (Hermes/Hercules) and so on indefinitely, and when this activity
became the rule rather than the exception,[20] we begin to sense something
frenetic in their rococo imaginings, as if the existing gods, already

multi-faceted, were not enough – as if the magi were rushing slightly hysterically to try every possible permutation of the psyche's myths and personifications and so exhaust imagination.

Was it some such exhaustion which at the height of the Renaissance led the citizens of Florence – scene of the most dazzling efflorescence of art, science, learning, invention, thought and fashion since Athens two thousand years before – to turn against their culture as if in disgust?

29

Syzygies

THE BONFIRE OF THE VANITIES

On the last day of the carnival in Florence, 1497, a huge pyramidal flight of stairs was built in the Piazza della Signoria. It was stacked, from the bottom step upwards, with the carnival paraphernalia – masks, disguises, false beards – then, more sinisterly, with volumes of Latin and Italian poetry. Women's ornaments were next: toilet articles, scents, mirrors, wigs (blonde ones were in fashion). Finally, paintings – especially paintings of beautiful women. It is said that Botticelli threw on some of his early works. Bells pealed, trumpets sounded, people sang as the great pile was set alight.[1]

The bonfire was lit in the third year of a Dominican monk's four-year rule over Florence. He was the charismatic preacher, Savonarola. Under his sway – he was only one of many such preachers with varying degrees of influence (Hieronymus of Siena, a holy hermit, later lorded it over Milan) – the populace renounced luxury and fashion and even their books and paintings. 'Savonarola carried the people so triumphantly with him that soon all their beloved art and culture melted away in the furnace which he lighted.'[2]

However, he was unsuited to government, unable to see further than a theocracy in which everyone simply bowed before God. He was what we now call a fundamentalist, uninterested in culture, learning, art; and so it is all the more incomprehensible how the urbane, sophisticated and cultured Florentines could submit to such a narrow puritan.

It was, we can only suppose, the very narrowness that appealed to them – the sudden longing for simplicity, unintellectual faith and a single

God. A sudden sickening, perhaps, of too much richness, like the uncontrollable crystallization of a super-saturated solution. Above all, a craving for escape from an imaginative life that had been wrought up to an overwhelming pitch.

Whatever its historical cause, the bonfire of the vanities is, psychologically, a striking example of a revolutionary change from 'soul' to 'spirit'. Jung called such revolutions – he got the word from Heraclitus – an *enantiodromia*, literally meaning a 'counter-running'. In fact, he reckoned it a psychological law: any extreme psychic one-sidedness is liable to reverse itself suddenly into its own opposite. The most famous example is the conversion of St Paul on the road to Damascus. Having persecuted Christians fanatically, he had a vision of Christ and thereafter embraced His teachings with equal fervour.

However, enantiodromia is not the universal law Jung thought it was. It applies only to individuals, and to cultures, whose monotheism and literalism has polarized them. A one-sided conscious stance is overwhelmed by, and converted to, its unconscious opposite because the psyche is already polarized into consciousness and unconscious. But such polarization is not characteristic of the traditional, daimonic organization of the psyche.

In Western culture it sometimes seems as if our whole psychological history, from the bonfire of the vanities onward, is a series of enantiodromia: the Enlightenment reaction against daimonic 'superstition' and 'imagination'; the Romantic counter-reaction; the rise of philosophical materialism and, at its height, the violent volte-face of Spiritualism. We have alternately demonized and divinized Nature instead of participating in that doubleness which reflects our own.

All sudden twists in the *Zeitgeist*, sudden surges of a nation's mood, sudden declarations of war, have their source, perhaps, in the reversing of the poles of a collective psyche. And we should remember, too, that just as polarizing is in large measure a result of literalizing, so the new stance is cast in the same literal mould as the old. Literalistic materialism is countered by a belief in literal spirits, instead of by a metaphorical psychology.

Even when there is no violent enantiodromia the tension between Many and One, soul and spirit, in both the individual and the collective psyche is always present and always seeking to maintain equilibrium. As early as the sixth century BC Xenophanes of Colophon was exasperated by the Many and 'tired of all the stories by all the poets about all the Gods and Goddesses'.[3] His longing to be free of Homeric polytheism was the impetus behind the philosophers' search for a principle of unity. At about the same time as Plato was unifying his multiplicity of Forms under the one Form of the Good, Gautama the Buddha was emptying the Hindu proliferation of daimons and gods into Nirvana, 'freedom from opposites' – that paradoxical Void which is also divine plenitude, where souls are released from the grinding wheel of perpetual death and reincarnation.

The tension between soul and spirit in the Elizabethan psyche – which became, as I have suggested, polarized and literalized in the English civil war – was embodied in the works of Shakespeare. He was writing at a time when the 'spirit' seed of puritanism was steadily growing up and through the soil – the 'soul' – of the old Catholic order, behind which stood an even older pagan order. Daimonic reality – imagination itself – suddenly seemed fragile, even unreal in the face of the certainty and literalism of puritan ideology; and Shakespeare wrote its epitaph in his last major play:

> The cloud-capped towers, the gorgeous palaces,
> The solemn temples, the great globe itself . . .
> . . . shall dissolve,
> And, like this insubstantial pageant faded,
> Leave not a rack behind. We are such stuff
> As dreams are made on; and our little life
> Is rounded with a sleep.[4]

As if he were Shakespeare himself retiring to Stratford-on-Avon, Prospero – the very type of the Renaissance magus – dismisses Ariel, his helping spirit; casts away his books of magic; and retires to Milan where 'every third thought shall be my grave'.[5] The daimonic age of high imagination and natural magic has come to a close. There is regret in Shakespeare's lines but perhaps also relief. Prospero's weary resignation reflects the sense of ennui unadulterated soul entails, where everything is image, an insubstantial pageant of metaphor – Yeats's 'mist and foam' – without the fixity and grip of the literal.

THE DAMNATION OF THE SIDHE

This is the trouble with the realm of soul which I have been so eager to defend. On its own, without the invigoration of spirit, it can become deadly. We are lost in its labyrinth, worn out by its unceasing cycles, exhausted by the sheer opulence of its imagery, prey to that fatalism of which 'soul' religions are accused, until, finally, we despair.

Something of this daimonic despair is conveyed in the recurring motif of Irish fairylore in which a priest travelling through the wilds of western Ireland is accosted by one of the Sidhe, who fixes him with those strange silvery eyes and asks: 'Can the Sidhe ever find salvation?'

The trembling priest is taken aback. He is not sure, he says; then, gathering courage and remembering that he is confronting an enemy of the Church, he proclaims that the people of Fairy will always lie outside Christendom. Nothing can be done for them. Whereupon the fairy goes sorrowing on his way.

This is more than a propaganda story put out by the early Christian missionaries to pagan Ireland. The longing of the Sidhe for 'salvation' is a longing for the hard certainty of our literal world, a sign of their weariness with their own world and a desire to enter time, to become mortal, to be able to die and to be saved. A longing for that human potential for transformation which they are denied. 'It is as if the daimons sorrowed for the sorrow of man, which they can never know.'[6]

To the daimons, it is we who are strange and alluring, just as, to daimonic cultures, it is the self-assured, rational, Bible-toting white man and his single-barrelled God who are uncanny and to whom many are drawn, even as they know it will be fatal to their old culture. Perhaps this was why St Patrick, as legend tells us, converted the Irish so painlessly to Christianity. Perhaps they secretly yearned for liberation from the besieging Sidhe, for a new spirit of literalness to give solidity to a world of mist and foam.

All pagan 'soul' cultures assume that the gods can appear to men and women. The response to them was not one of worship but of dazzlement and awe, the Irish before the Sidhe no less than Odysseus before Athene. The Christian God, on the other hand, does not appear but sends His

Son in an extraordinary disguise: He comes as a man. Not even a Herculean, heroic, messiah-like man, but a carpenter – who claims that He is the Way, the Truth and the Life, and that no one comes to His Father except by Him. He is not only God and man, therefore, but also an arch-daimon who mediates between us and God once and for all, thus superseding all other daimons.

The great drawback of the Incarnation, God made Flesh, is that it is perceived as God made literal, a God who erases myth, imagination and the daimons. Its strength is its impossibility, its absurdity (as Tertullian remarked). Christ is the Paradox whom no one could ever have dreamed up. A little carpenter announces that he is God – to the pagans this was foolishness; to the Jews, an offence. Far from lifting the Roman yoke, this God-man is crucified – by the Jews for the serious crime of blasphemy, by the Romans for the trivial crime of being a public nuisance. The pagans were quite used to the idea of a dismembered or sacrificed god or hero, but shocked by the idea that a god might be literally crucified.

It was a decisive event. Jesus stepped out of myth into history – in a sense He created history. Suddenly the old gods seemed to pale by comparison with His real red blood, red and shed for mankind. The realm of soul was called by the Spirit to wake from its dream of gods and daimons. They are false, said the Spirit, mere idols – even devils – and must be cast down before the one God.

At the same time, while God may very well have remained One, Jesus – as befits a paradoxical God-man – shape-shifts like a daimon. Not in Himself, but in the minds of Christians, each of whom believes that their understanding of Him is the true one. But there are almost as many Jesuses as there are believers. In the early days of the Church, when He had to compete with other gods and heroes, He was unhesitatingly identified with Apollo, Prometheus, Perseus, Orpheus, Dionysus, Adonis, Eros, Mithra, Osiris, etc.[7] Christ as Hercules was especially popular, and perhaps still is, to judge by the number of muscular Christian crusades, Actions and Reforms in which we see more Herculean ego than *imitatio Christi*.

Since then, Jesus has been variously characterized as the Teacher, the Divine Child, the Holy Fool, the Good Shepherd, the Meek Lamb, the Heroic Messiah, the Lilies-of-the-field Hippy, the first Communist, the robust Working Man and Class Hero, and so on. Lately he has been prevalent as the intimate Friend of born-again evangelists, whose familiarity with the Saviour strikes Christians of the old school as so unseemly.

THE SACRED MARRIAGE

At first sight it seems as though all the links in the Golden Chain are on the side of soul, the Many, polytheism, as against the monisms of spirit, whether Christian, philosophical or scientific. Actually they are only compensating for the monistic emphasis, redressing the balance. In themselves they are supremely adept at giving soul and spirit equal weight. Indeed, it is almost the defining feature of Golden Chain members that they reconcile the two perspectives, especially in their manifestation as One and Many, from Plotinus who brilliantly expounded the relationship of Plato's Forms to the ineffable One, to Jung who squared the many archetypes with the unity of the Self. All the alchemists, all the magi and most of the Romantic poets were Christians, who found imaginative ways of marrying their monotheism to Neoplatonism or pantheism.

It is one of the conundrums of Plato's works that they provide both the foundation for Western culture's rationalism, and for rationalism's subversion. The reason is, that there are two strands of thought in Plato, a *logos* and a *mythos*. The former pertains to reason and spirit; the latter, to imagination and soul. (Both Blake and Yeats, who came to Plato through the Neoplatonists, and therefore from his *mythos* side, were shocked by his other, rationalistic side and temporarily rejected him.)[8]

While the Neoplatonists held spirit and soul sublimely in tension, there were always attempts to unite them in concrete images. Favourite among these was the *hieros gamos*, or sacred marriage, between masculine and feminine in their various mythic configurations – not only god and goddess, king and queen, lover and beloved, but also mother and son, brother and sister, father and daughter.

Alchemy spontaneously threw up single images of the sacred marriage, such as an androgyne, a hermaphrodite, a Stone – unnatural images, perhaps because it is an 'unnatural' spirit notion to compress what is essentially paired into a singularity. Jung's self is a similar symbol of unity-in-multiplicity – a Mercurius-like 'complex of opposites'. But from soul's viewpoint, the psyche does not need these centres and goals. It is a dynamic polycentric totality, subject to perpetual flux and structured like a mythology. Its centre lies with whatever god or myth is currently constellated.

If there is one pairing – we recall from the work of Lévi-Strauss – which acts as a rubric for all the other pairs, it is Heaven and Earth. All the myths can be read as attempts to bring about their marriage, a return to a primordial state of unity.

The myth of original unity is usually expressed in symbols of a previous time or place: the Golden Age, Eden, Arcadia, Atlantis, the Dreamtime. Soul says: 'These are real places, but not literal – the earthly paradise lies always all around us and we have only, somehow, to see it.' Spirit says: 'The earthly paradise is not here, but elsewhere. We must leave immediately for Happy Valley, Shangri-la, Eldorado; or else we must build Utopia or New Jerusalem where everyone will be happy and good (or else).' The daimonic viewpoint says: 'Who knows what other worlds are possible for the truly daimonic human – the legendary shaman, the Zen master, the Taoist sage, the Christian saint, the visionary artist? Who knows where, after long and many transformations, light as thistledown they might be blown, body and soul, by the viewless winds of the spirit?'

The daimonic perspective does not polarize soul and spirit. It imagines by means of both, each reflecting the other. It does not think in philosophical mode, which so often means an oppositional mode; rather, it thinks in pairs, and paired images, like Jung's anima and animus. We cannot take a view of soul without taking into account the spirit which informs the view we are taking. So, for example, if the soul is variously pictured in dream or fantasy as mother, sister, fleeing nymph, destructive goddess, then a complementary spirit image is implied – hero-son, brother, pursuing Pan, god of light who must be sacrificed.

In a pairing of soul and spirit, the unity which spirit would impose on soul becomes merely a natural reflection of spirit, not a literal singleness but a sense that everything is infused with soul and all events are primarily psychic. Conversely, the multiplicity with which soul always threatens spirit is not a literal many-ness but a gentle reminder that God has many masks and many mansions.

We have no choice but to think in pairs – that is, to think mythologically, to imagine. This is why, instead of forever trying to separate the perspectives of soul and spirit, we should try and develop what Hillman calls 'syzygy consciousness' – a hermaphroditic way of thinking in which soul and spirit are co-present in any event.[9]

Whenever an image of soul appears we should be aware that the image is already determined by the perspective of spirit – usually, in Western culture, that of the ego – which, in turn, is determined by soul. Each reflects the other, and that is why we cannot think or imagine outside their doubleness, no matter how much the rational ego – that uncontrollable spirit! – tries to persuade us otherwise. For he always constellates an irrational and dangerous partner who, if he persists in his folly, will possess him or destroy him.

NEW AGES

The modern rational ego is a development of the spirit perspective. We have seen how it arose in the early seventeenth century, and how it achieved ascendancy or, at least, an orthodoxy which still prevails. The pessimistic view of this perspective, with its materialism, rationalism, scientism, technocratic tendencies and so on, is that it has become separated from soul to a disastrous extent. It has lost connection with the Earth and the 'feminine', both metaphorically and literally, and is laying waste (witness the impending ecological catastrophe) to everything around it. It is aggressive, greedy, exploitative in every sense. Its technologies are out of control. Its hubris will lead us to world destruction.

This sort of view is held by a loose coalition of otherwise quite different people, from strange New Agers to hard-core eco-warriors, to ordinary sensible liberals. Each has different ideas of how to change the prevailing orthodoxy but all of them, it seems, envisage some kind of enantiodromia in which current values are replaced by their opposites. For example, the New Agers long for a sudden access of 'higher consciousness' which will do away with materialism at a stroke – but their own brand of spiritual theosophy is equally literalistic. They do not see the myth in all their movements, nor the movement in myth. Many ecologically-minded people speak of the world as if it were literally a 'living organism' or a 'goddess' ('Gaia'), when they might do better to see it as ensouled, and ourselves individual expressions of soul.

Another 'New Age' view is, on the contrary, optimistic about the rational ego and sees its rise as a kind of cultural rite of passage. Just as we must separate ourselves from family at puberty and return to society reborn; just as the Hero must leave his Mother and his home to embark on the marvellous Quest from which he will return, after much tribulation, with the world-transforming secret, so (it is argued) the modern rational ego had to separate itself from the womb-like closure of the medieval world-view, divorce itself from Dame Kind and drive forward and upward, conquering and inventing and progressing until, at its furthest reaches and achievements, it voluntarily turns and reunites itself with soul, the goddess, the eternal Feminine, in a divine syzygy that will usher in a whole new state of consciousness in which Heaven and Earth are at last wed.

THE MYSTERY OF LOVE

Richard Tarnas takes this sort of view in his excellent book *The Passion of the Western Mind*. He reads the history of Western culture in a psychological way and perceives one over-arching and archetypal dialectic: the heroic masculine differentiation out of a primordial feminine unity, and its subsequent reunion with its matrix. From the ancient Greek subjugation of 'pre-Hellenic matrifocal mythologies', and the 'Judaeo-Christian denial of the Great Mother Goddess', to the Enlightenment's exaltation of a 'rational ego' over 'a disenchanted external nature', he sees 'a progressive denial of *anima mundi*', and an oppression of the feminine by the masculine. The '*crisis of modern man*', he emphasizes, '*is essentially a masculine crisis*'.[10]

Far from being pessimistic about this, however, Tarnas is optimistic, almost millenarian. A sacred marriage *is* at hand, he says – a fulfilment of 'the underlying goal of Western intellectual and spiritual evolution.

For the deepest passion of the Western mind has been to reunite with the ground of its own being.' (His italics.)[11] It has been the task of 'masculine consciousness . . . to forge its own autonomy' and then 'come to terms with the great feminine principle in life, and thus recover its connection with the whole'.[12]

If I demur slightly from this hopeful vision it is, firstly, because I wonder whether Tarnas is not taking masculine and feminine too literally, as if they meant male and female. Secondly, I wonder if he is not taking the idea of 'evolution' too literally. 'Evolution' is a spirit notion which soul does not recognize. Traditional societies do not evolve. They live within a mythology which contains all imaginative possibilities, Earth Goddesses no less than Heraclean egos. These are embodied or expressed in the sacred action called ritual, but they are not literally acted out. Because we are changing, we think of ourselves as evolving. We are not. We are literalizing the old myths. Since these always include symmetrical and inverted variants of each other, we are forced to act out these variants as enantiodromias – a swing to an equal and opposite literalism. Tarnas's resurgence of the 'feminine' looks a lot like this.

Besides, and thirdly, the mythic image of the sacred marriage is as old as myth itself and should not, surely and once again, be taken literally. What we are more likely to arrive at than a sacred marriage is another enantiodromia. If the rational ego is to disappear it is more likely to be destroyed by the ricochets of ideologies made in its own image. Scientism might well be deluged by a tide of belief in the literal reality of the paranormal or the occult. Religious fundamentalism might well rise up, Savonarola-like, and denounce science and technology as the work of the Devil; or else it might form sects that try and flee back to Nature, away from the technocracy of the modern world. Materialism might well be countered by a belief in literal spirits or angels or aliens, wrapped in a vague spiritualistic theosophy. But, of course, all this is already happening.

The sacred marriage belongs in myth, not in fact. Like 'the marriage of Heaven and Earth', it is the image we think of as the 'goal' of myth. It is not a literal goal, however, but rather an image which underlies the dynamics of Imagination as it constantly shifts contradictions it cannot reconcile on to different metaphorical levels. None of the pairings which constitute the basic elements of Imagination are ever quite allowed to 'marry' – they are simply held in tension by an analogical relation to another pairing, and another, so that they are always simultaneously teased apart and held together, but never united.

If, on the other hand, a sacred marriage could step out of myth into history, it could only do so (we are led to believe) by the mystery of love – but then only in an intimate way, through the love between two people, or between a person and God. Love might be able to be sustained between a few people – at most – through that special communal love called *agape*.

Christian *agape* presupposes a group of people selflessly united in a love of God – a group of individuals, that is, already transformed by a high degree of initiation. Such a community becomes impossible above a certain number. It makes no sense to think that it might by some 'evolution' become embodied in a culture larger than a small tribe. Besides, this image of community already sounds less like a sacred marriage than a monastic order – a spirit community very different from the community of soul, whose image is provided by daimons like the Sidhe, united in music, dancing, drinking, feasting and fun.

30

The Bear that Bites the Heart

As he travelled across the vast bleak steppe he could see in the distance
the Iron Mountain which propped up the sky like a tent-pole. Around
him lay a grim reminder of his journey's perils: the bones of unsucccessful
colleagues and their horses littered the approach to the mountain . . . As
he climbed towards the top of the mountain, he quailed in the face of
the sky which banged and flapped against its peak. Only during the split
second when it rose off the summit could he slip through with one finely
judged leap. There! Now he had to travel downwards, through the 'jaws
of the earth', down to a sunless sea straddled by a hair's-width bridge.
As he teetered across he could see yet more bones of those who had failed
gleaming palely in the depths below . . .[1]

THE WORLD-TREE AND THE SWORD-BRIDGE

This Altai shaman's otherworld journey is undertaken with reluctance,
if not involuntarily, because of its danger. Once through the narrow gap
or over the narrow bridge, he will be painfully initiated, usually by
dismemberment. But he will also learn the sacred songs and gain the
help of daimons which will enable him voluntarily to re-enact the journey
later, in order to retrieve souls lost in the Otherworld, and so heal their
owners' sickness.

The otherworld journey takes place in a trance or 'ecstasy', from the
Greek *ekstasis*, implying something which makes you 'stand outside'
yourself. It referred to any state of awe, stupefaction, hysteria or diabolic
possession;[2] but it was Plotinus who first applied the word to mystical

union with the One[3] – a condition he achieved on four occasions – and, from him, it passed via Gregory of Nyssa into Christian mysticism.

Shamanic ecstasy does not always involve an otherworld journey. It may be a straightforward communication with, or possession by, a spirit or spirits who speak directly through the shaman. This form of shamanism is especially common among women shamans, rare in Siberia for example, but numerous in south and south-east Asia – in Korea all the shamans are women (or, occasionally, men dressed as women).[4] It is, too, mostly women – the mediums and 'channellers' – who carry on this tradition in the West.

While the otherworld journey is not the only form of shamanism, it is the most resonant. When Joseph Campbell in *The Hero with a Thousand Faces* (London, 1988) analysed hero myths from across the world, he identified many universal elements, such as the call, summoning the hero to his adventure or mission; his reluctance or refusal; his acceptance and setting out; his crossing of the threshold into an Otherworld; encounters with supernatural helpers; his ascent or descent; his initiatory trials and ordeals, notably his 'death' by being dismembered or devoured; his resurrection and return with the treasure – the healing herb, elixir of life, Golden Fleece or Holy Grail.[5] This is also essentially the pattern of the shaman's otherworld journey.

For example, the ways he enters the Otherworld are as near-universal as they are among the heroes of myth: by flying, on a reindeer or horse, often symbolized by a drum; by climbing up to the skyworld on the world-tree, often symbolized by the central pole of the tent (yurt or ger) which Siberian shamans shin up, emerging through the smoke-hole as if into the celestial region (North American shamans climb trees, Australian Aboriginals, poles, in the same spirit);[6] or by a narrow bridge, which represents so well the hair's breadth between the literal and the metaphorical, the blink of an eye between sight and vision.

THE SHAMAN'S IRON BONES

According to the Tungus of Siberia, a future shaman falls ill and has his body cut in pieces and his blood drunk by 'evil spirits' – who turn out to be the souls of dead shamans, deliberately disguising themselves. The Avam-Samoyed shaman, Dyakhade, was initiated – as many Siberian and Mongolian shamans are – by a daimonic blacksmith.[7] The naked man seized Dyakhade with tongs the size of a tent, cut his head off, sliced his body into pieces and boiled the lot for three years. Then he put the head on an anvil and hammered it. He separated the muscles from the bones, and put them back together again. He covered the skull with flesh and joined it to the torso. Next, he pulled out the eyes and put in new ones. Lastly, he pierced Dyakhade's ears with his iron finger and said that now he would be able to hear the speech of plants.[8]

This all happened in a dream or visionary state. Dyakhade woke in his own tent.

A Yakut shaman described how his head watched the chopping up of its body: 'they hook an iron hook into the body and tear up and distribute all the joints; they clean the bones by scratching off the flesh . . . They take the two eyes out of the sockets and put them on one side.'[9] The bits of flesh are scattered on all the paths of the Underworld, or they are eaten by the nine spirits that cause sickness, whose ways the shaman will thereby know in the future.

Dismemberment is at the heart of the shaman's initiation. He is torn apart and reconstructed with 'iron bones'. In Australia, the Aranda initiate is lanced through the neck by a 'spirit' while sleeping at the entrance of the initiatory cave. Then he is carried into the cave by the spirit who tears out his internal organs and replaces them with new ones. Quartz crystals are inserted into his body, conferring powers on him, notably the power of flight. They are held to be of celestial origin and only quasi-material as if they were 'solidified light'.[10]

That pioneer in the study of comparative religion, Romanian-born Mircea Eliade, emphasizes that shamanic initiation is not so much a death and rebirth as a death and resurrection.[11] He is trying, of course, to convey that sense of a concrete experience (rather than an abstract 'spiritual' experience) which I have specifically appropriated the term 'daimonic' to describe. Only the concreteness of dismemberment can dissolve the obdurate literalistic perspective of the heroic ego.

Mythology attests to this. The death and resurrection of the Egyptian god and culture-hero Osiris is 'the basic myth of dynastic Egypt'.[12] He is trapped by his brother Set in a sarcophagus which is flung into the Nile and floats out to sea. His sister Isis roams the world looking for him, very much as Demeter searches for the daughter who has been abducted into the Underworld by Hades. Isis finally rescues her brother – only to see him torn by Set into fourteen pieces. She reassembles and revives him; and he becomes the ruler of the Underworld and judge of the Dead.

Throughout the ancient world, mythological hero-gods – Tammuz, Attis, Mithras, Adonis – died violently and were reborn. In Greek myth, Dionysus was torn to pieces as a child by titans, then boiled in a cauldron. He was rescued and reconstituted by his grandmother, Rhea.[13] His cousins, the three sons of his mother Semele's three sisters, all suffered similar fates, as if they were reduplications or variants of the Dionysian myth: Pentheus was hunted down and torn to pieces by his own mother and aunts, who had been turned by Dionysus into Maenads – 'raging' women; Melikertes was hurled into a cauldron of seething water; Actaeon was savaged and eaten by his own hounds.[14]

Death by animals is another initiatory motif. The initiation of Antdaruta, a Greenland *angakoq* (shaman), began as a straightforward 'fairy encounter'. He heard a mysterious singing from among some rocks, followed by the appearance of two 'inland-dwellers' – fairy-like daimons – who became his first 'helping spirits'. Next, he became apprenticed to an old 'magician' who took him one day to a cave by the sea. The magician took off his clothes and crept inside. Antdaruta waited. Before long a great bear came swimming by, crawled ashore, entered the cave and flung itself upon the magician, crunching him up and eating him. Antdaruta understood that this was something that had to happen to him; but, when it did, he was surprised that it did not hurt except when the bear bit him in the heart.[15]

All shamans among the Angmagsalik of Greenland are devoured by an *angakoq* bear, which is larger than an ordinary bear and so thin that its ribs are visible. Sanimuinak was eaten by one who came out of the sea and bit him in the loins. It hurt at first until sensation left him. He remained conscious, however, until his heart was eaten. Then he lost consciousness, and was dead. He woke later, naked, at the same spot. He walked by the sea. He heard something running after him. It was his breeches and boots and frock which fell down so that he could put them on.[16]

THE VISION QUEST

'All the wisdom is only to be learned far from the dwellings of men, out in the great solitudes, and is only to be attained through suffering.'[17] The words of the Caribou shaman Igjugarjuk are worthy of one of the Christian 'Desert Fathers'. They are especially applicable to the Native Americans; for, the further south in North America one goes, the more one finds that the motif of dismemberment which extends from Australia to the Arctic circle is replaced by the more familiar fasting, praying and initiatory vision of the Plains peoples, for example.

A characteristic Native American shamanic initiation is described by the Sioux medicine-man Leonard Crow Dog, who was only a boy at the time.[18] Before he sets off for the ancestral place on the hill where he will 'cry for a dream, ask for a vision' – the decisive qualification for a medicine-man – he is purified in a sweat lodge especially built for him by the elders out of simple but sacred elements: fire, rocks, earth, water, sage. The lodge itself is made out of twelve 'bones' (bent-over willow saplings) covered with the 'flesh' of blankets and a tarpaulin. It is called 'the whole universe' and, in the centre, a fire pit is dug and filled with hot rocks. When the water is poured on, the steam is 'the holy breath of the universe'. While the prescribed songs are sung, a sacred pipe is smoked and the sweat lodge fills with tobacco smoke.[19]

After his 'cooking' – steaming and smoking – in the lodge, where after hours of songs the presence of spirits is felt, Crow Dog climbs the hill to the ancestral spot and enters the vision pit dug into the ground. His aids on the vision quest include twenty pieces of flesh his sister has cut off herself as an act of self-sacrifice; a medicine bundle with a stone in it; and an eagle-bone whistle to blow in emergencies (but not to summon human help). He stays in the pit for two days and two nights without food and water. He prays until the tears stream down his face. Then at last he has the first of the visions that indicate he will be a medicine-man.

He sees on the evening of the second day a fiery hoop with a mouth and two eyes. He hears a voice in the darkness. It is not human, and the hairs stand up on his neck. 'Remember the hoop,' says the voice; 'this night we will teach you.' Many feet can be heard walking around the vision pit. And, suddenly, he is out of the hole, in another world – a prairie covered with wild flowers, covered with herds of elk and buffalo. A man floats out of the mist towards him. He is wearing an old-fashioned buckskin outfit and he tells Crow Dog: 'Boy, whatever you tell your people, do not exaggerate; always do what your vision tells you. Never pretend.' There follow further visions – of a cloud which becomes an eagle that confers power on him; a rider on a grey horse and holding a hoop made of sage; a hairy, pale, formless creature who tries to take his medicine, and whom he is forced to wrestle. Then somebody shakes him by the shoulder. It is his father. The two days and nights are over. His dream is interpreted for him, and he becomes a medicine-man.[20]

THE SACRED HEART

Margaret Mary Alacoque had a vision of a heart surrounded with rays of light more brilliant than the sun, and transparent like a crystal. A spirit took out her heart and, placing it inside the 'crystal' heart, inflamed it – before replacing it in her breast.[21] This spontaneous laceration did not happen to a shaman but to a nun. She identified the spirit as Christ, while the vision – the Sacred Heart – is a devotional image for Roman Catholics. Thus we see that even when shamanic experience has long disappeared as a social institution, it continues to appear spontaneously – we remember, too, the medieval accounts of near-death experiences where daimonic initiation has become punishment by demons; or modern accounts of 'alien abduction' where initiation is read as extraterrestrial invasion.

On the other hand, Sister Alacoque's vision was not as spontaneous as it would have been if it had appeared to a lay person, or even to another nun. For she was a nun who practised severe physical austerities. In common with many Christian mystics she believed that to imitate Christ's physical suffering before and during his Crucifixion was the way to purification and sanctity. It may also be seen as a kind of initiation by those who have a shamanic vocation but, lacking a visionary tradition of daimonic transformation, have to dismember themselves, as it were, praying for the intervention of Christ or his angels to raise them up.

The early fourteenth-century Dominican monk, Henry Suso, describes his self-initiation in graphic detail: he wore an iron chain until the blood ran off him. He had a secret undergarment made for himself in which 150 brass nails were fixed, so that the points drove into his flesh. Sleeping in this on hot summer nights, he would cry aloud and twist around in agony, 'as a worm does when run through with a pointed needle'. But it was not enough – he also devised two leather loops into which he put his hands and fastened one on each side of his throat so that even if his room had caught fire he would have been unable to help himself. Then he would cry to God, saying, 'What a dying this is! When a man is killed by beasts of prey it is soon over; but I lie dying here . . . and yet cannot die.'

Next, he had two leather gloves made, studded all over with sharp tacks lest he should try to release himself, while asleep, from his garment or from the lice which ceaselessly gnawed him. Often the tacks in the gloves would tear him while he slept so that his flesh festered. He continued this for about sixteen years, at which time 'there appeared to him in a vision . . . a messenger from Heaven, who told him that God required this of him no longer. Whereupon he discontinued it, and threw all these things away into a running stream. At the same time, he made himself a cross with thirty iron needles and nails protruding from it and he bore it on his bare back day and night, so that he was always bloody and seared.'[22]

There is more, and worse, to come but I will stop there. Suso was rewarded for his years of pain by a series of visions, including the Virgin Mary, the celestial landscape and his own soul lying entranced in the arms of God. Once he was given the Holy Child to hold by the Virgin.[23] But, while Sister Alacoque craved pain – 'Nothing but pain makes my life supportable,' she often said[24] – Suso never seemed to turn his torment into masochistic pleasure and so enjoyed no alleviation of pain for twenty-five years or more.

The initiation by daimons in the realm of soul is literalized into self-torture. This became inevitable once the middle realm of soul, intermediate between spirit and body, was lost. It was formally abolished in 689, at the Church Council of Constantinople; but it was already becoming unintelligible through Christianity's endemic literalism which, instead of seeing body and spirit as bound together by soul or as being the physical and non-physical aspects of soul, polarized soul into opposed principles. With no daimonic realm, psychic transformation is forced to manifest literally, as physical change (fasting, pain, self-denial) or as spiritual change (prayer, effort of will, self-discipline) or both at once.

3I

'The Night-mare Life-in-Death
was She'

THE ANOREXIC AND THE ASCETIC

It was while Francis of Assisi was in the wilderness, subjecting his body
to deprivation and suffering, that he was given stigmata, the wounds of
Christ in his hands, feet and side. We can see the paradox of this event:
the intense rejection of the body during the Middle Ages made it the
focus of attention, so that it also became the vehicle of soul's expression.

The paradox continues to pervade Western culture. The body still
holds centre stage. Soul and spirit struggle to express their perspectives
through it as best they can. Soul is perpetually hungry for the images
which spirit starves it of. The body tries to satisfy both in literal fashion
by moving between poles of obesity and anorexia; or else, as it were
bulimically, by eating and starving at the same time. 'Fitness' regimes –
the word is telling since it implies moral worthiness as well – simultaneously feed the body and waste it through exercise and strengthening
combined with dieting. Bodily strengthening and fitness can become a
Heraclean defence against the 'weakness' of soul, its illness, imperfection
and pathology, which draws sustenance, like the Sidhe, from our conscious and bodily life. But the latter, in turn, fears soul's subversive
bleeding of its strength, drawing it down towards the death that is also
imaginative life; for, as Heraclitus says, 'Dionysus and Hades are one.'

Whatever else anorexia nervosa is, it can be read as a spiritual condition
which has been medicalized. Since anorexia delays puberty, or returns
sufferers to a pre-pubescent state, it can be seen as a refusal to change
biologically until there is some accompanying meaning. It can be seen,
in other words, as soul's longing for initiation. Or perhaps some anorexics

are simply those who in another age would immediately be recognized as having a vocation for the ascetic or monastic life. The point is that as long as soul is ignored and spirit therefore literalized, the body has too much weight to carry and too much meaning to express.

THE SUBTLE BODY

For instance, it has to carry the whole burden of longing for an immortal 'subtle body' promised by the Elixir of Life and symbolized by the 'diamond body' of Chinese alchemy, or the resurrected body, crystalline or iron-boned, of the shaman. We literalize this body by acting out fantasies of physical renewal through diet ('you are what you eat'), and fantasies of eternal youth through drugs, cosmetics and plastic surgery.

The fantasy of immortality is one of the staples of scientism, taking three main forms: (a) Rip van Winkleism, or the notion that we can freeze our bodies cryogenically in order to awake in a better time in the future; (b) Pandorism, or the idea that we can produce a perfect human organism, like Pandora in the Greek myth, by genetically engineering embryos; (c) Mechanism, or the futuristic fantasy of the Really Mad Scientists that we will eventually, somehow, be able to transfer our 'consciousness' or 'intelligence' into deathless machines that will control the universe and 'store an infinite amount of information', thus enabling us to become omnipotent, omniscient and immortal, that is, God.

Unlike St Francis, who wished to achieve perfection in spite of the body, we try to reach perfection through the body, in a seamless process of spiritualization or its equivalent which, like all ego fantasies, is designed to avoid the imperative of death. Even when we take the opposite route, the way of St Francis, and attempt to abnegate the body altogether, we tend to avoid initiation through abstract prayer or bloodless meditation – another way, as I have suggested, of suppressing soul.

Besides, it is doubtful whether voluntary disciplines can ever do more than prepare the way for initiation – which, like the shaman's call, is, finally, involuntary. We cannot will to die to ourselves. The will is itself part of that egoism which clings to its own life. Thus we are initiated by what we cannot control. Our dreams, for instance, dismember the events of the day, re-imagine them, as our natural life is drained into the service of our spectral, psychic life. Sleep, the little death of the body, is also dreaming, the coming to life of the soul.

In the life of the body, it is loss that dismembers us. Our hearts are broken; we bleed, hurt, ache; we are gutted. Bereavement opens us up like a scalpel, we fall apart, we feel cut up into little pieces. Grief numbs us; our bodies feel odd and separate; we seem to be living in a dream, in another world.

These are the experiences we must not seek to cure or get over, so that we can return to the persons we were. Instead we must allow the deep energies they release to transform us. We ought not to fear the disintegration of our too, too solid selves; we ought to welcome the death of our heroic egos. It is not only loss that initiates us if we will but let it. It is also love, the prerequisite of which is that passionate attention which is death to egoism. Love is less reliable than loss as the generator of transformation because it is easily confused with attachment, wish, desire, and so may be unreal without our knowing it. The reasons for our suffering in loss may be equally unreal or deluded, but at least the suffering itself is real. 'A cry of pain is always irreducible.'[1]

Plato and his followers presented three paths to wisdom and self-realization: eros, dialectics and mania. The path of love we can understand. Perhaps, too, the idea of a deep intellectual engagement with truth implied by dialectics is also a path, like gnosis, we can comprehend. The path of madness, however, is more difficult to grasp in an age where the emphasis lies on 'mental health'; and I would be glad to leave it out, were it not intrinsic to soul.

But before I turn to madness, I will tell one more initiatory tale.

THE GREENLAND WIZARD

The flight to the Otherworld, the encounters with daimons, and the initiations inherent in dreams, are not a monopoly of the shaman. 'They are, in fact, the basic experience of the poetic temperament we call "romantic".'[2] In a shamanizing society, Shakespeare's *Venus and Adonis*, some of Keats's longer poems, Yeats's *The Wanderings of Oisin*, T. S.

Eliot's *Ash Wednesday* would all, says Ted Hughes, 'qualify their authors for the magic drum . . .'. And if many poets have an easy time of it compared to shamans, many do not. We think of Eliot's breakdown, of Yeats's transfixion by unrequited love and of Coleridge running naked through his house in a frenzy of delirium. Suffering, he wrote, 'with a shower of arrowy death-pangs . . . transpierced me, & then he became a wolf and lay gnawing my bones'.[3] His doctor diagnosed a nervous disorder, brought on by overwork and anxiety; but Coleridge suspected another, more exciting dimension to the experience.

He may have suspected that he was a shamanic type. In an early poem, 'The Destiny of Nations – A Vision', he transcribes an ethnographical account of a Greenland *angakoq*'s descent into the ocean where it is his task to persuade the hideous Mother of the Sea Creatures to release some of her children for hunting and food. It is probably the first reference to such a thing in English:

> . . . the Greenland Wizard in strange trance
> Pierces the untravelled realms of Ocean's bed . . .
> Over the abysm, even to that uttermost cave
> By mis-shaped prodigies beleaguered, such
> As Earth ne'er bred, nor Air, nor the upper Sea.[4]

Coleridge used the otherworldly sea-journey as a basis for his own great initiatory poem, 'The Rime of the Ancient Mariner'.[5]

As the Mariner's ship sails away, leaving the sun behind, hidden in a mist, it also leaves behind the sunlit world of sweet reason and of orthodox religion. Ahead is another world presided over by the 'fog-smoke white' moon; and it will seem to the Mariner, who sees it distorted by his conventional Protestant spectacles, as a kind of hell.[6]

The first encounter on a shaman's otherworld journey is often with a daimon of the threshold, a bird or animal perhaps, who is helpful or destructive. 'Either way, directly or indirectly, this creature gives place (by immolation, by self-sacrifice, by transformation, by acting as a guide) eventually to the prize – as if it were an aspect of that prize, the only aspect . . . visible to the untransformed adventurer in the opening phase.'[7] For the Mariner, it is the albatross who leads him through the traditional clashing rocks, in this case of ice. Then he kills it – and the ship breaks through to the Otherworld as if the bird's death had turned the key. 'We were the first that ever burst/Into that silent sea.'

This new world is a nightmare. Its sun is not like ours but 'like God's own head'. It turns bloody; the sea turns to a 'lifeless ocean, almost solid, rotting, burning as if with hellfire'. Slimy creatures with legs crawl on the surface. The whole crew is dying of thirst. This is the extreme point of the descent at which, were he an *angakoq*, the Mariner would meet the Mother of the Sea Creatures.[8]

Instead, a woman appears. She comes in a ship of bones. She is at once alluring and alarming – her lips are red, her looks are free, her locks as yellow as gold, but her skin is as white as leprosy. 'The Night-mare Life-in-Death was she, Who thicks man's blood with cold.' She has a companion, 'a Death', with whom she is playing dice. She cries out, 'I've won!' – and at once the sky darkens, her ship disappears, the sails begin to drip with dew, and the parched sailors begin to drop to the deck, all dead except for the Mariner.[9]

The woman is an ambiguous goddess, like the spirit of the sea. She is life to the pagan shaman and poet but death to the narrow Christian. The Mariner tries to resist her, the albatross still hanging like a cross round his neck; he tries to pray, but his heart is dry as dust. At last he is forced to give up his Christian spectacles, as it were, and adopt the viewpoint of the goddess.[10]

Immediately he sees how beautiful, not loathsome, the water creatures are. 'A spring of love' gushes from his heart, and he blesses them. At once the albatross drops from round his neck and he falls blissfully asleep. When he wakes, there is rain – water to drink – and a high wind that yet does not move the ship, which moves as if by itself. The crew is raised from the dead, not by their own souls but by 'a troop of spirits'. They are the spirit of the Mariner's old Christian self which refuses to lie down and die, and which wrests control of the ship from his new, effortless shamanic self. He is forced back into his rational, Christian persona to whom it seems that the spirit of the sea – which is ominously following the ship – is like a 'frightful fiend'. Nor can she be denied with impunity: as the ship reaches port she surges up and sinks it.[11] The Mariner is saved by the Pilot and his boy who are driven mad by his 'strange power of speech'. And so he returns to his former self, scarred and maimed and doomed to retell the tale of his searing encounter with the goddess.

'The Rime of the Ancient Mariner' is a poem so strange that much of it can only be made intelligible by understanding that it is, among other things, about a shamanic journey that failed, a 'call' to the young Coleridge by his personal daimon or poetic self. The first rule of shamans, as of poets, is that, once called, you must shamanize – or die. Coleridge refused his call; he refused the life-in-death and was condemned to death-in-life. His poetry dried up, he was tortured by screaming nightmares, he spent his days talking and talking, like the Mariner, in a flight from his enraged muse, his eloquent, elegant discourse growing emptier and emptier so that few who listened, though spellbound by his strange power of speech, could remember a word of what he said.

The initiatory experience, such as dismemberment, is the climax of the otherworld journey; the furthest point of descent, like King Lear's hovel on the blasted heath, whence the hero or shaman begins his return. But we should remember firstly that the whole journey is initiatory in the way that all contact with the Otherworld is a kind of dying, a daimonizing operation on the rational ego; secondly, that we are entitled to resist that operation, as the strong rational ego often does; and thirdly, that it is this strength which, on the one hand, makes the Otherworld seem weak and ghostly, and, on the other, precisely this resistance which, compelling the daimons to initiate the ego by force, makes it seem hellish and demonic.

32

The Myths of Madness

FOUR KINDS OF MADNESS

'Our greatest blessings', remarked Socrates in the *Phaedrus*, 'come to us by way of madness [*mania*]' – providing, he adds, that 'the madness is given us by divine gift'.[1] Although the Greeks did recognize an ordinary kind of mania, caused by organic disease, madness is not usually a 'mental illness' to which we should apply medicine. It is a gift from the gods. It frequently occurs in mythology, which means that it is an archetypal condition of the soul. Because it is a mythical, not a medical, condition, the psyche can never be wholly free of madness or its possibility.

Socrates distinguishes four kinds of madness.[2] The madness bestowed by Apollo is prophetic; by Aphrodite and Eros, erotic; by Dionysus, ritual madness; and by the muses, poetic madness. Apollonic madness seems to have been aimed at knowledge of the future or of the hidden present. Given to individuals, it was a kind of mediumship, foreseeing and oracular. Erotic madness is more familiar – lucky the man or woman who has escaped the obsessive, addictive frenzy of sexual love. Dionysian madness was not individual but collective, bringing the sort of release (even the mental healing) we can experience in wild communal rites involving drink and dance, or on the terraces at a three-day festival of Greek tragedy. The chief feature of Dionysus' cult was ecstasy, which meant anything from 'letting yourself go' at a party, to 'becoming possessed'. Apollonic, erotic and Dionysian manias all imply ecstasy; only poetic madness does not. 'Epic tradition represented the poet as deriving supernormal knowledge from the muses, but not as falling into ecstasy or being possessed by them.'[3]

Poetic madness is useful. Homer sought it, and contracted it, when he did not know what to say next in *The Iliad*. The Muses do not supply inspiration but information about the past – famous battles, for instance – which the poet cannot know first-hand. They extend memory. Their gift, as they told Hesiod on Mount Helicon, is that of true speech; but they admitted, too, that they would on occasion tell a pack of lies that looked like truth.[4] They are telling us not to put too much faith in memory (good advice, as we have seen), nor to set too much store by their communications. We should not, in other words, take them too literally.

ORPHEUS

According to Thomas Taylor (who made the first English translation of Plato and the Neoplatonists for the Romantics), the *Scholia of Hermeas* says that Socrates' four kinds of madness require each other and conspire together and all find a place in certain people.[5] He cites Orpheus – a telling example because Orpheus is the father of all shamans, combining as he does the function of poet and singer of sacred songs; prophet and seer; priest and theologian.

To put it another way, it is striking and a trifle unnatural the way the modern world has divided the shaman's role into specialized jobs, and even subdivided them, such that modern healing not only hives the body off from the soul, separating medicine and theology, but also divides body from mind, medicine from psychotherapy. The shaman's unity of function suggests that this is not a good thing.

The myth of Orpheus falls into four main parts which do not seem to relate to each other, even seem to contradict each other – until we understand them as each coming under the aegis of one of the gods of mania.

First of all, Orpheus is under the sway of the Muses – his mother is the Muse Calliope – who give him such a wonderful gift of poetry and song that he is able to enchant all the animals and birds, and even Death himself. His instrument is the Apollonic lyre rather than the Dionysian flute; but it is Hermes who teaches him to play – and, moreover, to play the music specific to each god. This image of differentiation and harmony was eagerly taken up by the Renaissance Neoplatonists who hailed Orpheus as the founder of polytheism, and who saw their own culture as a return of the religion of Orpheus whom the lyre-playing Ficino consciously tried to reincarnate.[6]

Secondly, it is Eros who drives Orpheus into the Underworld; but he is not trying to usurp it, like Heracles, nor learn from it, like Odysseus – he is trying to retrieve his beloved wife, Eurydice, who has died of a snake-bite. He succeeds in charming Hades with his music, and is given permission to take Eurydice back to this world. However, the Greeks were uncertain of the outcome:[7] in one version of the myth, Orpheus brings her back to life; in the better-known version he is allowed to retrieve her, providing that he does not look back. Failing to hear her footstep behind him, he does look back – and loses her.

Thirdly, like Dionysus, Orpheus is dismembered. Once again, it is not certain why. Some say that the Maenads tore him to pieces for being hostile to the worship of Dionysus; others, that he rejected the women's advances because he preferred young men. However, his cult was too Dionysian and his marriage too passionate for either 'reason' to be literally true.[8] Instead, they point to his affinity with Dionysus and his notorious 'effeminacy' – point, that is, to the androgynous nature of the god and to the bisexual structure of the psyche.

Fourthly, it is said Orpheus preached all his life that Apollo was the greatest of the gods. When he was torn to pieces, his head floated all the way to Lesbos, where it uttered prophecies and oracles. However, the head was placed in the sanctuary of Dionysus and was eventually silenced by Apollo.[9] In addition, Orpheus was credited with the founding of the Mysteries, those initiatory rites which were so secret that we know very little about them. The Eleusinian Mysteries were the most famous; but Orpheus instituted the Mysteries of Apollo in Thrace; those of Hecate in Aegina; and those of subterranean Demeter at Sparta. Above all, it seems, he founded the Dionysian Mysteries. Dionysus was the god of Orphic religion.[10]

Orpheus, then, stands at a crossroads of contradictions. He is both Apollonic and Dionysian; husband and homosexual; poet and theologian (founder of Mysteries); both a retriever of souls, represented by Eurydice, from the Underworld, and also one whose soul is always in the Underworld (she does not make it back). Shamans usually have this kind of contrariness, as befits daimonic men. They dress as women or have wives in the Otherworld. Daimons teach them sacred songs which give them control over the Otherworld. They retrieve lost souls, or sometimes they cannot. They are dismembered like Dionysus or possessed like the oracles of Apollo. Like Orpheus, the shaman is a marvellous complexity who can minister both to the individual and to the tribe, body and soul.

MADNESS AND INSANITY

Madness – as the Greek tragedies tell us – is the way the gods reach us.[11] The gods are in the diseases, said Jung. It is up to us how we treat that madness. As the Muses implied in their remarks to Hesiod, to treat madness as metaphorical is the way to truth – to treat it as literal is the way to falsehood. We must distinguish, that is, between madness and insanity. Whenever we take the god-given madness to ourselves, harness it to our egos, take credit for it, take it literally – we are in danger of insanity. We begin to believe that the thoughts and revelations that are sent to us are our own; or that we are the unique instrument of the gods, the Chosen One.[12]

Apollonic insanity, then, might consist of oneness at all costs (a-pollo = 'not many'), leading to paranoia, which sees the same hidden cause behind all events, and to monomania. The Eros that would connect us madly to the gods might become insanely fixed on one object or person whom we blindly worship as a divinity, no matter how unrealistic that is. The Dionysian madness that would liberate us temporarily from our individual prisons and pent-up feelings might abolish individuality altogether and manifest itself in 'collective hysterias' or dangerous mobs.[13]

The ancient Greek *Oreibasia* was a mid-winter rite dedicated to Dionysus in which the women left the city and went at dead of night into the mountains. There, in imitation of the Maenads, they drank wine and danced themselves into an ecstasy, thrashing their long hair about, and finally dismembering and eating raw a young goat which represented the god. The rite is both horrible and holy, a pollution and a sacrament, in which the devouring of the god becomes a communion, and murder becomes sacrifice.[14]

The myths tell us, however, about women who refused the rite. The daughters of King Minyas, for example, were extremely sober and industrious, and they scorned the women who worshipped Dionysus. The god appeared to them in person and warned them not to neglect his rites. They disobeyed. Whereupon he turned himself, like Proteus, into a bull, a lion, a leopard. The three prim women were so maddened that they tore one of their sons to pieces before running off to roam the mountains, out of their minds.[15]

The lesson is clear: let Dionysian madness in or you will be driven insane. Instead of sacrificing the god metaphorically, in animal form, you will kill literally – 'act out', as the psychotherapists say, what should remain as imaginative or ritual action. If the denial of divine madness leads to insanity, so, conversely, the cure for insanity is to convert it into madness, which is initiatory. It destroys the ego and the literalism that holds the madness in thrall to insanity, and connects us back to the gods.

For example, when King Lear divides his kingdom among his flattering daughters and rejects the truthful daughter – Cordelia, his very soul – he is sane in the eyes of the world but, more deeply, prey to an insanity which only his madness on the stormy heath can cure by stripping him down to his essential humanity and reuniting him with Cordelia.

There is madness in myth. Heracles goes mad and kills his sons, for which he is forced to do a penance of twelve labours. Odysseus goes mad when the oracle tells him that to embark on the Trojan War will take twenty years and leave him destitute and alone. He is senselessly and madly ploughing a field when his baby son is placed in front of the plough. He stops at once. Heracles was insane, not mad; Odysseus mad, not insane.

But if there is madness in myth, there is also myth in madness; and herein lies our fascination with madness and our sense that it conceals some larger imaginative dimension, like the myth that there is a genius – that is, a daimon – inside it.

Take, for example, the story of a young man called Charles who began to think he was a bit like Jesus. He sometimes called himself Son of Man, a play on his surname. But actually he was more like Dionysus, who was something of an outcast like himself. Both attracted a band of followers, mostly women, and roamed the hills, communing with Nature. Both were musical and both were 'gods of drugs' – in the one case, wine; in the other, hallucinogens. Both pursued an ideal of freedom, joy and ecstasy which, paradoxically, was bound up with extreme savagery. Dionysus, as we know, was dismembered; Charles, on the other hand, who should by rights have suffered a similar initiatory fate, decided to murder and dismember some other people of whom he disapproved.

In fact, it was his followers, his Maenads, who broke into a house and butchered the occupants, among whom was a celebrated actress called Sharon Tate. Charles Manson seems to have remained a god to his followers. 'To this day, the women who carried out the murders will not recant, even though to do so would result in their freedom', writes Dennis Stillings, the Jungian social analyst. 'Whatever we may think, they have seen God. In an essentially secular, godless, and meaningless society . . . their world was filled with meaning by Charlie.'[16]

33

Ungodly Messiahs

ACTION AND RITUAL

If Odysseus was mad when they placed his son in front of the plough, then he was not mad enough to run the child over. There is a kind of double vision in madness which is absent in insanity. One remains oneself while being another. It is possible, of course, that Odysseus was not mad at all, but only pretending to be mad in order to avoid signing up for war; and this is what his colleagues were testing when they put his son in danger.

The point is that there is a doubleness, even a duplicity, about madness which is analogous to play-acting, just as insanity is analogous to 'acting out' – which we might characterize as the literal enaction of essentially imaginative events, including myths, dreams and fantasies. This does not mean that all physical action is 'acting out' because of course many physical actions are not literal, but actually a concrete form of imagining. Ritual, for example. In fact, any action which is informed by imagination becomes ritual; and so, in traditional cultures, all activities, from cooking to gardening to hunting and dancing, are performed according to patterns established by the gods. Thus the whole of life is imbued with the meaning we associate with ritual.

Indeed, no activity takes place without taking the daimons into account lest they sour the milk or steal a cow, or worse. All they need is attention – a bit of food left out, a respect for the places they are said to inhabit, a place for them by our hearths and in our hearts. Nowadays we do not heed the daimons and so they reproach us from their current home, the unconscious, with unruly behaviour we try to quieten with secular rituals, such as stress management, psychotherapy, drugs, fitness regimes, relaxation techniques, recreational games and so on, none of which imaginatively accommodates – that is, enshrine – the daimons at their proper distance from us, and their proper nearness.

The analogy between madness and play-acting is apposite. Both require double vision. The origin of tragic drama (Greek *tragos*, 'goat') is supposed to lie in the song and dance 'in praise of Dionysus performed by singers dressed up as animals . . . and for the duration of the dance . . . the world of myth and material reality become one'.[1] Neither the shaman in his ecstatic goat-dance, nor his audience – however swept up in divine madness – ever believe that he is identical with the god. Neither, that is, becomes like the actor who thinks he is his character, nor like the person who writes abusive letters to the actor who plays a villain in a drama. Such people have lost the power to distinguish between what is metaphorical and what is literal, and so behave insanely.

We can now see that the madness of which the shaman has often been accused by Western anthropologists is not insanity but a 'divine', initiatory madness which may well cause the initiate to wander about in a state of dissociation for months. It is part of the 'softening up' of his ordinary self in order to shift its shape sufficiently to allow him to slip through the strait gate into the Otherworld. It is a madness he has voluntarily to return to when he is shamanizing, the madness of travelling 'outside himself' through the Otherworld. Sometimes he is not wholly outside himself, but travelling as if in imagination and relaying his itinerary to the audience; sometimes he is play-acting, sometimes pretending – he might be all these things in the course of a long seance – but he is not hoaxing his audience or lying to them, as Western rationalism often asserts.

We can easily understand this because we experience much the same thing at the performance of a gripping play. We do not, I think – as is often said – have to 'suspend disbelief'. On the contrary, disbelief is too easily suspended, and we have to 'suspend belief', remind ourselves that it is only a play if we are not to be completely swept away. Not that we rush on to the stage, rolling up our sleeves, when the heroine is attacked; but we do not think of her as an actress.

Our plays are detached affairs compared to the shamanic ritual in which audience participation is so much more intense, a communal Dionysian drama where anyone can potentially experience sympathetic ecstasy. Yet the crucial thing is that we still experience that enchantment which, on a good night, springs up between the actors and audience as a daimonic reality in which all participate.

THE VOCATION OF THE SERIAL KILLER

Like sex, violence and disease, madness is part of the psyche. Myths tell us this, and so do dreams which delight in crazing our everyday world (studies of dreams show that the majority of them are nightmares).[2] Imagination informs the soul by deforming and transforming, spawning monsters. We love monsters as much as we fear them. As we are taught less about myth, where monsters rightly dwell, we become proportionately more fascinated by human monsters. For example, at the end of the twentieth century serial killers featured prominently, both in fiction and in fact.

They are not like ordinary murderers who kill only once, usually someone known to them, and for comprehensible motives such as anger, greed or fear. Serial killers kill, by definition, many times, usually people unknown to them, and for reasons which are not immediately (if ever) comprehensible. They fascinate us perhaps because they seem to have a mythic dimension, as if they were acting out some archetypal pattern beyond themselves – making actual the sex and violence that should remain in the imaginative realm. If this is the case, they kill strangers because they are not killing persons, but images – or, rather, one image in many persons. It may be the image of the Mother, the Girl, the Whore, Womankind or whatever; but, finally, it is the soul from whose images serial killers yearn like Heracles to be free.

Soul demands of the serial killer what it demands of us all – that he metaphorically kill his ego in order that his soul might live. He chooses instead to literally kill his soul in order that his ego might live. Soul, however, cannot be killed. It is not only immortal, but it is also the very root from which the ego has sprung. Any attempt to uproot soul only makes it come back at us in distorted form, as a demonic image which has to be killed again and again.

Just as obsessive disorders and compulsive behaviours, such as Lady Macbeth's hand-washing, are literal enactments of recurrent rituals, such as ceremonies of cleansing, so the serial killer's repeated murders often conform to some pattern, like the monstrous shadows of ritual's decorous repetitions. Because he cannot move to another metaphorical level; because he cannot transform acting out into play-acting, insanity back into divine madness, he can only go on and on in the same way. A serial killer never voluntarily stops.

No attempt at a purely 'secular' explanation – bad parents, early traumas, hereditary taint, social conditioning – can account for the serial killer's sense of being possessed. For example, despite fervent prayer, the fourteen-year-old Joseph Bartsch had the feeling 'of no longer having any control over what I was doing';[3] and he went on to torture and kill little boys. Jeffrey Dahmer, who ate the flesh of his victims, chose to go to trial rather than plead guilty because he 'wanted to find out just what it was that caused me to be so bad and evil'.[4] Andrei Chikatilo, the Russian killer of some fifty adolescents, said that 'it was as if something directed me, something ouside me, something supernatural'.[5]

It was when I heard of the serial killer's awful lacerating and disembowelling that I was reminded of the gruesome initiation of so many shamans. I began to wonder whether serial killers are people who have a shamanic vocation but who, for some reason, have turned their back on the call. Tormented by the daimons who would perform the imaginative dismemberment their vocation requires, they can only quieten them (and only temporarily) by literally dismembering one victim after another.

Called by daimons, the serial killer subjugates this divine impulse under an ego which, according to the law of psychic energy, is inflated by delusions of its own divinity in exact proportion to the force with which it denies its calling. Unable to relate to the daimons, he feels himself to be possessed by a demon. The divine voice which calls him to shamanize is distorted into those 'voices' which command the serial killers to commit atrocities, and which they are strangely unable to disobey.

The sexual component in the acts of serial killers is often thought to be their cause. But it may only be a symptom of the deeper malaise. Dennis Nielsen's fondling of the boys he has killed, Dahmer's eating of his victims' flesh – such behaviour may be the only way they can have any sort of human intercourse.[6] While their killings are brutal acts of the egoistic will, their subsequent behaviour towards the bodies may be expressions of soul's desperate attempt to connect. Are not our own expressions of soul also distorted? Is not love, for example, frequently forced through tortuous channels so that it can only appear as rancour, hatred, perversion – all deadly, but all efforts nevertheless to connect with others? Can we not imagine the absolute zero of iciness in which the serial killer must live in order that caressing a corpse is the closest he can come to a warm relationship?

THE SACRIFICE OF ISAAC

A killer might claim that he was acting on orders from God. He might look from the outside just like the Patriarch Abraham who was commanded by Jehovah to kill his only child Isaac, the beloved son of his old age. In fact, Abraham would appear worse than a murderer because the killing of one's children was regarded by his society as the most heinous of crimes. Even if he pleaded, as killers often do, that he had been commanded by God to kill Isaac, he would not have increased his chances of leniency – he would probably have faced additional charges of blasphemy.

This situation is completely reversed when viewed from the inside. What society calls murder, Abraham calls sacrifice. His freely chosen decision to kill Isaac on God's command is an expression of his intimate and personal relationship with God. This relationship, comprising many factors including love and doubt, is called faith; and Abraham is justly known as 'the father of faith'. (God intervened to spare Isaac's life at the moment when Abraham was about to bring down the knife.)

Analogously, self-sacrifice resembles suicide. But whereas the first is an act of love by one who has died, or is willing to die, to himself, the second is an act of despair by one who will not die to himself and so, trapped in an ever narrowing ego-world, can see no exit except through physical extinction.

MAN-GODS

If serial killers are kinds of inverted shamans, perhaps the great tyrants of Western culture – Napoleon, Hitler, Stalin – can be described as false messiahs. Whereas Christ, the God-Man, set the importance of the individual in relation to God against all temporal power – both of religion (Judaism) and of the state (Roman imperialism) – the Man-god exalts the collective power of the state, embodied in himself, over every individual. It is arguable that the Man-god as we know him was only made possible by Christian monotheism, which both insisted on a single God and made that God literal in the person of Christ. There have been, and are, of course, monstrous tyrants in non-Christian societies; but I would suggest that they are all the product of that monotheism whose inversion leads to monomania. Even in polytheistic cultures, such as ancient Rome, the Man-gods (Caligula, Nero) selected a single god from the pantheon (Zeus, Apollo) with whom to identify.

Hitler and Stalin both possessed a sense of their historic mission to rescue their people, no matter what the cost in material and human sacrifice.[7] Hitler believed that, as Fuehrer, he was 'the saviour appointed by Providence' who 'performed his role as a ritual figure in the service of a myth . . .'[8] Stalin had to conceal his sense of personal destiny because of the Communist Party's disapproval of any cult of personality; but in the copy of Napoleon's *Thoughts* found in his library, Stalin had marked this passage:

It was precisely that evening in Lodi that I came to believe in myself as an unusual person and became consumed with the ambition to do the great things that until then had been but a fantasy.[9]

We can see how they were, in a sense, correct about their feeling of destiny. They believed in their invulnerability – Hitler was famous in the trenches of the First World War for leading a charmed life, and he was notoriously difficult to assassinate. This invincibility, like that of Siegfried, is also a sign of their refusal to sacrifice the ego. As a result, they suffer from the psychological 'inflation' I touched on earlier. The ego seizes on the divine vocation and wants to become a god. The more the Man-gods become puffed up with this sense of divinity, the harder it becomes to die to themselves and the more they feel the threatening presence of the void left by the soul they have reviled.

Nothing can be allowed to live outside the tyrannical ego – that is, nothing can be allowed to have autonomy, to have its own soul. The Man-god must subjugate and dehumanize everybody. He must continually ward off the annihilating void, or seek to fill it, with acts of power – which only makes the void emptier and hungrier. It cannot be filled with people because people have souls – the very things the Man-god cannot abide – and so he tries to fill it with unsouled people: slaves and corpses. Stalin continuously killed his rivals and so-called friends alike, as if he wanted everyone but himself dead; Hitler imprisoned more and more groups of people including, by the end of the war, thousands of Aryan Germans, as if he secretly wanted everyone but himself in a concentration camp. 'To be the last man to remain alive is the deepest urge of every real seeker after power.'[10] The messianic figure who will not die to himself must lay waste to the world.

The corollary of megalomania is paranoia. It was paranoia that aroused Hitler's nationalistic consciousness in the first place and took him into politics – he saw Germany as besieged by enemies, and this vision was shared by Germans who also detected a conspiracy of unseen enemies: capitalists, social democrats, Marxists, Bolsheviks, Slavs and Jews. 'A mass of potential converts waiting for a messiah to liberate and focus their energies.'[11] This belief in his messianic role helped Hitler in the early days when he felt invulnerable and his intuitive brilliance brought him military success. But it was also the hubris which did not allow him to look at what was actually happening, and which brought about his downfall. He was destroyed by his own image of himself, which blinded him to any shortcomings or mistakes.[12]

Stalin was also paranoid from the beginning. It took the form of 'chronic suspicion, utter self-absorption, jealousy, vindictiveness, hypersensitivity, megalomania',[13] writes Alan Bullock in *Hitler and Stalin; Parallel Lives*. He could not abide any criticism of, or opposition to, anything that might disturb his image of himself. Anyone who gave him unwelcome facts was accused of lying, malice and sabotage; anyone he wished to betray and kill, he always accused of treachery. He combined delusions of grandeur with the conviction that he was the victim of persecution and conspiracy.[14]

No matter how absolute the power of the Man-god, there is always a suspicion that there are still autonomous powers – people who have not yet fallen under his thrall, people who still have souls – individuals – who are plotting against him. In fact, paradoxically, the more powerful he is, the stronger the suspicion. But conspiracy is really the literalization of the whisper of the daimons in his own blighted soul. They can never be wholly blotted out, and will always come back at him, demonized, as unseen enemies. His only defence is through his own train of equally literalized daimons: the spies who foster his need for omniscience and the secret police who promulgate his omnipotence, abducting us like demons at dead of night.

34

The Cure of Souls

THE KORE IN THE UNDERWORLD

'The soul at the point of death has the same experience as those who are being initiated into the Great Mysteries', wrote Plutarch.[1] He cannot speak of these Mysteries in any detail because it was forbidden to do so. But he intimates that the soul wanders about and is beset by terrors before being struck by a marvellous light and then received into paradisal regions.

'Hear then and believe, for what I tell you is true', says Lucius in Apuleius' *Metamorphoses*, which is reckoned to be a thinly disguised description of the Mysteries. 'I drew near to the confines of death, treading the very threshold of Proserpine [that is, Persephone]. I was borne through all the elements and returned to earth again. At the dead of night, I saw the sun shining brightly. I approached the gods above and the gods below, and worshipped them face to face. See, I have told you things which, though you have heard them, you still must know nothing about . . .'[2]

The most famous Mysteries, at Eleusis, were founded on the myth of Demeter and the Kore (meaning 'daughter') who, one summer's afternoon, was dreamily picking narcissi and poppies in the drowsy meadows when suddenly the ground opened up and she was snatched into the brazen chariot of Hades, Death, and carried down to the Underworld.

We are all Kores, innocently dreaming in the sunlit fields, until we are hit by disaster, despair, depression, grief – any sudden event which violates our natural consciousness and opens it to the unnatural perspective of death.

This is not the way of humanistic psychology which, following Aristotle, identifies psyche with life and psychology with the study of human nature. It is the way of archetypal psychology which, following Plato, examines 'soul in relation with death, the psychologizing of dying out of life'.[3] This is not a literal death but a deathly perspective on life, a sense of the invisible presence of Hades in the midst of life, where Hades does not mean extinction but means both a god and the place where he dwells – the vast underground realm of imaginative richness.

Contact with death, or with any of the little deaths which life throws at us, turns our point of view upside down. We see things from the perspective of soul rather than ego. We see that soul is not only ours. We see that, in fact, our souls project us as literal realities and that the 'I' we thought we were is not real. We move from mortal fear of death to a kind of love for it, just as the violated Kore grew to love Hades and became Persephone, 'Bringer of Destruction'.

The rape of the Kore 'never happened; it is always', like all myths. This means that it is not just a single event in our psyches but is always going on as a basic pattern of psychodynamics. And because it is the central myth of the Eleusinian Mysteries, 'Hades' rape of the innocent soul is a central necessity for psychic change.'[4]

THE VIRUS OF IMAGINATION

The rejection of Hades' advances – the resistance to death – is the hallmark of modernity, and especially of our approach to medicine. Of all the technological developments which have changed our lives since the Renaissance, medical technology is perhaps the one we can point to with most confidence and say: 'There, at least, things are getting better.' Medicine can now regularly perform what the newspapers somewhat inaccurately call miracles. Compared to Victorian urban life in England, with its industrial diseases, its killing smogs, its awful infant mortality, its terrible infections – TB, cholera, typhoid fever, diphtheria – and even its strychnine-laden beer and lead-ridden tea, we are the picture of health, better and longer-living than ever before.

The progress that industrialization brought also brought a dark age for the health of the majority. But sometimes we get a tiny sharp reminder that, before this time, things were not so uniformly dire. We are glad to live in an era of toothpaste, anaesthetics and proper dentistry; but the teeth of skeletons found on board the sunken Elizabethan warship, *Mary Rose*, were all but perfect (perhaps because there was no sugar back then, and lots of gnawing of meat?). However, on the whole, when we concede that people may have been healthier than us in some small respects in the past, and that the Elizabethans were probably healthier than the Victorian urban poor, we feel relieved that we are unlikely to be wiped out by bubonic plague, or polio, smallpox or appendicitis.

We are better than ever – so why do we so often feel iller? Why does spending on health increase every year, but we do not seem happier? Why are we beginning to question the benefits of longevity? Why are we now plagued by complaints which may not be life-threatening but which make our lives a misery and which doctors can do little about – unexplained headaches, chronic backache, stomach disorders; anxiety attacks, stress disorders and depressions; plus a host of ills that seem to hover on the border between mind and body, such as ME, MS, chronic fatigue, hyperactivity, allergies, asthma, eczema and other 'nervous' disorders? Why can we never rid ourselves of Big Killers – we may have done away with the Black Death, but now we have Cancer and Heart Disease?

There are lots of answers to these questions; but the single most neglected answer (it will not surprise you to hear) is that we have neglected soul, especially in the field of mainstream medicine whose materialistic presuppositions tell us that the body is all we have; that it is more or less a machine – complicated, yes, but still essentially a machine; and that it includes the 'mind' which is complicated, yes, but no more complicated than the brain with which it is identical, and which will eventually be completely understood.

The daimonic tradition, on the other hand, tells us that the body is the physical expression of an individual soul connected to the Soul of the World and, as such, it is – like Nature – a citadel of metaphors. None of its expressions, including its symptoms and diseases, is merely biological. They are also imaginings which invite us to see heart disease, for example, as a sickness of the emotions, perhaps of the imagination itself, since these are traditionally seated in the heart; which invites us to see cancer as a revolt against the materialistic conception of the body itself, because cancer is like the body's madness, the body turning on itself, eating into itself, as if to free itself from itself or free it from its own literalistic conception of itself.

From the daimonic point of view, the tiny agents of disease such as bacteria and viruses are, like subatomic particles, daimonic entities whose existence was postulated hypothetically – that is, imagined – before they were 'discovered'. This is not to say that they do not exist; it is only to say that their existence is not only literal, even though we demonize them, ward them off and exorcize them in the literalized rituals we call vaccination, disinfection, etc. Viruses in particular have been fashionable in recent times. They are blamed for more and more diseases whose causes are uncertain. They may be different viruses – or, more alarmingly, they may be the same viruses which have mutated. The elusive, shape-changing nature of viruses suggests that they are the usual literalized daimons.

Moreover, there is a dark suspicion that the mass of 'wonder' drugs we have invented do not necessarily cure diseases but suppress them. According to this view a disease is then driven deeper into the body, only to reappear later in another, more virulent guise – exactly like the daimons we repress at our peril lest they mutate into demons. The high incidence of cancer would, from this viewpoint, be 'conceived as the suppressed form of diseases that we no longer manifest'.[5]

THE RAISING OF THE DEAD

Despite all our medical triumphs, a groundswell of grumbling has grown in volume over the last forty years, a dissatisfaction with the materialistic and technological approach to our bodies, which has encouraged a lot of people to experiment with 'alternative' medicine and 'holistic' therapies – many of which are administered in as literal a way as conventional medicine, using a kind of spiritual 'technology' which equally ignores soul.

Nevertheless they do point to a growing feeling that it is insane to treat the body in isolation, as if it were the only thing we consist of. We watch the holy grail of Total Health recede ever further from us as we increasingly understand that soul will never let us be totally well. Psyche constantly makes itself felt in psychosomatic disorders, in hypochondriacal feelings of dis-ease, in anomalous symptoms which chronically subvert the quality of our lives. It will always prise open a crack in our armour of health to let in sickness or to leach health, like a wasting disease, towards death.

Of course we should do what we can to avoid sickness and to cure it; but we should not let our Heraclean efforts blind us to the inner meaning of sickness, the opportunities it is offering us for psychic transformation, for initiation, which is an engagement with death rather than its denial. Many of the daimons a shaman encounters are called by the names of diseases. He engages with them in order to know them and to enlist their help in the care, and cure, of souls.

The tendency of medicine to deny soul is present in its mythic foundations. Asclepius was the first doctor, taught medicine by his father, Apollo, and (some say) by the centaur Cheiron. But when Asclepius began raising the dead, Hades complained to his brother, Zeus, that Asclepius was robbing him of his subjects. Zeus killed Asclepius with a thunderbolt, but later restored him to life.

Here, in Hades' complaint, we see medicine's predilection for affirming natural life, denying the life of the psyche and refusing the soul its connection with death. Hence medicine's emphasis on preserving life, raising up bodies at all costs, cheating Hades by depriving soul of its underworld dimension and keeping it in the upper daylight world.

THE INITIATION OF MEDICINE

The strength of modern medicine, which was made possible by the polarizing of soul into the literalized extremes of spirit and body, is also its weakness. The more we concentrate on the body alone, the more medicine will be shadowed by spirit. It is, for instance, a truism to remark how the medical profession has set itself up as a secular cult, with its reverence-inspiring white coats and arcane jargon, its priestly hierarchy and dogma, its purification rituals of sterilizing and hygiene (Hygeia, 'Health', was Asclepius' daughter). But I did not notice its affinity with traditional shamanism until my own father, dying of motor neurone disease and semi-delirious in Intensive Care, described how he had been carried off by masked daimons, thrust into a narrow, stifling cave and painfully pierced through the arms and tongue by sharp instruments. I recognized at once an Aboriginal initiation rite, and marvelled that my old dad should have spontaneously envisioned such a thing.

However, it turned out not to have been a vision: he had indeed been taken by surgically-masked hospital staff to one of those whole-body scanners and subsequently, as part of various tests, been repeatedly pierced with needles. At once we begin to see how many medical procedures resemble initiatory operations – drugs begin to look like shamanic substances taken to induce altered states of consciousness; surgery begins to resemble a literalistic dismembering; prosthetics, literalized 'iron bones'; X-rays and fibre optic probes, the seer's insight.

THE RAT BENEATH THE SKIN

All traditional cultures attribute the causes of illness to daimons, in the form either of the Dead, or of daimonic humans such as witches, sorcerers or bad shamans. They do not necessarily claim that witchcraft alone caused the illness. They may well subscribe to what E. E. Evans-Pritchard called 'dual causality', which incorporates both 'mystical and natural causation'. For example, among the Zande people whom he was studying, a granary weakened by termites collapsed on a group of people, causing injury. Witchcraft was blamed. The termites were acknowledged as the natural cause of the collapse, but they did not explain *why* the structure fell – why this granary at this time when these persons were underneath.[6] Occult action is a metaphor for hidden meaning.

And so it is with illness. There is no such thing as a simple 'organic' disease – there is not even such a thing as a 'natural' death. Sickness and death occur through occult harm, which takes two forms: either it steals the soul, or it implants disease in the body. Consequently, medicine-men, shamans and witch-doctors perform only two main cures (although both are supplemented by plant, herb and talismanic treatments): the first is the retrieval of the lost soul; the second is the physical removal of the disease. What is dug or sucked out is 'usually a thorn, crystal or feather . . . as in tropical America, Australia, and Alaska'; or sometimes a 'worm', a 'bone', or a 'stone'.[7] In the Philippines it is a 'rat'.[8]

Western medicine is committed to the view that these procedures are not merely unpromising, but futile. They cannot work, and so, if they appear to, the patient was not ill in the first place or there was a placebo effect or the illness was psychosomatic or there was some medicinal virtue in the herbal part of the treatment. Traditional medicine distinguishes between, but does not divorce, body and soul. To retrieve the soul is to restore the body which, until then, is like a zombi, as we saw earlier. Whatever is removed from the body is physical; but whether it is produced by conjuring or by magic, it is not literal – it is a daimonic object which does not so much represent the disease as concretely embody it. There is no question, as Western wiseguys claim, of fraud – the shaman's duplicity is that of the Trickster and the actor, not that of the con-man.

The nearest equivalent we have to the shaman's Otherworld journey to retrieve lost souls, is psychoanalysis and its descendants. Jung's psychology was forged out of his battle with what he thought was a psychosis, but which, when he surrendered to it, turned out to be a 'divine madness' which cast him down into the Underworld where he encountered both his personal myth and the myth of our times.[9]

Although Freud never encountered the collective unconscious in so striking a way, even he had a *nekyia* – a descent to the Underworld – of a kind: his book on dreams. He called it a reaction to his father's death – the most important event, and loss, of his life. The book was not only a venture into the forbidden Underworld of dreams (albeit expressed in the language of rational science), but an expression of the initiatory experience of loss which had connected him to death.[10]

If modern psychology is therefore founded on myths of descent into the Underworld, it ought to resemble shamanism. At first sight this does not appear to be the case. We picture the patient on the couch and the silent analyst in the private room. Then we picture the shaman treating his patient in the midst of the whole community or, at least, as many as will fit into the hut or tent. There is music, singing, perhaps dancing and, above all, an intense audience participation, even to the point where members of the audience themselves become possessed by spirits.[11] In the course of his performance the shaman generally re-enacts the events that constituted his 'call', and describes his Otherworld journey. More than this, he relives it in all its immediacy. But then, so to a large extent do his patient and the audience, who are embraced by the story, dramatized as it is by songs, percussion and the voices of the daimons ringing out of the shadows cast by firelight.

This reliving of past events in all their vividness and violence is, we remember, what psychoanalysts call 'abreaction' – the decisive moment in the treatment when patients resurrect the original event from which their disturbance stems. In psychoanalysis, then, the patient is active and talks and abreacts, while the analyst is passive, listens and does not abreact.[12] In shamanism it is the other way round: the patient is passive, listens and abreacts, if at all, by proxy. The shaman is active, talks (chants, sings) and 'abreacts'. He makes the otherworld journey on the patient's behalf, while in psychoanalysis patients make it on their own behalf.

Moreover, they travel through a personal Otherworld and construct from within an individual myth out of personal history. Shamanism turns this around: it is the shaman who travels through the impersonal Otherworld, the topography of the tribe's mythology, and gives to patients from outside a collective myth which is, by definition, beyond their personal history. Analysands are first integrated with themselves, and so become ready to join society; the shaman's patients are integrated into the group, and so become themselves again.[13] So we see that psychoanalysis and shamanism are not as different as they seem, but are, like myths, sort of symmetrical and inverted versions of each other.

Psychotherapy is an art of double vision, which sees the metaphor in a patient's literal story, the myth behind his history. It tries to dissolve the blocks and fixities in the patient's psyche, to re-imagine the traumas that can only be seen in one way; and this means guiding the patient towards seeing through the literalisms which are preventing the free flow of imagination. Once the psyche is unblocked (once the soul is freed from its imprisonment by hostile daimons, a shaman might say), the patient can find a way back to his own deepest self (his soul can be retrieved). He is not necessarily cured because his deepest self might lie in sickness or madness. They might be his vocation.

The weakness of psychotherapy is its personalism – it does not connect the patient to myths beyond his personal history; and, secondly, its individualism – it does not connect the patient to the tribe. It has been argued, with justice, that psychotherapy ultimately encourages self-centredness: we sit in little rooms 'dealing with' our rage when, by rights, we should be turning it into righteous *out*rage against society's ills.[14] It is about me-me-my soul, while it should be about the Soul of the World. Thus, while the worthiest souls come to terms with themselves, the world goes to the dogs.

35

The Waste Land

LOSS OF SOUL

The primary cause of illness in traditional societies is 'loss of soul'. Here, the word 'soul' refers to what we think of as our sense of ourselves, our ability to say 'I'. It refers to what we call the ego. But it is nothing like our rational ego – if anything it is pretty much the opposite of it. In traditional cultures the ego is a soul, an ego-soul or daimonic ego. It is far more fluid and vulnerable than our ego. It is a soul that can wander off; or be violently abducted; or be lured away by an erotic attraction for a fairy or mermaid, such as those who live at the bottom of the Amazon, and hold the souls of fishermen in the Otherworld.[1]

Loss of soul can even be fatal. The *British Medical Journal* for 1965 reported several cases of death by hex, or witchcraft, in Africa. There is never any obvious medical cause of death – the victims claim that their souls have been stolen or lost, and they simply lie down and die. Post-mortem examinations show that the adrenal glands are drained, pointing to a massive release of adrenalin – through fear, perhaps – followed by a critical drop in blood pressure, followed by death. If the victims of witchcraft do not die, they are nevertheless reduced, we recall, to the condition of the 'living dead'. They are 'away', as the Irish say. The remaining body is a 'log'; or the 'likeness of a body'; or a zombi.

Westerners are not so prone to loss of soul in this sense. Our egos are not at all fluid and vulnerable; nor are they susceptible to getting lost in the Otherworld. Our problem is the reverse: we lose the Otherworld. We do not lose the ego-soul of traditional cultures, but soul[2] – the realm of soul, the unconscious, anima, our personal daimon, our own deepest self. We lose the dimension of imagination which gives depth, colour, connection and meaning to our lives. In extreme cases we suffer from a condition which psychology calls depersonalization.

William James, in his book on varieties of religious experience, wrote that the principle which transfigures the world during mystical experiences is the same principle which operates in depersonalization – but as it were in reverse.[3] Depersonalization is not, in other words, a medical condition. It is like a vision – but one in which the world becomes 'weary, stale, flat, and unprofitable',[4] as Hamlet perceives it. Such a vision seems to have been an inevitable accompaniment to the *via negativa*. The Desert Fathers' wilful denial of soul and its images brought on a state called *acedia*, or accidie, a kind of apathy they often described in terms of spiritual dryness. It was like St John of the Cross's Dark Night of the Soul, when the supplicant feels the remoteness of God and the waste of the world.

The depersonalized individual no longer recognizes himself as a personality. He observes his own actions as if from outside, an onlooker to himself. He is not depressed exactly; rather, he suffers from that deadness, emptiness, apathy and sense of monotony[5] for which dryness is the most apt metaphor. Loss of soul is also loss of world-soul, so that he is not only estranged from himself, but also from the world, which seems alien and unreal. It is flat, lacking the three-dimensionality that double vision imparts; and it is dead, lacking the imagination that would animate it.

Depersonalization is a kind of despair, and more common perhaps than we suspect. The reason why chronic sufferers do not, like hexed Africans, lie down and die is, I suppose, owing to the very strength of the ego and its engines which keep our machinery on its feet and drive it through its routines. We feel like automatons operated by invisible powers; and this is analogous to the reverse feeling that we are part of a larger pattern, in the hands of the gods, and our lives are deep and meaningful rather than superficial and meaningless. Thus, paradoxically, nothing gives us a stronger demonstration of soul's autonomy than depersonalization because it convinces us that our own self-important egos are personifications whose reality depends on something other than our consciousness, will or reason.[6]

Depersonalization can be seen as the logical goal of the soul-destroying, depersonifying, anti-daimonic rational ego which wants to turn us all, like poor Darwin, into 'machines for grinding out facts'. Because it takes away our ability to personify, it turns soul into an abyss of deep space, unmediated by the personified images I call daimons. At the same time it deprives the world of depth, rendering it flat and without perspective. The chilling thing is that this is exactly the universe which cosmologists hold up to us as being the case. The world of depersonalization is the world of scientism – whose refusal of initiation and denial of death, whose maintenance of the rational ego at all costs, leads us into an empty and soulless dystopia. I am struck by a pang of fear that I am, Westerners may be, so far depersonalized as a matter of course that we are only half alive. I wonder whether we have even an inkling of how our lives might be if our momentary contacts with the Soul of the World – those little flashes of truth and beauty – were to become as continuous as the air we breathe.

THE HOLY GRAIL

It is no coincidence that the poem hailed as the first great modern poem – T. S. Eliot's *The Waste Land* (1922) – is precisely about the crisis characteristic of the twentieth century: loss of soul. Or, as Ted Hughes puts it in *Winter Pollen*, 'the convulsive desacralization of the spirit of the West'.[7]

The poem describes the aftermath of the catastrophe which Shakespeare had tried to avert by dramatizing the consequences of exalting the new rational puritan ego at the expense of soul. Born out of 'both the depression and the violent collapse of ego'[8] which Eliot like a shaman had suffered, *The Waste Land* depicts an 'unreal' urban world whose inhabitants are anxious, empty, indifferent and rather sordid. The figure of Tiresias, the blind androgynous seer of Greek myth, moves in the background, acting as our conductor through modernity and out into the desert where there 'is no water but only rock' and 'dry sterile thunder without rain'.[9] There is almost no possibility of poetry any more, only odd quotations from past poetry whose riches lie scattered through *The Waste Land* like glittering shards in the dust.

E. M. Forster remarks somewhere that the poem is about 'the failure of the regenerating waters to arrive'. And what are these waters? They are the waters which will return fertility to the Waste Land. The title is a deliberate echo of Arthurian myth, in which the incurably wounded King presides over a barren land, a perpetual winter. It can only be revitalized by the Holy Grail – which will provide the waters, not in the literal sense of fertility, but in the spiritual sense. The Holy Grail is the Soul of the World. Its fertility is the superabundant generation of all imaginative life.

Thus the myth of Demeter and the Kore, which I mentioned earlier as being paradigmatic of the individual soul's initiation, is also a myth about the loss of the world-soul. Demeter lays waste to the world, forbidding the trees to fruit and the crops to grow, because she is so angry at Zeus for allowing his brother Hades to take her daughter. Nor will she restore the world until the Kore is returned. But the return of the Kore is precisely the restoration of the world-soul. The fact that she eats some pomegranate seeds and is thereby forced to remain in the Underworld for three months every year is not simply a myth about the origins of winter – it is also a metaphor for the way that natural life, the green growing life of Demeter, is always connected to Hades, to death, through soul.

Without soul, without imagination and its daimons, the world is laid waste. And this is what Eliot fears has happened to the modern world. *The Waste Land* implies what William Blake foresaw: that 'the apocalypse that kills the soul of the world is not at the end of time, not coming, but apocalypse now; and Newton and Locke, Descartes and Kant are its horsemen'.[10]

At the turn of the twentieth century, the soul that had been so long estranged by materialism and rationalism signalled its return through the physical symptoms which Freud observed in the neuroses of his patients. Ever since, we have confused soul with the place where it was rediscovered – as if our lost soul could only be regained in psychotherapy. Moreover, we have tended as a result to locate soul, now called the unconscious, exclusively within individuals. We have forgotten that soul is in everything and that everything is in soul, and that soul is as much collective and impersonal as individual and personal. We have neglected

Anima Mundi – which now, at the beginning of the twenty-first century, cries out for our care and attention with physical symptoms analogous to the ones psychoanalysis noticed in individuals.

Everything we once cherished as the basis of life, everything we could always turn to if all else failed, has seemingly turned against us: air, sunlight, rainfall – they are all polluted, carcinogenic, acid, harbouring poisons. Part of the pollution is the way that, even if literal pollution is not certain, we feel it to be so. Paranoia is a way of life, as we sense attack from unseen agents all around us – germs, viruses, invisible 'rays' (such as microwaves) in the air and even poisons in food full of putative pesticides and chemicals and dangerous genetic modifications.

This paranoid sense of the world conspiring against us is also, of course, a symptom of the world reviving. We have declared it dead for so long that when it comes back to life, ensouled and animated as of old, it comes back apparently as death itself. The outcast daimons return as the vengeful demons of lethal pathological symptoms.

If we wish to reinstate the Soul of the World in her original glory, we will have to do more than introduce environmental remedies, which, however well-meaning, tend to stand at an equal and opposite pole – that is, to be as literalistic as the damage we do. We have to cultivate a new perspective, or seeing through; and a sense of metaphor, a seeing double. We may even, if we are to shift our obdurate literalism, have to let in a bit of madness, give ourselves up to a spot of ecstasy. We can always make a start by trying to develop a better aesthetic sense, an appreciation of beauty, which is the first attribute of soul. For the way we see the world can restore its soul, and the way the world is ensouled can restore our vision.

If, on the other hand, we continue to ignore the gods and daimons, and to live behind the barricades of the heroic rational ego, we know what will happen. We know what will happen because we know what happened, and is always happening, to Heracles who embodies above all that perspective; and I append his story here, well-known though it is, by way of a final, and cautionary, tale.

THE SHIRT OF NESSUS

Heracles' wife, Deianeira, is unhappy at her husband's neglect of her. When he asks her to weave him a special shirt to be worn at a sacrifice, she sees her opportunity to recapture his interest. For she has a love-potion, given to her by a centaur called Nessus and made out of his blood. She dips the shirt in the potion and sends it off.

As is often the case with the wives of heroes, Deianeira represents Heracles' soul. Like all our souls, she is constant and goes on loving, no matter how we neglect her, or whether we even know it or not. But if we are dead set on denying her, her love can only reach us in a distorted, even a destructive, form.

Nessus' blood in which the shirt is dipped is, unknown to Deianeira, not a love-potion but a poison; for Nessus the centaur is a vengeful daimon whose comrades Heracles has (as part of his war on all daimons) killed. One version of the myth tells us that Nessus' blood is poisonous because he was shot and wounded by one of Heracles' poisoned arrows in the past. This has a poetic truth and justice because it is Heracles himself who has really poisoned love. Poison is sometimes the only way love can reach us. It is a metaphor for the corrosive force love is perceived to be by the impervious Heraclean ego – which, if it will not die to itself, must finally consume itself. And so, Heracles puts on the shirt and, insane with agony, tears himself to pieces.

Epilogue

And what of the Philosophers' secret fire? The aim of a secret is to evoke a sense of mystery, to mobilize all our faculties and to put us on our mettle. It lures us on, even deceives us into embarking on a prospective quest whose ordeals would otherwise deter us. We set out in search of the hidden knowledge and power we believe the secret will confer – only to find on the way that these things are images of a wisdom and glory we did not dream of in the beginning.

The secret I have tried to reveal on every other page of this book is in a sense no secret – it is an open secret passed along a Golden Chain of initiates, like the secret of the Greek Mysteries. 'And as to the philosophy, by whose assistance these mysteries are developed', Thomas Taylor assures us,[1] 'it is coeval with the universe itself; and however its continuity may be broken by opposing systems, it will make its appearance at different periods of time, as long as the sun himself shall continue to illuminate the world.'

To reveal a secret is self-defeating because its power depends on the silence and darkness in which it incubates and grows until it permeates our entire being, and we find ourselves transmuted. Thus, although I may uncover the secret fire, the secret of the secret fire remains a matter for one's self.

References

Further details of referenced authors are in the 'Selected Bibliography'.

Abbreviations

CW: Collected Works;
frg.: fragment

Prologue

1. Quoted in Taylor, p. 89

1 *Shape-Shifters*

1. Ellis Davidson (1989), p. 133
2. Ibid., p. 137
3. Gregory (1976A), pp. 9–10
4. See Hutton, pp. 124–5
5. Kirk, pp. 31–2
6. Dodds (1965), pp. 37–8
7. Hutton, p. 202
8. Ibid.
9. Medhurst, p. 4
10. Ibid.
11. Ibid., p. 12

12. Campbell (1988), p. 74
13. Ibid.
14. Lévi-Strauss (1972), p. 37
15. Williams, Noel, 'The Semantics of the Word *Fairy*: Making Meaning out of Thin Air' in Narváez, p. 458
16. Ibid., p. 465
17. Plato (1970), XI, 3
18. Quoted in Gregory (1976A), p. 338
19. Medhurst, p. 12
20. I Corinthians 10–20
21. See Chaucer, Geoffrey, 'The Tale of the Wife of Bath', lines 8–18
22. Quoted in Dodds (1965), p. 37
23. Dodds (1965), pp. 53–4
24. Jung (1967), pp. 208–9
25. Ibid.
26. Evans-Wentz, p. 47
27. Bord, pp. 62–3
28. Evans-Wentz, pp. 208–9

29. *Transactions of the Devonshire Association*, vol. 60, pp. 116–7
30. McManus, pp. 45–6
31. Ibid.
32. Larsen, pp. 77–8
33. Bord, pp. 60–61
34. Hansen, Kim, 'UFO Casebook', in Evans and Spencer, pp. 75–9
35. Ibid.
36. See, for example, Hopkins (1988A and 1988B); and Strieber

Shadows on Stone (RCA Records, 1996)
20. Lévy-Bruhl, op. cit., p. 41
21. See Barley (1983)
22. Picard, pp. 194f
23. Quoted in Lévi-Strauss (1969), p. 37
24. See Gregory (1976B)
25. Hughes (1994), p. 268
26. Jung (1967), p. 390
27. Yeats (1959), p. 335
28. Cf. Halifax, op. cit., p. 120
29. Vitebsky, p. 93

2 The Seal-Woman's Skin

1. Evans-Wentz, p. 218
2. Lévy-Bruhl (1965), pp. 234–5
3. Ibid., p. 299
4. Gregory (1976A), p. 9
5. Lévy-Bruhl, op. cit., p. 278
6. Halifax (1991), p. 122
7. Homer, *Odyssey*, Book XI
8. Medhurst, p. 29
9. Ibid., p. 37
10. Ibid., p. 37
11. Rojcewicz, p. 490
12. Briggs, pp. 131–2
13. Lévy-Bruhl, op. cit., p. 299
14. Ibid., p. 45
15. Ibid., p. 286
16. Ibid., pp. 158–9
17. Ibid., p. 170
18. Graves, vol. 2, p. 274
19. Quoted by Merrily Harpur, album notes to Matt Molloy's

3 Concerning Zombis

1. Intro. to Kirk, The Reverend Robert
2. Bennett, Margaret, 'Balquidder Revisited: Fairylore in the Scottish Highlands 1690–1990', in Narváez, pp. 98f
3. Ibid.
4. Quoted by Bord, pp. 62–3
5. Narváez, Peter, 'Newfoundland Berry Pickers "In the Fairies"', in Narváez, pp. 357–8
6. Evans-Wentz, p. 73
7. Narváez, op. cit., pp. 345–6
8. Ibid., pp. 347–8
9. Ibid., pp. 348–9
10. Gregory (1976A), pp. 9–10
11. See Cohn, Chapter I
12. Needham (1978), pt 2, 'Synthetic Images'

13. Gregory, op. cit., pp. 9–10
14. Ibid.
15. Ibid., p. 11
16. Quoted in ibid., p. 364
17. Cf. Hopkins (1988A and 1988B)
18. This discussion is taken from Littlewood, R., and Douyon, C., 'Clinical findings in three cases of zombification', *Lancet*, 11 Oct. 1997, [350 (99084): 1094–6]. It also draws on 'To the Ends of the Earth: Interview with a Zombie', a TV programme made by the authors, Channel 4, 20 April 1997
19. Ibid.
20. Ibid.
21. Ibid.
22. Lévy-Bruhl (1965), pp. 170–71
23. Ibid., p. 267

11. See *Eyrbyggja Saga*, quoted in Ellis Davidson (1989), p. 134
12. Gregory (1976A), pp. 9–10
13. Metzner, pp. 200–201
14. Lévy-Bruhl, pp. 301–2
15. Ibid.
16. Ibid., p. 304
17. Ibid., pp. 303–4
18. *Odyssey*, Book XI
19. Blake, p. 150
20. 'Finscéalta agus Litríocht', in *Béaloideas* (1992–3)
21. Ibid., p. 122
22. Ibid., p. 124
23. Onians, p. 100
24. 'Under Sirius' in Auden (1971), p. 245
25. Heraclitus, frg. 15, quoted in Hillman (1979), p. 44
26. For example, Plotinus, I, i, 9
27. Blake, p. 154
28. Plato (1970), Book VII

4 St Patrick's Purgatory

1. Curtayne, p. 79
2. Ibid., p. 99
3. Zaleski, p. 36
4. Hopkin, pp. 87–9
5. Zaleski, p. 77
6. Curtayne, p. 45
7. Ibid., p. 44
8. Zaleski, *passim*
9. McManus, p. 99
10. ibid., p. 100

5 The Soul of the World

1. Alderson Smith, p. 179
2. Coleridge, p. 167
3. Auden (1963), pp. 54–5
4. Blake, p. 605
5. The expression is repeated from Thales to Proclus's *On the Sacred Art*
6. Blake, p. 793
7. Jung (1967), pp. 199–205
8. Jung, *CW* 5, para. 388

9. Proclus's commentary on Plato's *Republic*, quoted in Raine and Harper, p. 376

10. Hillman (1975), p. 151

11. Hillman (1979), p. 23

12. Jung (1967), pp. 182–3

13. Hillman (1975), p. 104

14. Hillman (1979), p. 134

15. Heraclitus, frg. 45

16. Hillman (1975), p. x

17. Ibid., p. 23

18. Hillman (1979), p. 12

19. Ibid.

20. Ibid., p. 55

21. Ibid., p. 124

22. Ibid., p. 127 (his italics)

23. Ibid.

24. *De Anima*, 47, 2, quoted in Dodds (1965), pp. 46–7

25. Hillman (1979), pp. 61–2

26. Dodds (1952), p. 109

27. Hillman (1979), pp. 60–61

28. Ibid., p. 99

6 *Inside Out*

1. Trans. and quoted in Dodds (1965), p. 37

2. Dodds (1952), pp. 104–5

3. Ibid., p. 41

4. Jung, *CW* 14, para. 410

5. Jung, *CW*, 9, I, para. 291; cf. *CW* 10, para 13

6. Murdoch (1978), p. 50

7. Jung, *CW* 13, para. 75

8. Whyte, p. 27

9. Plotinus, IV, 4, 4, quoted in Hillman (1986), p. 183

10. Dodds, E. R., 'Tradition and Personal Achievement in the Philosophy of Plotinus', in *The Ancient Concept of Progress and Other Essays*, (Oxford, 1973), p. 135, quoted in Hillman (1986), pp. 150–51

11. Descartes, 2, 4

12. Rojcewicz, p. 496

13. Wordsworth, p. 149

14. 'A Vision of the Last Judgement', in Blake, p. 617

15. 'The Everlasting Gospel', ('d' version) lines 103–6, in Blake, p. 753

16. Poem in a letter to Thomas Butts, 22 Nov. 1802, lines 27–30, in Blake, p. 817

17. Auden (1963), p. 438

18. Quoted in Midgley (1992), p. 59

19. Ibid., p. 37

20. Dawkins, p. 1

21. Hawking, p. 13

22. Midgley (1991), pp. 48–9

7 *Matter and Spirits*

1. Midgley (1992), p. 77 (my italics)

2. Hillman (1979), p. 69

3. Ibid., p. 71

4. Desmond and Moore, p. 526
5. Ibid., pp. 607–8
6. Crookes, pp. 7–26
7. Davies and Gribbin, p. 210
8. Davies, p. 102
9. Davies and Gribbin, p. 136
10. Ibid., p. 139
11. Ibid., p. 249
12. Ibid., p. 250
13. Malcolm, pp. 313–23
14. Davies and Gribbin, p. 15
15, Quoted in Davies, p. 219
16. For example, Jones

8 *'How Natives Think'*

1. Needham (1980), Chapter 2
2. Ibid., cf. Needham (1981), I
3. Poole, Roger C., Intro. to Lévi-Strauss (1969), p. 22
4. Trans. Lilian A. Clare, London, 1926
5. Jung, *CW* 8, para. 329
6. Cf. ibid.; ibid., para. 127
7. Lévi-Strauss (1969), pp. 83f
8. Lévy-Bruhl (1965), p. 283
9. Lévi-Strauss (1972), p. 263
10. Lévy-Bruhl, Lucien, *La Mentalité Primitive* (The Hubert Spencer Lecture, 1931), quoted in Avens, p. 25
11. Evans-Pritchard, E. E., *The Theories of Primitive Religion* (Oxford, 1965), pp. 86–92, quoted in Avens, p. 26

12. Tillyard, p. 38
13. Ibid., p. 44
14. Ibid., p. 103
15. III, 1, 10
16. Lewis, C. S., p. 122
17. Ibid.
18. Lévi-Strauss (1969), p. 162

9 *The Daimons' Tales*

1. Yeats (1961), p. 107
2. Lévi-Strauss (1970), p. 12. The translation is from *Yale French Studies* (1966; New York, 1970)
3. Hughes (1994), p. 41
4. Harpur (1994), pp. 272f
5. Hillman (1975), p. 130
6. Ibid., p. 132
7. Ibid., p. 163
8. López-Pedraza, *passim*
9. Needham (1978), p. 55
10. Kirk, G. S., p. 19
11. Ibid., pp. 71–2; cf. Needham (1978), p. 64
12, See Leach, pp. 72–4
13. Lévi-Strauss (1970), p. 13
14. Hughes (1994), p. 152
15. Lévi-Strauss (1977), p. 209
16. Fordham, p. 178
17. Hillman (1979), p. 148
18. Lévi-Strauss (1970), p. 240

10 The Hero and the Virgin

1. Tertullian actually said: 'The Son of God died; it is by all means to be believed, because it is absurd. And he was buried, and rose again; the fact is certain because it is impossible.'
2. Sallust, *Of Gods and the World*, quoted in Hillman (1979), p. 182
3. Eliade (1989B), pp. 40f
4. Ibid., p. 34
5. Hughes (1994), p. 152
6. Tarnas, p. 319
7. Lienhardt, G., 'Modes of Thought' in *The Institution of Primitive Society* (Oxford, 1959), p. 49
8. Barfield, pp. 73–4
9. Ibid., p. 75
10. See Auden, W. H., Introduction to *Shakespeare's Sonnets* (New York, 1964)
11. Murdoch (1978), p. 79
12. Quoted in Barfield, p. 128

11 Rites of Passage

1. Meade, Michael, Foreword to Eliade (1995), pp. xxiii–iv
2. Halifax (1991), pp. 70–7
3. Eliade (1995), p. 31
4. Ibid; cf. Lévy-Bruhl (1965), p. 214
5. Meade, op. cit., pp. x–xiii
6. Eliade (1995), p. 129
7. van Gennep, Arnold, *Les Rites de Passage* (1909)
8. Barley (1986), p. 103
9. Ibid.
10. See Barley (1983), final chapter
11. Lévi-Strauss (1970), pp. 336–8
12. Eliade (1989A), pp. 35–8, 158f
13. Meade, op. cit., pp. xxii–iv

12 The Animals Who Stared Darwin in the Face

1. Desmond and Moore, p. 188
2. Wilson, p. 136
3. Desmond and Moore, p. 122
4. Sheldrake, pp. 55–6
5. Ibid.
6. Desmond and Moore, p. 119
7. Wilson, p. 136
8. Ibid., p. 141
9. Wilson, p. 134; Desmond and Moore, p. 187
10. Wilson, p. 135
11. Desmond and Moore, p. xvi
12. Ibid., p. 191
13. Ibid., p. 261
14. Ibid., pp. 635–6
15. Ibid., p. 251

16. Wilson, p. 136
17. Desmond and Moore, p. 283
18. Milton, pp. 156–9
19. Ibid.
20. By Sir Gavin de Beer
21. Quoted in Milton, p. 156
22. cf. Milton, p. 149
23. Desmond and Moore, p. xix
24. Wilson, p. 133
25. Desmond and Moore, p. 631
26. Wilson, p. 132

13 The Transmutation
of Species

1. In *New Statesman and Society*,
28 Aug. 1992
2. Milton, p. 15
3. For example, Desmond and
Moore, pp. 40, 186
4. Milton, p. 297
5. Ibid., pp. 123–4
6. Ibid., p. 128
7. Ibid., p. 130
8. Michell, John, 'When Feathers
Fly: A Case of Fossil Forgery?' in
Fortean Times 52 (1989), p. 47
9. Ibid.
10. Ibid., p. 49
11. Cf. Milton, p. 130
12. Wallis, p. 131
13. For example, in Plato's
Timaeus, 35A
14. Sheldrake, p. 55
15. Quoted ibid., pp. 56–7

16. Hillman (1975), p. 124
17. Ibid.
18. Midgley (1985), p. 6
19. Desmond and Moore, p. 378
20. Ibid., p. 526
21. 'The Marriage of Heaven and
Hell' in Blake, p. 151
22. Plato (1970), *The Republic*,
11, 3
23. Barfield, p. 64
24. Midgley (1991), p. 202
25. For a detailed discussion of
this, see Harpur (1994),
pp. 40–43
26. Quoted in Sheldrake, p. 80
27. Quoted in Midgley (1985),
p. 123
28. Quoted in ibid.
29. Quoted in Lewontin, p. 13
30. Ibid.
31. Ibid., p. 100

14 The Composition of
the Magi

1. Yates (1964), p. 1
2. Quoted in French, p. 94
3. Walker, pp. 75–6
4. Ibid., p. 82
5. Yates (1964), p. 8
6. Ibid., p. 66
7. Walker, pp. 82–3
8. Burckhardt, pp. 350–1
9. Quoted in Hillman (1986),
p. 155

10. Ibid.
11. Ibid., pp. 155–6
12. Augustine, St, X, 8
13. Hillman (1975), p. 196
14. Letter to George and Georgiana Keats, 21 April 1819, in Keats, p. 336
15. Hillman (1975), p. 194
16. Quoted in Tarnas, pp. 214–5
17. Ibid.
18. Yates (1964), p. 116
19. Yates (1983), p. 25
20. Scholem, p. 40
21. Yates (1964), p. 92
22. Hughes (1992), p. 21
23. Scholem, pp. 100, 135. See also Scholem, G., *On the Kabbalah and its Symbolism, passim*
24. Ibid., p. 100
25. Ibid., p. 17
26. Murdoch (1993), p. 185
27. Ibid., p. 187
28. Ibid., p. 198
29. For example, by Hughes (1992), pp. 19f

8. Ibid.
9. Quoted in Hughes (1992), pp. 22–3
10. Cf. Fideler, David, review of Antoine Faivre in *Alexandria* 2, p. 396
11. Cf. Yates (1964), p. 151
12. Ibid., p. 244
13. Tarnas, p. 295
14. French, p. 162
15. See Rossi, pp. 1–35
16. Yates (1964), p. 147
17. Tarnas, p. 293
18. French, p. 94
19. Yates (1964), pp. 440–41
20. French, p. 164
21. Yates (1964), p. 149
22. Cf. Lewis, C. S., p. 138
23. Yates (1964), p. 92–3
24. Ibid., p. 435
25. Ibid.
26. Ibid., p. 436
27. Hillman (1975), p. 4
28. Ibid., p. 5

15 *Conjuring Angels*

16 *The Boar from the Underworld*

1. French, p. 5
2. Ibid., p. 6
3. Hughes (1992), p. 22
4. Quoted in French, p. 129
5. Yates (1964), p. 258
6. Ibid., p. 265
7. Ibid., p. 266

1. Hughes (1992), pp. 74–5
2. Ibid., p. 75
3. Hughes (1994), pp. 109–10
4. Hughes (1992), pp. 86–7
5. Ibid., p. 88
6. Ibid., p. 89
7. Lines 701–2

8. Line 719
9. Hughes (1992), p. 83
10. Ibid.
11. Yates (1983), pp. 156, 160
12. Hughes (1994), p. 118

17 *Mercurius*

1. See Acherjee, Joyanta, 'Red for Danger' in *Fortean Times* 127, October 1999
2. Sieveking, Paul, 'Deadly Alchemy' in *Fortean Times* 69, June/July 1993, pp. 44–5
3. 'The Pocket Neutron Bomb', *Dispatches*, TV Channel 4, 13 April 1994
4. Jung (1967), p. 230
5. Ibid., p. 231
6. Ibid., p. 235
7. Ibid.
8. See *Nicholas Flamel, His Exposition of the Hieroglyphicall Figures, which he caused to be painted upon an arch in St Innocent's churchyard in Paris*, trans. Eirenaeus Orandus (London 1624), quoted in Harpur (1990), pp. 428–30
9. Quoted in Harpur (1990), p. 461
10. Ibid.
11. Ibid., p. 296
12. *Gloria Mundi* (1526), quoted in Harpur (1990), p. 13

13. Ibid.
14. Ibid., pp. 49–50
15. Taylor, pp. 77–8
16. Yates (1964), p. 150
17. Quoted in Harpur (1990), p. 132
18. Ibid., pp. 132–3
19. Ibid.
20. Jung, *CW* 12, para. 375
21. Ibid., para. 394
22. Ibid.
23. Ibid., para. 396
24. Ibid., para. 394
25. Quoted in Nicholl, p. 29
26. Ibid.
27. Cf. Hillman (1975), p. 137
28. See Waite, A. E., *The Hermetic Museum Restored and Enlarged* (London, 1893), 2 vols., quoted in Nicholl, pp. 94f
29. Medhurst, pp. 16–17
30. See Valentinus, Basilius, *Practica una cum duodecim clavibus . . .* [The Twelve Keys] in *Musaeum Hermeticum* (Frankfurt, 1678), X, pp. 403f. Also quoted in Jung *CW* 12, para. 444
31. I, 4, 10; IV, 3, 29, quoted in Hillman (1986), pp. 151–2
32. See chapter on Heraclitus in Kirk and Raven
33. Quoted in Raine, p. 118

18 The Philosophers' Retorts

1. Sheldrake, p. 69
2. Ibid , p 70
3. Jung, *CW* 12, para. 394
4. Quoted in Dobbs
5. Ibid.
6. Quoted in Jung, *CW* 12, para. 378
7. Trans. W. Cooper (London, 1673)
8. Quoted in Harpur (1990), p. 473
9. Ibid.

19 The Cosmos and the Universe

1. Fideler, David, 'Cosmology, Ethics and the Practice of Relatedness . . .' in *Alexandria* 4, 1997, p. 103
2. Quoted ibid.
3. Yates (1964), p. 154
4. Barfield, pp. 49–50
5. *De Caelo*, 279A
6. Cf. Tillyard, pp. 55–6
7. Quoted in Barratt, p. 8
8. Gribbin, p. 76
9. Davies, p. 116
10. Malcolm, p. 384
11. Davies, p. 159
12. Davies and Gribbin, p. 161
13. Yates (1964), p. 93

14. Davies and Gribbin, p. 167
15. Ibid.
16. Sheldrake, p. 74
17. See Overbye, Dennis, 'The Shadow Universe' in *Discover*, May 1985: 13, quoted by Stillings, pp. 17–18

20 The Weight of the World

1. Quoted in Midgley (1985), p. 2
2. Weinberg, Steven, *The First Three Minutes; A Modern View of the Origin of the Universe* (London, 1977), p. 155, quoted ibid., p. 75
3. Hillman (1975), p. xiv
4. Ibid.
5. See Hughes (1992), pp. 351f
6. Quoted in Sheldrake, p. 62
7. Ibid.
8. Kuhn, p. 163
9. Midgley (1992), pp. 81–3
10. Sheldrake, pp. 63–4
11. Plotinus, IV, 3, 9
12. Fideler, David, 'Neo-platonism and the Cosmological Revolution: Holism, Fractal Geometry, and Mind in Nature', in *Alexandria* 4, p. 145
13. Davies and Gribbin, p. 302
14. Davies, p. 210
15. Ibid.
16. Midgley (1992), p. 123

21 Fafnir's Blood

1. Dubos, René, *The God Within* (New York, 1973), p. 264
2. Hillman (1979), pp. 110–117
3. Harpur (1994), p. 268
4. Hillman (1979), p. 115
5. Graves, vol. 2, p. 280
6. Metzner, p. 127
7. Ibid., pp. 127–8

22 The Myths of Machinery

1. Midgley (1992), pp. 12–13
2. Lévi-Strauss (1978), p. 319
3. Ibid.
4. Ibid., p. 322
5. Ibid., p. 321
6. Ibid., p. 317
7. Stillings, Dennis, 'Electricity, Alchemy and the Unconscious', in *Artifex* 10, pp. 29f
8. Murdoch (1978), p. 5
9. Ibid.
10. Ibid., p. 65
11. Halifax (1991), p. 158
12. Quoted in Stillings, Dennis, 'Helicopters, UFOs, and the Psyche' in *ReVision: the Journal of Consciousness and Change* 11, 4, Spring 1989, p. 25
13. Ibid., p. 26
14. Picard, pp. 163f

23 The Invention of Walking

1. Holmes, p. 148
2. Ibid., p. 38
3. Coleridge, p. 87
4. Ibid. Also Holmes, p. 120
5. Holmes, p. 149
6. Ibid., pp. 149–50
7. Ibid.
8. Raine, p. 265
9. Ibid.
10. Coleridge, p. 167
11. Ibid.
12. Auden (1963), pp. 54f
13. Quoted ibid., p. 55
14. Ibid., pp. 56–7
15. Sutherland, p. 3
16. Ibid., p. 2
17. Ibid.
18. See Harpur (1994), p. 62
19. Holmes, p. 60
20. Quoted in 'Rousseau', The Open University, BBC TV 2, 12 Aug. 1996
21. Holmes, p. 66
22. Quoted in Sheldrake, p. 51

24 The Romantic Philosophy

1. Introduction to Locke, p. 17
2. Locke, p. 89
3. Warnock, p. 21

4. Tarnas, p. 343
5. Ibid., p. 359
6. Ibid., p. 397
7. Gellner, Ernest, *The Legitimation of Belief* (Cambridge, 1975), pp. 206 7, quoted in Tarnas, pp. 421–2
8. Warnock, p. 30
9. Book I, para. 234, quoted in Warnock, pp. 32–3
10. Ibid.
11. Ibid., p. 30
12. Ibid.
13. Tarnas, p. 433
14. Ibid., p. 434
15. Berlin, p. 42
16. Collins English Dictionary (London, 1982), entry for 'Schelling'
17. Cf. Tarnas, p. 381
18. Warnock, p. 66
19. Ibid., p. 92
20. Ibid., p. 68
21. Quoted in Warnock, p. 84
22. Ibid., pp. 77–8

25 *Boehme and Blake*

1. Urban, Hugh, 'Imago Magia, Virgin Mother of Eternity: Imagination and Phantasy in the Philosophy of Jacob Boehme' in *Alexandria* 2, p. 233
2. Ibid., p. 234
3. Weeks, p. 7

4. Ibid., p. 1
5. Ibid., p. 2
6. Urban, op. cit., p. 236
7. Ibid., p. 237
8. Ibid., pp. 239–40
9. Ibid., p. 248
10. Ibid., p. 244
11. Frye, p. 12
12. Yeats (1961), p. 114
13. Ibid., p. 113
14. Raine, p. xxx
15. Ibid., p. 119
16. Ibid.
17. Yeats (1961), pp. 112–13
18. Frye, p. 85
19. Ibid., p. 13
20. Ibid., p. 14
21. 'A Vision of the Last Judgement', 95, in Blake, p. 617
22. Quoted in Frye, p. 14
23. Cf. ibid., p. 16
24. Cf. ibid., p. 20
25. Letter to Cumberland, 12 April 1827, in Blake, p. 878
26. 'The Marriage of Heaven and Hell', 8, in Blake, p. 151
27. Poem in a letter to Thomas Butts, 22 Nov. 1802, lines 87–8, in Blake, p. 818
28. López-Pedraza, p. 18; cf. Hillman (1979), pp. 180–81

26 *Remembrance of*
Things Past

1. Proust, I, p. 60
2. Ibid., p. 61
3. Ibid.
4. Ibid.
5. Spence, p. 138
6. Yates (1984), pp. 191–2
7. Hillman (1975), p. 92
8. Bettelheim, Bruno, *The Uses of*
Enchantment (London, 1978),
p. 320
9. For a discussion of this, see
Harpur (1994), pp. 226f
10. Cf. Hillman (1975), p. 18
11. Harpur, op. cit., pp. 275f
12. Hillman, op. cit., p. 99

27 *The Still Sad Music*
of Humanity

1. Yeats (1961), p. 79
2. Murdoch (1993), p. 320
3. Wordsworth, p. 164, line 49
4. Ibid., lines 41–9
5. Ibid., lines 89–91
6. Ibid., lines 100–102
7. Proust, I, p. 59

28 *The Desert and the*
Rose Garden

1. Quoted in Underhill, Evelyn,
'The Mystic as Creative Artist' in
Woods, p. 408
2. Ibid.
3. Ibid.
4. Williams, p. 61
5. Ibid., p. 59
6. Ibid., p. 58
7. Cf. Hillman (1975), pp. 67–70
8. Tarnas, p. 19
9. *Phaedrus*, 249b
10. Murdoch (1978), p. 4
11. Miller, p. 27
12. Quoted ibid., p. 75
13. Quoted in Sheldrake, p. 21
14. Wind, p. 133
15. Ibid., p. 218
16. Plotinus, IV, 3, 11f
17. 'The Statues', lines 20–23, in
Yeats (1967), p. 375
18. Wind, p. 19
19. Ibid., pp. 128–9
20. Ibid., p. 200

29 *Syzygies*

1. Burckhardt, p. 305
2. Ibid., p. 297
3. Miller, p. 30
4. *The Tempest*, IV, i, 151–8
5. Ibid., V, i, 311

6. Harpur (1994), p. 266
7. Tarnas, p. 110
8. Raine, pp. 73–4
9. Hillman (1985), pp. 173–8
10. Tarnas, p. 442
11. Ibid., p. 443
12. Ibid.

30 *The Bear that Bites the Heart*

1. Adapted from Vitebsky, pp. 74–5
2. Dodds (1952), p. 72
3. VI, ix, 2
4. Eliade (1989A), pp. 461–2
5. Campbell (1988), pp. 47f
6. Halifax (1982), p. 17
7. Vitebsky, p. 84
8. Ibid., pp. 60–61
9. Halifax (1991), p. 14
10. Eliade, op. cit., pp. 137–8
11. Ibid., p. 65
12. Campbell (1991), pp. 424f
13. Kerenyi, p. 254
14. Ibid., pp. 262–4
15. Halifax (1991), pp. 108–9
16. Ibid., p. 112
17. Ibid., p. 69
18. Ibid., p. 77
19. Ibid., pp. 81–2
20. Ibid., pp. 83–5
21. James, pp. 343–4
22. Ibid., pp. 307f
23. Cox, Michael, *Mysticism; the*

Direct Experience of God (Wellingborough, 1983), p. 114
24. James, p. 310

31 *'The Night-mare Life-in-Death was She'*

1. The thought is Simone Weil's. See her *Notebooks*, 2 vols (London, 1976)
2. Hughes (1994), p. 58
3. Holmes, p. 128
4. Quoted in Hughes, op. cit., p. 412
5. Holmes, p. 140
6. Hughes, op. cit., pp. 422–3
7. Ibid., p. 423
8. Ibid., pp. 425–6
9. Ibid., pp. 427–31
10. Ibid., p. 431
11. Ibid., pp. 431–2

32 *The Myths of Madness*

1. Dodds (1952), pp. 70f
2. See Thomas Taylor's note at the end of his translation of Iamblichus's *On the Mysteries of the Egyptians, Chaldeans and Assyrians* (London, 1821), pp. 350f
3. Quoted in Dodds, op. cit., pp. 81f
4. Ibid.

5. Ibid., p. 76
6. Cobb, Noel, 'Who is behind Archetypal Psychology? An Imaginal Inquiry', *Spring*, 1988, p. 140
7. Graves, I, p. 115. Also Cobb, ibid., p. 151
8. Cobb, op. cit., p. 146
9. Ibid.
10. Guthrie, p. 127
11. Hillman and Ventura, pp. 109–10
12. Ibid.
13. Dodds, op. cit., p. 76
14. Ibid., Appendix I: 'Maenadism'
15. Kerenyi, pp. 260–61
16. Stillings, p. 5

33 *Ungodly Messiahs*

1. Snell, p. 92
2. Hillman (1979), p. 92
3. Hillman (1996), p. 236
4. Ibid., p. 237
5. Ibid.
6. Ibid., p. 234
7. Bullock, p. 370
8. Ibid., pp. 366–7
9. Quoted ibid., p. 370
10. Canetti, p. 515
11. Bullock, p. 378
12. Ibid., pp. 392–3
13. Ibid., p. 384
14. Ibid., pp. 384–5

34 *The Cure of Souls*

1. *On the Soul*, quoted in Eliade, Mircea, *From Primitives to Zen* (London, 1967), p. 302
2. XI, 1–26, quoted ibid., pp. 306f
3. Hillman (1975), p. 208
4. Ibid.
5. Sardello, Robert J., 'The Illusion of Infection: A cultural psychology of AIDS', *Spring*, 1988, p. 20
6. Evans-Pritchard, p. 475
7. Lévi-Strauss (1977), p. 19
8. James Hamilton-Paterson, personal communication, 6 Feb. 1992
9. See Harpur (1994), pp. 290–5
10. Hillman (1979), p. 21
11. Lewis, I. M., p. 53
12. The following analysis was suggested by Lévi-Strauss (1977), pp. 180f
13. Ibid., pp. 198f
14. Hillman and Ventura, p. 11

35 *The Waste Land*

1. Vitebsky, p. 100
2. I discuss these distinctions in detail in Harpur (1994), pp. 257f
3. Cf. Zaleski, p. 201
4. *Hamlet*, I, ii, 133
5. Hillman (1985), pp. 105–7
6. Hillman (1975), p. 49

7. Hughes (1994), p. 271

8. Ibid., p. 273

9. Eliot, p. 76, lines 331, 342

10. Quoted in Hillman, James, 'Anima Mundi: the Return of the Soul to the World', *Spring*, 1982, p. 90

Epilogue

1. Taylor, Thomas, *A Dissertation on the Eleusinian and Bacchic Mysteries* (London, 1790)

Selected Bibliography

Alderson Smith, Peter, *W. B. Yeats and the Tribes of Danu* (Gerrards Cross, Bucks. Eng., 1987)

Alexandria: The Journal of the Western Cosmological Traditions, ed. David Fideler (Phanes Press, PO Box 6114, Grand Rapids, Michigan 49516)

Artifex: The Journal of Archaeus Project, ed. Dennis Stillings (2402 University Avenue, St. Paul, Minnesota 55114)

Auden, W. H., *The Dyer's Hand* (London, 1963)

——*Collected Shorter Poems 1927–1957* (London, 1971)

Augustine, St, *Confessions* (London, 1961)

Avens, Roberts, *Imagination is Reality* (Dallas, 1980)

Barfield, Owen, *Saving the Appearances; A Study in Idolatry* (London, 1957; Wesleyan Univ. Press, 1988)

Barley, Nigel, *Symbolic Structures; An Exploration of the Culture of the Dowayos* (Cambridge, 1983)

——*A Plague of Caterpillars* (London, 1986)

Barratt, William, *Death of the Soul* (Oxford, 1987)

Béaloideas, The Journal of the Folklore of Ireland Society, Department of Modern Irish, Galway University, County Galway, Eire

Berlin, Isaiah, *The Crooked Timber of Humanity; Chapters in the History of Ideas*, ed. Henry Hardy (London, 1990)

Blake, William, *Complete Writings*, ed. Geoffrey Keynes (Oxford, 1966)

Bord, Janet, *Fairies; Real Encounters with Little People* (London, 1997)

Briggs, K. M., *The Fairies in Tradition and Literature* (London, 1967)

Bullock, Alan, *Hitler and Stalin; Parallel Lives* (London, 1993)

Burckhardt, Jacob, *The Civilization of the Renaissance in Italy* (London, 1990)

Campbell, Joseph, *The Hero with a Thousand Faces* (London, 1988)
——*The Masks of God: Primitive Mythology* (London, 1991)
Canetti, Elias, *Crowds and Power* (London, 1984)
Cohn, Norman, *Europe's Inner Demons* (Sussex Univ. Press, 1975)
Coleridge, Samuel Taylor, *Biographia Literaria* (1817; London, 1965)
Crookes, William, *Researches in the Phenomena of Spiritualism* (Manchester, 1926)
Curtayne, Alice, *Lough Derg; St Patrick's Purgatory* (London and Dublin, 1944)
Davies, Paul, *God and the New Physics* (London, 1990)
Davies, Paul, and Gribbin, John, *The Matter Myth* (London, 1992)
Dawkins, Richard, *The Selfish Gene* (London, 1978)
Descartes, *Discourse on Method and Other Writings*, trans. F. E. Sutcliffe (London, 1968)
Desmond, Adrian, and Moore, James, *Darwin* (London, 1992)
Dobbs, B. J. T., *The Foundations of Newton's Alchemy; or 'The Hunting of the Greene Lyon'* (Cambridge, 1975)
Dodds, E. R., *The Greeks and the Irrational* (Berkeley, 1952)
——*Pagan and Christian in an Age of Anxiety* (Cambridge, 1965)
Eliade, Mircea, *Shamanism: Archaic Techniques of Ecstasy*, trans. Willard R. Trask (London, 1989A)
——*The Myth of the Eternal Return; Cosmos and History* (London, 1989B)
——*Rites and Symbols of Initiation* (Woodstock, Connecticut, 1995)
Eliot, T. S., *Collected Poems 1909–1962* (London, 1963)
Ellis Davidson, H. R., *Myths and Symbols in Pagan Europe; Early Scandinavian and Celtic Religions* (Manchester, 1988)
——'Myths and Symbols in Religion and Folklore', in *Folklore*, 1989, ii
Evans, Hilary, and Spencer, John, eds., *UFOs 1947–1987* (London, 1987)
Evans-Pritchard, E. E., *Witchcraft, Oracles and Magic among the Azande* (Oxford, 1937)
Evans-Wentz, W. Y., *The Fairy-Faith in Celtic Countries* (Oxford, 1911; Gerrards Cross, Bucks., Eng. 1977)
Folklore; The Journal of the Folklore Society (University College, Gower St., London WC1 6BT)
Fordham, Michael, *The Objective Psyche* (London, 1958)

Fort, Charles, *The Complete Books of Charles Fort* (New York, 1974)
Fortean Times; The Journal of Strange Phenomena, eds. Bob Rickard and Paul Sieveking (IFG Ltd, 9 Dallington St, London EC1V 0BQ)
French, Peter J., *John Dee; The World of an Elizabethan Magus* (London, 1984)
Frye, Northrop, *Fearful Symmetry; A Study of William Blake* (Princeton Univ. Press, 1969)
Graves, Robert, *The Greek Myths*, 2 vols (London, 1960)
Gregory, Lady Augusta, *Visions and Beliefs in the West of Ireland* (1920; Gerrards Cross, Bucks., Eng. 1976A)
——*Gods and Fighting Men* (1904; Gerrards Cross, Bucks., Eng. 1976B)
Gribbin, John, *Spacewarps* (London, 1983)
Guthrie, W. K. C., *Orpheus and Greek Religion* (Princeton Univ. Press, 1993)
Halifax, Joan, *Shaman; The Wounded Healer* (London, 1982)
——*Shamanic Voices* (London, 1991)
Harpur, Patrick, ed. *The Timetable of Technology* (London, 1982)
——*Mercurius; or, The Marriage of Heaven and Earth* (London, 1990)
——*Daimonic Reality; A Field Guide to the Otherworld* (London and New York, 1994)
——*The Good People* (unpublished novel)
Hawking, Stephen A., *A Brief History of Time* (London, 1988)
Hillman, James, *Revisioning Psychology* (New York, 1975)
——*The Dream and the Underworld* (New York, 1979)
——*Anima; An Anatomy of a Personified Notion* (Dallas, 1985)
——*Loose Ends* (Dallas, 1986)
——*The Soul's Code* (London, 1996)
Hillman, James, and Ventura, Michael, *We've Had a Hundred Years of Psychotherapy – and the World's Getting Worse* (San Francisco, 1992)
Holmes, Richard, *Coleridge; Early Visions* (London, 1990)
Homer, *The Odyssey*, trans. E. V. Rieu (London, 1971)
Hopkin, Alannah, *The Living Legend of St Patrick* (London, 1989)
Hopkins, Budd, *Missing Time* (New York, 1988A)
——*Intruders* (London, 1988B)
Hughes, Ted, *Shakespeare and the Goddess of Complete Being* (London, 1992)

——*Winter Pollen; occasional prose*, ed. William Scammell (London, 1994)

Hutton, Ronald, *The Pagan Religion of the British Isles; Their Nature and Legacy* (Oxford, 1995)

James, William, *The Varieties of Religious Experience* (London, 1985)

Jones, Roger, *Physics as Metaphor* (London, 1983)

Jung, C. G., *Memories, Dreams, Reflections* (London, 1967)

——*Symbols of Transformation*, CW 5 (London, 1967)

——*The Archetypes of the Collective Unconscious*, CW (*Collected Works*) 9, I, (London, 1968)

——*Psychology and Alchemy*, CW 12 (London, 1968)

——*The Structure and Dynamics of the Psyche*, CW 8 (London, 1969)

——*Mysterium Coniunctionis*, CW 14 (London, 1970)

——*Alchemical Studies*, CW 13 (London, 1983)

Keats, John, *The Letters of John Keats* (Oxford, 1935)

Kerenyi, C., *The Gods of the Greeks* (London, 1992)

Kirk, G. S., *The Nature of Greek Myths* (London, 1974)

Kirk, G. S., and Raven, J. E., *The Presocratic Philosophers* (Cambridge, 1957)

Kirk, the Revd Robert, *The Secret Commonwealth* (1691), ed. Stewart Sanderson (Cambridge, 1976)

Kuhn, Thomas, *The Structure of Scientific Revolutions* (Univ. of Chicago Press, 1970)

Larsen, Stephen, *The Shaman's Doorway* (Barrytown, NY, 1988)

Leach, Edmund, *Lévi-Strauss* (London, 1970)

Lévi-Strauss, Claude, *Totemism*, trans. Rodney Needham (London, 1969)

——*The Raw and the Cooked* (London, 1970)

——*The Savage Mind* (London, 1972)

——*Structural Anthropology*, 1 (London, 1977)

——*Structural Anthropology*, 2 (London, 1978)

Lévy-Bruhl, Lucien, *How Natives Think*, trans. Lilian A. Clare (London, 1926)

——*The 'Soul' of the Primitive*, trans. Lilian A. Clare (London, 1928; 1965)

Lewis, C. S., *The Discarded Image* (Cambridge, 1964)

Lewis, I. M., *Ecstatic Religion* (London, 1978)

Lewontin, R. C., *The Doctrine of DNA: Biology as Ideology* (London, 1993)

Locke, John, *An Essay Concerning Human Understanding*, ed. A. D. Woozley (London, 1964)

López-Pedraza, Rafael, *Hermes and his Children* (Einsideln, Switzerland, 1989)

McManus, Dermot, *The Middle Kingdom* (Gerrards Cross, Bucks., Eng. 1959)

Malcolm, Andrew, *Making Names: An Idea of Philosophy* (Brighton, 1992)

Medhurst, W. H., *A Dissertation on the Theology of the Chinese . . .* (Shanghae [*sic*], 1847)

Metzner, Ralph, *The Well of Remembrance* (Boston, 1994)

Midgley, Mary, *Evolution as a Religion; Strange Hopes and Stranger Fears* (London and New York, 1985)

——*Wisdom, Information, and Wonder* (London and New York, 1991)

——*Science and Salvation; a Modern Myth and its Meaning* (London and New York, 1992)

Miller, David, *The New Polytheism* (Dallas, 1981)

Milton, Richard, *The Facts of Life* (London, 1994)

Monod, Jacques, *Chance and Necessity*, trans. Austryn Wainhouse (London and Glasgow, 1977)

Murdoch, Iris, *The Fire and the Sun* (Oxford, 1978)

——*Metaphysics as a Guide to Morals* (London, 1993)

Narváez, Peter, ed. *The Good People: New Fairylore Essays* (London and New York, 1991)

Needham, Rodney, ed. *Right and Left: Essays on Dual Symbolic Classification* (Univ. of Chicago Press, 1973)

——*Primordial Characters* (Univ. of Virginia Press, 1978)

——*Reconnaissances* (Univ. of Toronto Press, 1980)

——*Circumstantial Deliveries* (Berkeley, 1981)

——*Against the Tranquillity of Axioms* (Berkeley, 1983)

Nicholl, Charles, *The Chemical Theatre* (London, 1980)

Onians, R. B., *The Origins of European Thought about the Body, the Mind, the Soul, the World, Time and Fate* (Cambridge, 1981)

Picard, Barbara Leonie, *Tales of the Norse Gods and Heroes* (Oxford, 1953)

Plato, *The Republic*, trans. H. D. P. Lee (London, 1970)

——*Timaeus and Critias*, trans. H. D. P. Lee (London, 1971)

——*Phaedrus and Letters VII and VIII*, trans. Walter Hamilton (London, 1973)

Plotinus, *The Enneads*, trans. Stephen MacKenna (London, 1991)

Proust, Marcel, *Remembrance of Things Past*, 12 vols, trans. C. K. Scott Moncrieff (London, 1966–70)

Raine, Kathleen, *Blake and Tradition*, vol. I (London, 1969)

Raine, Kathleen, and Harper, George Mills, eds. *Thomas Taylor the Platonist: Selected Writings* (London, 1969)

Rojcewicz, Peter M., 'Between One Eye Blink and the Next: Fairies, UFOs, and Problems of Knowledge', in Narváez, pp. 479–514

Rossi, Paolo, *Francis Bacon: From Magic to Science*, trans. Sacha Rabinovitch (London, 1968)

Samuels, Andrew, *The Plural Psyche: Personality, Morality and the Father* (New York and London, 1989)

Scholem, Gerschom, *Major Trends in Jewish Mysticism* (New York, 1961)

Sheldrake, Rupert, *The Rebirth of Nature* (London, 1990)

Snell, Bruno, *The Discovery of Mind: The Greek Origins of European Thought*, trans. T. G. Rosenmeyer (New York, 1960)

Soskice, Janet Martin, *Metaphor and Religious Language* (Oxford, 1985)

Spence, Jonathan D., *The Memory Palace of Matteo Ricci* (London, 1985)

Spring: A Journal of Archetype and Culture (PO Box 222069, Dallas, Texas 75222

Stillings, Dennis, 'Images of High Numinosity in Current Popular Culture', in *Artifex* 6, 2 (April 1987)

Strieber, Whitley, *Communion* (London, 1988)

Sutherland, James, *A Preface to Eighteenth Century Poetry* (Oxford, 1963)

Tarnas, Richard, *The Passion of the Western Mind* (New York, 1991)

Taylor, F. Sherwood, *The Alchemists* (London, 1976)

Tillyard, E. M. W., *The Elizabethan World Picture* (London, 1963)

Vitebsky, Piers, *The Shaman* (London, 1995)

Walker, D. P., *Spiritual and Demonic Magic from Ficino to Campanella* (London, 1958)

Wallis, R. T., *Neoplatonism* (London, 1972)

Warnock, Mary, *Imagination* (London, 1980)

Weeks, Andrew, *Boehme* (Univ. of New York Press, Albany, 1991)

Whyte, L. L., *The Unconscious before Freud* (New York, 1978)

Williams, Charles, *The Descent of the Dove* (London, 1963)

Wilson, Jason, 'Darwin's Nausea' in *Harvest*, vol. 34, 1988–9, pp. 132–41: *The Journal for Jungian Studies*, Karnac Books, 58 Gloucester Rd., London SW7 4QY

Wind, Edgar, *Pagan Mysteries in the Renaissance* (London, 1967)

Woods, Richard, ed. *Understanding Mysticism* (London, 1981)

Wordsworth, William, *Poetical Works* (Oxford, 1971)

Yates, Frances A., *Giordano Bruno and the Hermetic Tradition* (London, 1964)

——*The Occult Philosophy in the Elizabethan Age* (London, 1983)

——*The Art of Memory* (London, 1984)

Yeats, W. B., *Mythologies* (London, 1959)

——*Essays and Introductions* (London, 1961)

——*Collected Poems* (London, 1967)

Zaleski, Carol, *Otherworld Journeys* (Oxford, 1988)

Index

Index

Sioux 89
skin-shedding, tales of 15–16
Socrates 8, 258, 259
Sophia, myth of 166–7
soul(s) 37, 114, 276, 284–5
    cure of 272–80
    and ego/rational ego 132, 161–2,
        240, 266
    and gravity 167
    Greek notion of 33
    and imagination 42, 114
    loss of 26, 281–3
    neglect of in field of medicine
        274
    and spirit 226–8, 229, 234–5, 238,
        239–40, 252, 266
    see also psyche
Soul of the World 37–44, 38, 46, 107,
    143, 167, 168, 185, 201, 220,
    222, 228, 236, 283, 285
Spencer, Herbert 98
spirit
    and soul 226–8, 229, 234–5, 238,
        239–40, 252
Spiritualism 55–6, 234
Stalin, Joseph 269, 270–71
stars
    Ficino and astral magic 111–14
statue-magic 113–14
Stillings, Dennis 263
Stoicism 111
subatomic world 57–8, 59
subject
    relationship with object 48
Sufism 41
suicide 268
superstrings 58
Suso, Henry 250–51
sweat lodges 89
Swedenborg, Emanuel 227–8

tabula rasa 199
Tarnas, Richard
    The Passion of the Western Mind
        241–2
Tate, Sharon 263
Tauler, Johann 225
Taylor, Thomas 259, 287
technology 180, 184–5, 187
    and myth 189
    rejection of by tribes 182–4
tekhne 184, 187, 190
telescopes 160, 185
Teleuts 17
television 186–7
Tempest, The 133
Tertullian 43
Thales 228
Theatrum Chemicum (Chemical
    Theatre) 139–40
Thonga 25
Thor 3
Thoreau 197
thymos 33
Tintern Abbey 221–2
Tolkein
    The Lord of the Rings 3
Torah 117
Torres Straits 30
totemism 63–5, 69
tragic drama 265
transmutation of species 100–109
transvestism 18
tribes 66
    and puberty rites 86–8
    rejection of technology 182–4
    relationship with Nature 183
    and totemism 63–5, 69
Trithemius, Abbot 112
Trobriand Island 15–16, 25
truth 220

A NOTE ON THE AUTHOR

Patrick Harpur studied English literature at Cambridge University, traveled in Africa, worked at part-time jobs, and became an editor in a publishing house. He left it in 1982 and has been writing since. He is the author of three novels—*The Rapture; The Serpent's Circle*; and *Mercurius; or, The Marriage of Heaven and Earth*—and *A Field Guide to the Otherworld*. He lives in Dorchester, England.